JOSEPH SMITH AND ABRAHAM LINCOLN

DEFENDERS OF
Religious Freedom

JOSEPH SMITH AND ABRAHAM LINCOLN

DEFENDERS OF
Religious Freedom

Ron L. Andersen

DIGITAL
LEGEND

ISBN: 978-1-944200-50-3

Digital Legend Press and Publishing
Salt Lake City, UT, and Rochester, NY
www.digitalegend.com
Send inquiries to: info@digitalegend.com or call 877-222-1960

Cover and interior designed by Jacob F. Frandsen

Contents

Foreword

WITH THE THOUSANDS of publications regarding the life, contributions and unique characteristics of Abraham Lincoln, (including three of my own) it is perhaps a curiosity that yet another book would be published concerning his singular, if not presumptuous mission to repair a flawed Constitution for the United States of America.

Notwithstanding, this book makes two unique, if not controversial claims. First, that the Constitution—that heaven-inspired document—arrived fresh from the signers with at least two serious flaws in its structure, and second, that heaven would require the best blood of the 19th century to fix and restore the original intent of that political masterpiece. *God would raise up two men for that special assignment—Joseph Smith, the Mormon Prophet, and Abraham Lincoln, America's sixteenth president.*

Although some may argue that any inherent discrepancies or oversights might have been corrected through the passage of time and the regular legislative process, the author compellingly asserts that absent the timely actions and sacrifices of these two valiant patriots, the nascent union might have splintered upon the rocky shoals she came so dangerously close to.

Perhaps Benjamin Franklin characterized this critical place in history most succinctly when he expressed the thought as a proverb:

> For the want of a nail the shoe was lost,
>
> For the want of a shoe the horse was lost,
>
> For the want of a horse the rider was lost,
>
> For the want of a rider the battle was lost,

For the want of a battle the kingdom was lost,

And all for the want of a horseshoe-nail.

Fortunately for every American, as well as every other person who has reaped the blessings of liberty which derive from the U.S. Constitution, the battle was *not* lost, and the *kingdom* did not perish from the earth.

Readers are invited to engage with the dialogue as if they were living in the times of the Prophet and the President, experiencing the very real abuses his co-religionists were suffering as well as the terrible blight of slavery which affected both the slavers and the slaves.

When faced with the realities of the time, including depredations done in the name of a confused and misinterpreted concept of "liberty and freedom," neither of these men was spared the throes of agony and helplessness, as they sought to end persecution and instill a sense of justice for the oppressed.

Somehow in the economy of heaven, grand souls are raised from obscurity to accomplish great, if not impossible tasks, seemingly with the sacrifice of their own comfort, happiness and even their very lives. Glory be to God, they fought the good fight, they finished their course, they kept the faith.

—Timothy Ballard
Founder of Operation Underground Railroad
and Bestselling Author

Introduction

AFTER JOSEPH SMITH was commanded by God to importune at the feet of judges, governors and presidents, Joseph traveled to Washington and met with President Van Buren, "who treated me very insolently, and said, 'Gentlemen your cause is just, but I can do nothing for you;' and 'If I take up for you I shall lose the vote of Missouri.'"[1] It was a fateful moment in the eternities when the Prophet of the Restoration, like Abinadi, stood before the President, the principle steward of the sacred Constitution, and in the name of God, importuned that the "just and holy principles"[2] of God's Constitution be honored and that His saints be recompensed for the wrongs committed against them. The President of the United States rejected the Prophet of God, and the vexing judgments of God awaited this condemned nation.

Now there is a question of great importance to be asked here. Did the Constitution justify the inaction of President Van Buren? Remarkably, the United States Constitution was, at that time, unclear as to the whether he was actually responsible for the protection of the Mormons from the intense religious persecutions which they had endured.

The reason: The U.S. Constitution was broken from the moment it was ratified. It contained two significant and costly flaws, which literally brought the condemnation of God to this country in the form of the Civil War, "beginning at the rebellion of South Carolina."[3] We know

---

1. B. H. Roberts, *History of the Church*, Salt Lake City, 1976, vol. 4 p. 80.
2. Doctrine and Covenants 101:77
3. Doctrine and Covenants 87:1

that God raised up men for the very purpose of establishing the extraordinary government for the people and by the people. But a careful study of the actual proceedings of the Constitutional Convention reveals that some of the men in that convention of 1787 were not among those whom God raised up. These few delegates were wary of a strong federal government and preferred that the states not be obligated to follow the Constitution, but rather follow it when they thought it expedient. These opposing Constitutional Convention delegates: Elbridge Gerry, Alexander Martin, John F. Mercer and Luther Martin prevailed, resulting in a compromise—each state's compliance to the sacred principles in the Constitution would be optional.

This was the first of two major flaws in the original Constitution. It would take 81 years to repair the damage when the Fourteenth Amendment to the Constitution was ratified in 1868. This meant that when the lawless mobs in Jackson and Caldwell Counties of Missouri, twice drove the Mormon citizens from their homes, then burned and stole their property, the Federal Government was powerless to require that the State of Missouri be brought to justice for not abiding by the "just and holy principles"[4] of the Constitution.

The second flaw was the allowance of slavery in the Constitution, a contemptible hijacking by a few convention delegates forced this compromise. These two flaws in the Constitution legitimized further erosion of the freedoms ostensibly guaranteed in this Promised Land. As sacred and inspired as our Constitution was designed to be, Satan's influence—like the proverbial camel's nose—insidiously inserted itself. In order to rescue, salvage and purify this sacred gift of liberty, the dross must be purged out. That ominous lot would fall to the two great mar-

---

4. Doctrine and Covenants 101:77

tyrs of the 19th century: Joseph Smith, the Prophet and Abraham Lincoln, the President.

This book explores in unprecedented detail, the thesis that it was these Constitutional flaws which compelled Joseph Smith, Jr. to run for the office of President of the United States. Standing before the highest leaders of the land, he prophetically warned of the vexing tribulations that would visit this nation if they did not make the provisions required to correct these damnable flaws. Inasmuch as Joseph the Prophet was assassinated in the attempt, another "humble instrument of the Hands of God," was raised up to complete the work that he would have corrected had he been elected. That man was Abraham Lincoln.

The argument cites the various references made by both these great Americans regarding the erosion of religious freedoms in America—a corrosion spawned by these Constitutional flaws. It will demonstrate how remarkably similar Abraham Lincoln's political platform and religious convictions were to those of Joseph Smith the Prophet and presidential candidate.

Today, apostles of the Lord Jesus Christ are covering the globe with warnings regarding threats to the long treasured freedom of religious expression. This is not the first attack on the great Constitution's protection of this sacred right. Joseph Smith's run for President of the United States was a noble attempt to end slavery and preserve religious freedom, cut short by his martyrdom. Abraham Lincoln also fought and succeeded in changing the flaws in the original Constitution to preserve these freedoms. How important are the religious freedoms guaranteed by the Constitution of this land? Important enough for God to sacrifice some of the most precious blood of that generation toward their preservation.

Thousands of books have been written about Lincoln, including my previous three books about this great president, but none has targeted his key role—his deep and oft expressed desire to protect the right to the free exercise of religion, a theme championed by our modern-day apostles and prophets—the way this one does.

—*Ron L. Andersen*

Rebellion

LINCOLN LOOKED NERVOUSLY at the large White House door that would soon open to hundreds of unknown guests. They would all politely congratulate him for his new role as the nation's new President, and welcome this new intruder to their city of Washington. Their well wishes he would graciously accept; yet he knew most of them were unhappy that he, rather than any of the other three candidates for the office was now the occupant of the Executive Mansion in Washington.

Lincoln also knew at the time of the election four months earlier in November 1860 that most in America thought well enough of him, but he was not their first choice for President. Stephen A. Douglas, John Breckenridge and John Bell, these men voters knew through their vast political success and high positions in Washington. But Lincoln had not held any political office, not even locally, for the previous eleven years. Unlike these other candidates, he had not been a governor or a judge or even a mayor.

His only political experience on the national scale was a rather unimpressive two-year term in the House of Representatives in 1847 to 1849. These well-informed guests also knew that their new President had very little formal education. In fact, his campaign managers, keenly aware that Lincoln had few distinguishing accomplishments, settled on touting him as the Rail Splitter, a fence builder, a common self-made man. Indeed, he was a stranger in this city, and to most Washington residents, an unwelcome one.

Never before had an inauguration taken place in such a tense and dangerous atmosphere. Riflemen lined the rooftops and cannon were set near the capital to nervously guard the life of the new United States President as he made his way from the Willard Hotel toward the Capitol in a cavalry flanked horse-drawn carriage accompanied by the outgoing and worn-out President, James Buchanan.

Many of Washington's residents were overwhelmingly sympathetic to the South and unabashed in their opposition to Lincoln. Wild rumors swirled, fed by many of the discontented Southerners who now felt trapped in Washington and fearful of their planned return to their home Southern States. They speculated about eminent attacks on Washington, about assassination attempts on the president-elect, and about plans for reinforcing Ft. Sumter to keep the US Army from preventing their intended, illegal and treasonous confiscation of the fort at the mouth of the Charleston, South Carolina harbor.

These Southern sympathies were firmly entrenched in many of Washington's social and political circles. For the first seventy-two years of the Federal government, Southern leaders had been dominant in Congress. Washington was a slaveholding city and even though both Abraham and Mary Lincoln were technically Southerners, having both been born in Kentucky, their new domicile was dangerously hostile territory for them. The citizens of Washington City had tolerated the Democrat Buchanan, but Lincoln, the first Republican President was viewed by many locals as a most undesirable interference. Even though he won the election, it was done with an overwhelming majority of electoral votes from the North and not one from south of the Mason-

Dixon Line. Inauguration Day 1861 was far different from the fifteen previous; this one was tense and subdued, with the Capitol City sparsely decorated compared to years past.

Opposites

Lincoln was rarely comfortable in formal socio-political settings but he knew them to be necessary—he would now need to collaborate with these honored guests who consisted of members of Congress, military officers and the like. Mary Lincoln, on the other hand had looked with great anticipation to this grand traditional Inaugural Ball. In the days preceding the event, she had made a trip to New York to meet the most renowned dressmakers and interior designers in America.

And she made purchases, many of them on the government's tab and without her husband's knowledge. She brought to her new home the finest materials for the numerous additional dresses that her full-time dressmaker would make in Mary's coming White House years. She also brought along curtains, carpets and wallpapers to upgrade the much-degraded interior of the White House, which had fallen into disrepair and neglect under previous administrations.

While Lincoln had little interest in being a part of Washington's elite social circle, Mary was consumed with it. In spite of Mary's unabashed efforts to impress and excel among the Washington women in the next four years, in the end, she only succeeded in being a painful embarrassment to herself and her husband. She never attained the respect and admiration she so blatantly and awkwardly pursued. Her husband understood that true respect and admiration comes only through the accomplishments of those who do not pursue such respect for themselves—it is earned. Mary, on the other hand, believed that her new station as Madam President, which she insisted on as her title should demand it.

Her husband was right in this regard, and she was woefully wrong. In the next four years, those who would approach Lincoln as Mr. President would routinely but kindly be corrected with "Call me Lincoln."[1] He would avoid referring to his new residence as the White House, calling it instead, "the place."[2] And the White House staff would repeatedly hear the President clarify that there was to be "no smell of royalty in this establishment."[3]

Earlier on that day of March 4, 1861, he was sworn in as President of the United States and had delivered his Inaugural Address. This night he and his family would sleep in the same house in which every American President since John Adams had slept. But first he had to face the throng of the sophisticated elite of American society. Almost all of these guests would conceal their sentiments that he and Mary were far from qualified to join their honored circle in society, but even worse, so regrettably ill-prepared to address this nation's worst crisis.

Little of this national calamity would be mentioned tonight. The Inaugural Ball was neither the time or the place, but they fully intended to, in the coming days, make clear to the new President their dissatisfaction with the positions and policies he brought with him to the White House from the loathsome prairie out west. Yet Lincoln knew the secession crisis was on the minds of all, and none more than his.

The White House doors eventually opened to the guests—dressed in tuxedos, military uniforms and elegant evening gowns—here Abraham

---

1. Compiled by Alexander Kelly McClure, *"Abe" Lincoln's Yarns and Stories*, Copyright by Henry Neil, 1901, pp. 276, 277

2. Ibid., pp. 276, 277

3. Ward Hill Lamon, *Recollections Of Abraham Lincoln*, University of Nebraska Press, 1994, p 6

and Mary Lincoln, fresh from Springfield, Illinois, cordially received and welcomed them to their new home.

Secession Crisis at the Door

When the last guest finally exited the White House very late that night, the exhausted couple shuffled to their new living quarters for a much needed rest. But just before the President could enter his living area, he was handed a note saying that Fort Sumter, South Carolina, was in grave danger. This nation's darkest days had now arrived on his first day as President. There would be little rest for the Lincoln that night and for the following four years.

The next morning, he received the detailed message from Major Robert Anderson, commanding officer at Ft. Sumter, stating that he had only enough provisions for his small detachment at the fort to last about six more weeks. Major Anderson also reported that, based on the massive firepower that the South Carolina militias now had aimed directly on Ft. Sumter, it would take an additional 20,000 men to keep the new Confederacy from taking the fort. Lincoln soon discovered that he only had some 17,000 in the entire U.S. Army and many of them had been dispersed throughout the west, 5,000 of whom were stationed at Camp Floyd in Utah, keeping watch on the Utah Mormons. Fort Sumter was one of only two remaining Federal forts residing in the Southern half of the Union that had not already been wrested from the government by the rebels.

The future of the nation centered on Ft. Sumter and all eyes, North and South, were on it. Lincoln could simply order Anderson to abandon the fort and concede that the Southern State's unlawful taking of federal forts and arsenals would be allowed and by so doing they would have their Confederate Nation, as was their desire. Or, if he and the government were to defend its right to exist, to retain its territory and possessions, Ft. Sumter suddenly became the looming target of its defense. The crisis was augmented by Lincoln's clear message in his inaugural address, earlier the day before, that the recent taking of all of the forts and installations from the government of the United States was done unlawfully and that he intended to keep them in the Union.

The daring rebellion in South Carolina by a small group of Southern rebels had completely overwhelmed the North and heartened the leaders in the other southern states with the genius and success of their plan. Six states followed South Carolina in secession; their hope for a peaceful separation was in sight and they saw no need, nor did their plans call for war. The government was hardly prepared for such a monumental crisis. The House of Representatives had just adjourned and the Congressmen were heading home. Lincoln's cabinet had not yet been approved or assembled. Add to this, Lincoln had never worked at an executive level. The only management experience he had was operating his two-man law practice in Springfield.

He had always worked on his own. The delegation and coordination between massive government departments was foreign to him. It had been ten years since he was even a government elected official when he completed his only term in the House of Representatives, and now he found himself as the inexperienced Chief Executive with the nation on the brink of civil war. This lack of administrative experience became quickly evident and did not inspire confidence in those around him. The new President was well aware of his own inexperience. At first he attempted to do everything himself, as he had always conducted his own business for years. Later he admitted to an Illinois friend that, "when he first commenced doing the duties, he was entirely ignorant not only of the duties, but of the manner of doing the business of the presidency."[4]

It is stunning that the colossal events of secession, which took place on President James Buchanan's watch in the 118-days between Lincoln's November 6, 1860 election and his inauguration on March 4, 1861, were done with Congress in session and with them seemingly powerless to stop the disintegration of the nation. President Buchanan made some tacit overtures in opposition but in the end he too turned spectator, saying, "Congress alone has power" to decide the legality of secession.[5] "But," observed Lincoln's friend and body guard, Ward Hill Lamon,

> Congress behaved like a body of men who thought the calamities of the nation were no special business of theirs.[6] Those Congressmen from the deep South were merely looking for the proper time to resign their elected office and return to their home states; those from the middle slave states could but watch to see how these movements would impact them, and, as the French minister observed, the leaders from the Northern states were a "mere aggregation of individual ambitions."[7]

Lamon continued:

> In the philosophy of their politics it [secession] had not been dreamed of as a possible thing. Even when they saw it assume the shape of a fixed and terrible fact, they could not comprehend its meaning. The nation was going to pieces, and Congress left it to its fate. The vessel, freighted with all the hopes

---

4. The Eloquent President, Ronald C. White, Jr., p 100
5. Recollections of Abraham Lincoln, Ward Hill Lamon, p 57
6. Recollections of Abraham Lincoln, Ward Hill Lamon, p 57
7. Recollections of Abraham Lincoln, Ward Hill Lamon, p 57

and all the wealth of thirty millions of free people was drifting to her doom, and they who alone had power to control her course refused to lay a finger on the helm.[8]

Lincoln believed many in the South opposed secession from the Union and would be coerced to support it. He also believed that it was the design and actions of a minority of Southern radical yet influential men, almost all slave owners and particularly in South Carolina, who were the authors of this national crisis.

Clear and Decisive Inauguration Speech

Lincoln went on in his Inaugural speech to clearly state the gravity of their actions and to plainly express his determination to do his sworn duty as President of the United States to protect the Constitution. To these Southern radicals he firmly declared: "In *your* hands, my dissatisfied fellow countrymen, and not *mine* is the momentous issue of civil war. The government will not assail you. You can have no conflict, without being you yourselves the aggressors. *You* have no oath registered in Heaven to destroy the government, while I shall have the most solemn one to "preserve, protect and defend it."[9]

"Plainly," Lincoln warned them, "the central idea of secession, is the essence of anarchy. No state, upon its own mere motion, can lawfully get out of the Union…and acts of violence, within any State or States, against the authority of the United States, are insurrectionary or revolutionary…"[10] With this clarity he extinguished any hopes of compromise. He would act on his duty to defend and uphold the Union.

---

8. Ibid., p 58
9. The Eloquent President, Ronald C. White, Jr., p 87
10. The Eloquent President, Ronald C. White, Jr., p 62

In plaintive warmth and sincerity, he brought his speech to its conclusion:

> I am loath to close. We are not enemies, but friends. We must not be enemies. Though passion may have strained, it must not break our bonds of affection. The mystic chords of memory, stretching from every battlefield, and patriot grave, to every living heart and hearthstone, all over this broad land, will yet swell the chorus of the Union, when again touched, as surely they will be, by the better angels of our nature.[11]

At the conclusion of the speech, eighty-four year old Chief Justice, Roger Taney, stepped forward to swear in the new President. With his left hand on an open Bible, and right hand raised to the square, Lincoln repeated the oath of office:

> I, Abraham Lincoln, do solemnly swear that I will faithfully execute the office of President of the United States, and will, to the best of my ability, preserve, protect, and defend the Constitution of the United States.[12]

Lincoln's inaugural message prompted a scathing response from South Carolina Governor Pickens where he warned,

> Nothing can prevent war except the acquiescence of the President of the United States in secession... Let your President attempt to reinforce Sumter, and the tocsin [alarm] of war will sound from every hilltop and valley in the South.[13]

---

11. Ibid p 62

12. The Eloquent President, Ronald C. White, Jr., p 92

13. Carl Sandburg, *The Prairie Years and the War Years*, New York, Harcourt, Brace & World, Inc., 1954, p. 224

To the astonishment of the Fire-Eaters in the South, as they were pleased to be called, unlike Buchanan, and the U. S. Congress, Abraham Lincoln was determined keep his solemn oath of office. To this new President, the preservation and protection of the Constitution was paramount. In his view, its safety could only be assured by surrounding it with a strong Union of all states. He could not consent to their secession because it would place in jeopardy the peoples' Constitutional civil and religious rights.

Even though talk of secession had been mounting in America during the previous 30 years, the nation had no plan on how to address it should it ever occur. This partly explains how the Congress and President Buchannan seemed utterly baffled as to how to respond to the crisis when it did occur. The ramifications of any action from the government were potentially catastrophic. The Buchanan administration's paralysis on the matter seemed to help President-Elect Lincoln formulate his own course of action. When he arrived at the White House he was prepared to do what had to be done to protect the civil and religious freedoms embodied in the Constitution that were in grave danger. Inaction was no longer an option.

The Sacred Constitution

At this juncture, it is vitally important to bring to remembrance God's Divine will concerning this nation, its Constitution and the secession crisis that President Lincoln now faced. God spoke with clarity on the matter to Joseph Smith in December 1833 just weeks following the saints' illegal and violent expulsion from their homes and farms in Jackson County, Missouri.

In revelation, He instructed Joseph Smith to importune for the re-dress and redemption for the losses of their homes, property and live-stock. These appeals for redress and justice were to go to the "rulers" who are "in authority over you" and continued:

> According to the laws and constitution of the people, which I
> have suffered to be established; and should be maintained for
> the rights and protection for all flesh, according to just and
> holy principles;[14]

Here God offers the remarkable revelation that the United States Constitution, which was developed by our founding fathers in 1787, was a work established under his Divine guiding hand. And it was his intent that the fair and righteous laws advocated in this Constitution were laws that He expected to be obeyed in this country, for they were His laws based upon "just and holy principles."[15]

Unfortunately, the unlawful events in Jackson County in 1833 were in stark disobedience to these laws, the foremost of which was that no religious expression or practice would be interfered with under this in-spired government. In Jackson County it was the religious practice and devotions of the Mormons in that area that were despised by the local leaders and citizens. The rights and protection of the Latter-day Saints were not being maintained, as God had instructed in this verse, and the mobs' actions were in complete defiance of the laws, which were founded upon "just and holy principles."[16]

In this revelation God introduced yet another remarkable compo-nent—even a government in this promised land. Through all the course

---

14. Doctrine and Covenants 101:76,77

15. Doctrine and Covenants 101:76,77

16. Doctrine and Covenants 101:77

of history and the myriad of inept and unjust governments and king-doms that had risen and fallen through the centuries, this government for the United States of America, would be unlike any other in history. It would have a constitution, founded upon unbiased and sacred princi-ples and it would be an unspeakable gift from the Great God in Heaven. This gift was not only proffered to the citizens of this chosen nation but to liberty loving people throughout the world whose countries would adopt similar constitutions that offered civil and religious freedoms.

The Lord continued to reveal more of His extraordinary involve-ment in the establishment of this nation and its government:

> That every man may act in doctrine and principles according to mortal agency, which I have given unto him, that every man may be accountable for his own sins in the day of judg-ment. Therefore, it is not right that any man should be in bondage one to another.

> And for this purpose I have established the Constitution of this land, by the hands of wise men whom I have raised up unto this very purpose, and redeemed the land by the shed-ding of blood.[17]

Elder Dallin H. Oaks had this to say about the inspired United States Constitution,

> It was a miracle that the Constitution could be drafted and ratified. It was the first written constitution in the world. Ev-ery nation in the world except six have adopted written con-

---

17. Doctrine and Covenants 101:77-80

stitutions, and the U.S. Constitution was a model for all of them.[18]

Somehow, Abraham Lincoln recognized the sacred nature of this Constitution and the republican form of government of the people that it inspired. He also saw it, not just for this nation, but spoke often about it benefitting mankind throughout the world. He used phrases like the "last best hope of earth" in referring to this government "of the people, by the people, and for the people."[19]

Adoption of similar principles in these constitutions (in all but six nations of the world) inspired leaders to embrace civil and religious freedoms for their citizens, opening the doors for the army of Latter-day Saint missionaries who have, and continue to cover the earth with their message of hope and salvation. The gift of the United States Constitution was meant for all nations of the world, and President Lincoln recognized the "formidable internal attempt to overthrow it"[20] that was taking place. He was not going to allow that to happen on his watch.

Rebellion

With South Carolina now viewing itself as no longer part of the United States, its leaders began demanding that the Federal Government turn over Ft. Sumter. The sight of the Stars and Stripes flying over the fort in Charleston harbor was now seen as a foreign presence and an affront to their presumed national sovereignty. They first appealed to President Buchanan, who surprised them by refusing to surrender Ft. Sumter or any other Federal arsenal or installation residing in the South. In fact, he sent a merchant steamer, *Star of the West,* with tons of

18. The Ensign, February 1992
19. Abraham Lincoln, The Gettysburg Address, November 22, 1863
20. President Lincoln's address to Congress July 4, 1861

supplies and two hundred additional men to reinforce Major Anderson's small contingent. Upon entering the Charleston harbor, shore batteries on both sides of the harbor awaited anxiously for orders to fire on the unarmed vessel.

The order finally came by Major P.F. Stevens, to 39 eager Citadel cadets manning the artillery on the Morris Island battery. Young G.W. Haynes had the dubious honor of firing the first shot of the Civil War, as he sent a cannon ball roaring over the top of the *Star of the West*. Others opened fire and forced the ship back out to sea. On March 1st, the newly installed President of the Confederacy, Jefferson Davis, ordered General Pierre Beauregard, ironically a friend and former West Point pupil of Major Anderson's, to take command of the Charleston defenses.

To be sure, Lincoln had laid out his intentions in his Inaugural Address earlier in the week. He told Americans that he intended to maintain the complete Union and all of the forts and other government possessions and resources therein. But he also said that he would not use force unless those in the South themselves "become the aggressors."[21] These commitments left him few options; but they left him the one option he intended to use. To Lincoln, not surrendering Fort Sumter was a required measure to preserve the Union. The Union had to remain strong to protect the Constitution. He would send a message of his peaceful intent to resupply the garrison at Fort Sumter with food and supplies, which the small garrison badly needed.

Unlike Former President Buchanan's attempt to hold the fort, Lincoln's ship would have no soldiers, ammunition or guns—no implements of war—only the needed provisions to sustain the lives of the 60 soldiers stationed there. His plan did not include an official declaration

---

21. Abraham Lincoln's First Inaugural Address, March 4, 1861

to the nation, just a simple letter to the governor of South Carolina. This letter would not be addressed to the newly elected President of the Confederacy, Jefferson Davis, whom Lincoln would not, and never did recognize as a leader in the Southern Confederacy.

We the People

Later in his July message to a special session of both houses of Congress, he succinctly described the global implications to this crisis of secession.

> It may be affirmed…that the free institutions we enjoy have …improved the condition of our whole people beyond any example in the world. Whoever…proposes to abandon such a government would do well to consider…what better he is likely to get in its stead; whether the substitute will give…so much of good to the people.

> Our adversaries have adopted some declarations of independence in which, unlike the good old one penned by Jefferson, they omit the words "all men are created equal." Why? They have adopted a temporary national constitution, in the preamble of which, unlike our good old one signed by Washington, they omit "We, the people," and substitute "We, the deputies of the sovereign and independent States." Why? Why this deliberate pressing out of view the rights of men and the authority of the people?

Lincoln continued by describing his interpretation of the Lord's "just and holy principles" embodied in this government of the *people, not deputies.*

> This is essentially a people's contest. On the side of the Union it is a struggle for maintaining in the world that form and substance of government whose leading object is to elevate the condition of men; to lift artificial weights from all shoulders; to clear the paths of laudable pursuit for all; to afford all an unfettered start and a fair chance in the race of life. ...this is the leading object of the Government for whose existence we contend.

Then, referring to the patriotic instinct of the common American, he said,

> They understand without an argument that destroying the Government which was made by Washington means no good to them. Our popular Government has often been called an experiment. Two points in it our people have already settled— the successful establishing and the successful administering of it. One still remains—its successful maintenance against *a formidable internal attempt to overthrow it* [emphasis added]. It is now for them to demonstrate to the world that those who can fairly carry an election can also suppress a rebellion.[22]

The New Commander In Chief

General Winfield Scott, Commander of the U. S. Army, and all members of Lincoln's new cabinet except one, pressed him to abandon

---

22. Lincoln's address to Congress July 4, 1861

his plan for Fort Sumter. They were willing to let it go into the control of the Confederacy. They simply didn't have the military forces to defend it—and no one wanted war. They believed that surrendering the fort would signal the North's peaceful intentions. While he agreed with them on the depleted military, and the anxious desire for peace with their southern brothers, Lincoln seemed to be looking far beyond these immediacies.

To him, the fort was symbolic, the place where he would put up a mild and measured resistance to the insurrections and treasons committed by the Fire-Eaters in the South—he would send a shipment of food to the small garrison that held the fort. By this simple measure he managed to frame for his country and the world to see for all time, that this peaceful gesture was justified. At the end of the new administration's first Cabinet meeting on the Fort Sumter matter, Lincoln asked them to ponder all options and further their discussion in their next meeting.

In the Cabinet meeting that followed, Lincoln listened intently as three Cabinet members had independently arrived at the conclusion that the new President's solution was the better option. It was with some difficulty that these seasoned Washington men now had to look to this inexperienced newcomer to address the greatest crisis this nation had ever faced. Nevertheless, one by one they began to see the wisdom of Lincoln's position.

Surprisingly, in the third meeting on the matter, the majority of the Cabinet came to agreement with the new Commander In Chief. With their backing, Lincoln ordered that a supply ship be readied to set sail for Fort Sumter. On April 6, 1861, after a very anxious first month in office and many accusations of ineptitude, the ever-deliberate President Lincoln would take his first action against the rebellion. He penned a brief and cordial letter to South Carolina Governor Pickens informing him that the ship would soon be arriving at Fort Sumter with supplies. It would contain no soldiers, no weapons no ammunitions, only food and supplies. Pickens was angry, but Jefferson Davis was incensed.

2

States' Rights and Slavery

T HE NOTION OF SECESSION was not new in this country in Lincoln's day. Some thirty years before the Civil War, Joseph Smith sat with some friends in his Kirtland, Ohio home on Christmas day in December 1832. The discussion turned to the issue of slavery in America, which had flourished and swelled for more than two hundred years. This issue was brought to national attention when the state of South Carolina chose to nullify or refuse to pay the tariffs that Congress recently imposed upon all states in the Union. They had had enough of Federal government intervention into their vibrant economy and they felt no real need to be a part of it any longer.

Planters in South Carolina and adjoining Southern states were experiencing exploding wealth with the rice and cotton commodities produced cheaply and in abundance on the backs of enslaved Africans who outnumbered the white populations in some of their states. Slave owners in South Carolina felt they could go it alone, and wanted to keep profits to themselves instead of feeding the Federal government through taxes and now tariffs. Earlier in 1832, South Carolina had decided to secede from the Union and this threat prompted Joseph Smith's Christmas day conversation.

States' Rights

There was a somewhat noble yet critically damaging condition shared by many early Americans up to the time of the Civil War, and yet this condition is much more subdued today. It is the strongly embraced notion of states' rights. The states' rights stand was a major stumbling block for the Founding Fathers, some of whom were suspicious of a new unified national government. Most early Americans felt that the states were best suited to govern themselves; and this stance persisted in spite of the near disaster that followed the winning of their independence from England where disagreements and strife between states nearly brought this country to utter ruin.

This deep allegiance to one's home state was widely celebrated in early America as demonstrated by many patriots, including Thomas Jefferson. Jefferson's love of his home state of Virginia ran much deeper than his devotion to the United States. He referred to his fellow Virginians as his countrymen and to Virginia as his country. For a time, he spoke of the United States Congress as a foreign legislature, and even referred to the Union as a Confederacy. These sentiments continued to be held by early Americans for more than four score years since the Declaration of Independence. It was this same devotion to one's state that influenced Robert E. Lee's decision to refuse President Lincoln's request that he lead the Union Army when his home state of Virginia joined the rebellion, even though Lee was opposed to secession and slavery. He could not go against his state of Virginia.

"Until his dying days, Thomas Jefferson regularly propounded local self-government above all else, supporting states' rights against the Union."[1] He was a strong proponent of the Tenth Amendment to the

1. April 1865, Jay Winik, p 11

Constitution that limited federal power in relation to the states. "In 1800, he soberly warned that a 'single consolidated government would become the most corrupt government on earth.'"[2]

While Jefferson was President, some states in New England were dissatisfied with the string of U.S. Presidents elected from the state of Virginia. It was the strong economies of these New England states that was carrying the nation's slow but gradual prosperity. When some of President Jefferson's, (another Virginian) economic policies appeared to be unfavorable to them, they took dangerous steps toward secession. To which Jefferson responded, "Whether we remain in our confederacy, or break into Atlantic and Mississippi confederacies, I do not believe very important to the happiness of either part," adding, "separate them if it be better."[3] Fortunately, better heads prevailed and the states remained in the Union.

Such states' rights sentiments were again expressed in 1832 over disagreements with President Andrew Jackson's tariff policies, when South Carolina made a near break from the Union. In response, President Jackson threatened to send 40,000 U.S. troops there to help clear their heads of the notion of nullification—it worked. Jackson's administration responded further by making "nullification" or secession from the Union illegal; a point to which Lincoln often referred. But these opinions persisted until December 1860, when South Carolina became the first of eleven states to actually secede, based on the perceived right of a state to leave the Union when dissatisfied with it.

---

2. Ibid., p 11

3. Ibid., p 11

Beginning at the Rebellion of South Carolina

In the course of that Christmas day conversation regarding slavery in America, Joseph Smith received one of his more than 130 revelations during his shortened life. It is recorded in Doctrine and Covenants section 87 and is referred to as the revelation and prophecy on war; the opening summary describes the setting for the revelation.

> At this time disputes in the United States over slavery and South Carolina's nullification of federal tariffs were prevalent. Joseph Smith's history states, 'Appearances of troubles among the nations' were becoming 'more visible' to the Prophet than they had previously been since the Church began her journey out of the wilderness.[4]

Doctrine and Covenants Section 87:

> 1 Verily, thus saith the Lord concerning the wars that will shortly come to pass, beginning at the rebellion of South Carolina, which will eventually terminate in the death and misery of many souls;

> 2 And the time will come that war will be poured out upon all nations, beginning at this place.

> 3 For behold, the Southern States shall be divided against the Northern States, and the Southern States will call on other nations, even the nation of Great Britain, as it is called, and they shall also call upon other nations, in order to defend them-

---

4. Doctrine & Covenants Section 87, Summary

selves against other nations; and then war shall be poured out upon all nations.

4 And it shall come to pass, after many days, slaves shall rise up against their masters, who shall be marshaled and disciplined for war.

6 And thus, with the sword and by bloodshed the inhabitants of the earth shall be made to feel the wrath, and indignation, and chastening hand of an Almighty God...

7 That the cry of the saints, and of the blood of the saints, shall cease to come up into the ears of the Lord of Saboath, from the earth, to be avenged of their enemies.

From this revelation it can be concluded that some 29 years before the first cannon fired upon Ft. Sumter in 1861, the Prophet Joseph Smith and his followers knew that South Carolina would indeed rebel and separate from this nation, along with other "Southern States." And that rebellion would culminate in a civil war that would lead to the "death and misery of many souls."[5]

"I am Utterly Unable to Shake from Myself the Conviction that I shall be Involved in that Tragedy."

There was another man in America, a contemporary and fellow Illinois resident with Joseph Smith, who also carried within him a foreboding and troubling premonition that slavery in America would finally be ended through a bloody civil war.

On a late summer Sunday in 1837, young Abraham Lincoln, age 28, jumped into a bandwagon in company with six other lawyers and two

---

5. Doctrine & Covenants Section 87:1

doctors, headed for nearby New Salem, Illinois to attend a camp meeting. One of the most notable of Illinois traveling preachers, Dr. Peter Akers would be addressing the evils of slavery—a theme that would kindle the ire of the majority of the listeners, and this rowdy Illinois crowd was more than ready to express their displeasure toward any orator whose theme was not to their liking.

Young Lincoln could scarcely be in any informal setting without someone calling for him to entertain them with his stories, and on this hot August day he did not disappoint. As the wagon rolled to New Salem, he cracked jokes and spun yarns about the wagon, the horses, lawyers, doctors and anything else that caught his attention during the fifteen-mile excursion. A good time was enjoyed by all.

When they arrived, as expected a large crowd had gathered to hear the renowned Methodist preacher expound on his sermon entitled, "The Dominion of Jesus Christ." Dr. Akers characterized himself as a student of Biblical prophecies and his message centered on the theme that Jesus Christ would certainly come again to his footstool here on earth, but not until the curse of slavery was eradicated from this nation's fabric. For three hours he quoted biblical scripture and noted prophecies and their fulfillment with the intent of disquieting many a devout believer for embracing both a faith in God and the evils of slavery.

Interestingly, during the course of his sermon he made some prophecies of his own. The first was that slavery would in fact be stamped out through a bloody American civil war, a far-fetched notion in 1837. Not stopping there, he exclaimed over the din of a growing number of hecklers that, "I am not a prophet nor the son of a prophet, but a student of the prophets. As I read prophecy, American slavery will come to an end in some near decade, I think in the sixties."[6] T. Walter Johnson's biography of Dr. Akers further states:

> After discussing the subject of slavery at some length he approached the pulpit stand with a gravity which hushed the audience to a breathless stillness, placed his long forefinger upon the page of the open Bible, and with all the solemnity of a Jeremiah said, "I cannot give you the exact date but in the latter part of 1860 or the early part of 1861 there will arise in this nation the greatest internecine war known to the history of the world. It will be brother against brother, family against family, and thousands of hearthstones will be made desolate. But through this bloody baptism we must pass for the deliverance of the slave from bondage."[7]

He then punctuated his revelation by saying that some of those present would live to see his prophecies fulfilled. Dr. Akers was surprisingly accurate with his predictions—civil war in America commenced in early 1861 and many in the audience would have still been living to see it, including Lincoln. But what made his three accurate prophecies even more astonishing was his fourth declaration. As the crowd began to surge toward him in angry disapproval, he exclaimed at the top of his voice so as to be heard, "Who can tell but that the man who shall lead us through this strife may be standing in our presence!"[8] A stunned Abraham Lincoln stood just 30 feet away.

---

6. John Wesley Hill, *Abraham Lincoln Man of God,* (New York and London: G.P. Putnam's Sons, 1920), p. 51.

7. T. Walter Johnson, Journal of the Illinois State Historical Society, vol. XXXII, number 4, Dec. 1939, p. 433.

8. Ibid., p. 52.

The impassioned sermon did not disappoint and on the return to Springfield, Lincoln's friends had much to debate as they deliberated on the minister's talking points. The group had gone some distance before they realized that Lincoln, who had always been a ready entrant into any discussion, had been unusually silent and seemed almost unwilling to share his impressions of the sermon. One by one the traveling companions took note of Lincoln's deep absorption into his own thoughts as they rolled along. At length he was called upon to report his impressions and his hesitation to respond was sensed by all, which only increased their determination to hear his thoughts.

After a long pause he said, referring to Dr. Akers' powerful message, "I never thought such power could be given to mortal man. Those words were from beyond the speaker. The doctor has persuaded me that American slavery will go down with the crash of a civil war."[9] Then for a few more moments he was silent and his friends remained so as well, detecting that Lincoln had even more solemn impressions to reveal. Lincoln continued, "Gentlemen you may be surprised and think it strange;" he paused again, "Do you know that all the time he was describing the overthrow of slavery in war and blood, it seemed to me that somehow or other, I was inseparably mixed up with it all, and so strong and deep was the impression, and so strange, that I cannot shake it off. I do not understand why it should be so."[10]

That night Lincoln had difficulty sleeping and when he arrived late into his law office the next morning his partner, John Todd Stuart without looking up, informed him that someone had come by to see him. Then glancing up at Lincoln's haggard face Stuart exclaimed, "Why

9. Ibid., p. 52
10. Ibid., p. 53

Lincoln, what's the matter with you?" To which Lincoln recounted the sermon from the day before and its relentless impression on him. He concluded by telling his law partner, "I am utterly unable to shake from myself the conviction that I shall be involved in that tragedy."[11]

Standing Alone

President Abraham Lincoln could have averted the Civil War, but he did not. Why? Many in the North were willing to let the southern states with their slaves, separate from the Union and become two nations. They were tired of the three decades of wrangling over slavery. The northern states had already freed themselves of the abomination of slavery—their blacks were free. Lincoln would have received only minimal opposition to allowing the southern demands for secession. But few saw the future chaos that would result with the division. At the beginning of his administration, Abraham Lincoln was quite alone in his unwavering resolve to protect the Constitution by preserving the Union.

For many years after the war, the south blamed President Lincoln for the carnage that they all had endured. They claimed that he had tricked them into firing the first shots of the war at his ship of food to Fort Sumter. As unthinkable as the secession was to most people in the nation, war was what they feared most. A large contributor to Congress's inability to act as the rebellion was taking place was their dread of a civil war and the bloodshed that would follow in its wake.

It was during the four months from Lincoln's November 1860 election to his inauguration in the following March, that South Carolina and six other southern states seceded from the Union. While this occurred, he made no public statements or formal addresses. Instead, he

---

11. Ibid., p. 53.

quietly watched the unraveling of this nation while President Buchanan finished out his term. Undoubtedly, the impassioned words of Dr. Peter Akers, spoken more than two decades earlier passed repeatedly through his mind.

> I cannot give you the exact date but in the latter part of 1860 or the early part of 1861 there will arise in this nation the greatest internecine war known to the history of the world. It will be brother against brother, family against family, and thousands of hearthstones will be made desolate. But through this bloody baptism we must pass for the deliverance of the slave from bondage.[12] "Who can tell but that the man who shall lead us through this strife may be standing in our presence![13]

The Oath of Office

Politicians in Washington could not agree on how to respond to the startling secession of the states to the south. So fearful were they of war, that some disregarded their Oath of Office as Senators and members of the House of Representatives by calling for a Constitutional amendment to offer even more appeasements for the Southern slave-owners' grievances. Their proposed concessions would have caused severe damage to the Constitution of the United States and this nation's freedoms, which they had sworn never to allow.

In the U. S. Constitution, it states, "The Senators and Representatives before mentioned, and the Members of the several State Legisla-

---

12. T. Walter Johnson, Journal of the Illinois State Historical Society, vol. XXXII, number 4, Dec. 1939, p. 433.
13. Ibid., 1, p. 52.

tures, and all executive and judicial Officers, both of the United States and of the several States, shall be bound by Oath or Affirmation, to support this Constitution; but no religious Test shall ever be required as a Qualification to any Office or public Trust under the United States."[14]

The Oath of Office for members of Congress prescribed by our Founding Fathers is this:

> I, _____ do solemnly swear (or affirm) that I will sup-
> port and defend the Constitution of the United States against
> all enemies, foreign and domestic; that I will bear true faith
> and allegiance to the same; that I take this obligation freely,
> without any mental reservation or purpose of evasion, and
> that I will well and faithfully discharge the duties of the office
> on which I am about to enter. So help me God.[15]

The Oath for the office of President was simply:

> I, _____ do solemnly swear or affirm (as the case may be)
> that I will support the Constitution of the United States.

When George Washington took this presidential oath of office, he added the words, "So help me God" at the end of his oath. Other Presidents followed Washington's example by adding the same supplication for God's blessing and guidance in the execution of their office as President. This ending phrase was also expressed by Lincoln in his swearing into office. It was during his administration in 1862, that "So help me God" was officially added to the oath of office for non-presidential offices, and has been used to this day.

---

14. U.S. Constitution, Article VI, clause 3

15. Title 5, Section 3331 of the United States Code.

The oath used today has been the same since 1966. What has not changed is the keystone of both oaths from the very beginning. The pledge in all cases has been, and is, to protect and defend the Constitution of the United States. The oath does not pledge to protect and defend property ownership, or the treasury, or the civil rights or even safety of its citizens. It does not pledge to defend the state governments or the right to pursue education or individual fulfillment. The oath in all cases is to defend the Constitution of the United States, which, in Lincoln's words establishes and defends "the civil and religious liberty"[16] of all citizens. All of the civil and religious rights held most dear to the majority of citizens of this country are embodied in the Constitution.

Defending Constitutional Freedoms

In spite of being faced with these overwhelming crises Abraham Lincoln saw far beyond many of the seasoned public servants and military leaders who surrounded him. Protection of the Constitution, the key element in his recent Oath of Office, was clearly his prime presidential objective. The Constitution could probably survive a civil war and clearer heads could, along with his veto power, prevent rash and unwise amendments to make slavery a legitimized cornerstone of this free republic. The irony was beyond comprehension for the new President who had decried the evil practice of slavery his entire life.

What threatened the Constitution most among these crises was secession, a divided and weakened republic, which he believed could not survive half slave and half free. Separations from the Union would result in the new nation-states developing their own modified Constitutions, just as the Confederacy was demonstrating. Over time these

16. Philip L. Ostergard, *The Inspired Wisdom of Abraham Lincoln,* (Carol Stream, Illinois, Tyndale House Publishers, Inc, 2008), 18,19

Constitutional dilutions and territorial divisions would tend to erode the strength and endurance of the original and divinely inspired Constitution. Or possibly new governments could be formed without constitutions altogether.

Eventually, the unspeakable gift of the original Constitution, written by "wise men whom [God] raised up"[17] would be left to be defended by a small consortium of the few scattered states that remained loyal to it. There would be no peace-loving global superpower that the United States has become to preserve civil and religious freedoms around the world. Lincoln somehow perceived that this and future assaults by short sighted special interest minorities, like the pro-slavery movement, would continue their battering against the inspired Constitution. By sending a ship of food to 60 beleaguered soldiers garrisoned in Fort Sumter in Charleston harbor, Lincoln was focused on preserving the Constitution and the civil and religious rights that it guaranteed. This is what he stated clearly just days earlier in his first inaugural address—that he would save the Union to protect the Constitution before he would address horrors of slavery or war.

Dangerous Amendments

In 1860, in response to South Carolina's rebellion and before Lincoln took his oath of office, the House of Representatives made the startling recommendation for a Constitutional amendment that would prohibit any further interference with slavery in hopes of placating the slave states. Six weeks after Lincoln's election, on December 18, 1860, (but before his inauguration) John J. Crittenden of Kentucky proposed six amendments to the Constitution in an effort to avoid civil

---

17. Doctrine and Covenants 101:80

war. This "Crittenden Compromise" was widely accepted by southern Congressmen. These Constitutional amendments would guarantee the permanent existence of slavery in the existing southern states. Future states in the southern half of the continent running west to California would also be constitutionally declared as slave states as well. Another amendment would legalize slavery in the District of Columbia. The final amendment declared that these new amendments *could never be appealed or amended.*

One must pause for a moment to visualize the future of the United States of America *and the world* under these appalling conditions. And some U.S. Congressmen were actually willing to drive this country to the precipice of disaster by making slavery a foundation principle of the first true republic in history. It is important to note that in the verse preceding God's declaration that it was He who established this Constitution by wise men whom he raised up, He states: "Therefore, it is not right that any man should be in bondage one to another."[18]

Think of the implications of this travesty. If one class of people could continue to be excluded from the civil and religious liberties protected in the Constitution, surely other classes or groups of people such as Mormons could be similarly ostracized and oppressed. Consider the horrible persecutions already inflicted with impunity upon the Latter-day Saints up to that point—not once did any level of this government come to their aid. And given the fact that President Buchanan had a large portion of the U.S Army under General Albert Sidney Johnston, camped and waiting for orders just forty miles from Salt Lake City, these proposed Constitutional amendments were a great danger to the Saints and to this nation.

18. Doctrine and Covenants 101:79

Somehow these southern elected officials had lost sight of the power and inspiration of the original Constitution where "We the people," meaning the majorities of the populace would determine their destiny through the power of the ballot box, not through powerful or wayward minorities. In this case a potent and sinister southern aristocracy, very much a minority in America, fueled by unrequited greed, wealth and ambition, was willing to jeopardize these liberties in favor of their own nearsighted economic prosperity.

The guiding and holy principles in the development of the Constitution by our Founding Fathers were eloquently expressed in the Declaration of Independence: "We hold these truths to be self-evident, that *all* men are created equal, that they are endowed *by their Creator* with certain inalienable *Rights*, that among these are *Life, Liberty and the pursuit of Happiness*" (emphasis added).

One thing was certain in the newly presumed independent state of South Carolina and the other states that would join their rebellion— they wanted no part of this Declaration of Independence. They were resolute in trashing the original Declaration of Independence and rewriting their own. In their Confederacy, all whites would be endowed with a haughty superiority to men and women of other races—especially blacks, on whose scarred backs their enormous wealth depended.

Among others, Abraham Lincoln had long lamented the sorry condition of slavery in America that stood in the face of these inalienable rights endowed to all men by their Creator. Nevertheless, he made it clear in his inaugural address that ending slavery was not his objective during this crisis, but rather saving the Constitution by preventing disunion. "I have no purpose, directly or indirectly, to interfere with the institution of slavery in the States where it exists. I believe I have no lawful right to do so, and I have no inclination to do so."[19]

This Crittenden Compromise, which may have forestalled the civil war some years, had the power to completely dismember the Constitution and the strength of this nation to uphold and defend these rights. It is a frightful thought that the halls of Congress held representatives of the people who promoted and fought for such inhumane conduct.

When the proposed pro-slavery amendments were tabled while Lincoln awaited his inauguration, we can assume he was relieved by the lack of support to move them forward. In response to this defeat, senators and representatives for the Southern states walked away from their elected offices in Washington and their solemn oaths to protect the United States Constitution and returned to Richmond, Virginia. There in the new and illegally declared capital of the Confederacy, they accepted military and political appointments for their new government, which would stand in bloody opposition to the one they had just deserted.

God's "Wrath and Indignation"

At the time of Lincoln's election, there were an estimated four million African slaves in America. Numerous times Abraham Lincoln expressed his fear that God was angry at the violent abuse of these men, women and children by slave owners and by the state and federal governments who passed bushels of grossly discriminatory laws to preserve Negro subjugation. He believed that God did not approve of wealthy merchants and slave owners—driven by greed—who had taken upon

---

19. The Eloquent President, Ronald C. White, Jr., p 81

themselves to carve up and weaken this "almost chosen nation,"[20] as Lincoln called it, by seceding from the Union for their own personal gain.

Lincoln himself believed it was Divine design that placed him at the helm of this nation at its most critical hour of civil war—an awkward, self-educated backwoodsman who possessed a singularly remarkable humility and intellect. A man whom, from his early years, appeared to be molded and prepared to become the most powerful and influential President to ever lead a nation in human history. As President, Lincoln relied on the Bible to a remarkable degree, and he repeatedly addressed the people of this nation with messages that one would expect to hear from the mouth of a prophet, not from a politician.

Referring to God, on whom Lincoln so completely relied, he said:

> I have had so many evidences of His direction, so many in-
> stances when I have been controlled by some other power
> than my own will that I cannot doubt that this power comes
> from above. I frequently see my way clear to a decision when
> I am conscious that I have not sufficient facts upon which
> to found it. But I cannot recall one instance in which I have
> followed my own judgment founded upon such a decision,
> where the results were unsatisfactory; whereas, in almost every
> instance where I have yielded to the views of others I have had
> occasion to regret it. [21]

---

20. Collected Works of Abraham Lincoln, IV, Roy Basler, p 236
21. Abraham Lincoln—Man of God, John Wesley Hill, p 124

Fort Sumter

The crisis of Fort Sumter that was before this new administration was one of many instances when, though he had listened intently to their reasoning as to why the fort should be surrendered, his prayerful impressions told him that it was not the right thing to do. It is remarkable that in the tense discussions regarding the dilemma at Fort Sumter, that Lieutenant General Winfield Scott and Lincoln's Cabinet gradually assented to his plan to send food to Major Anderson and his small force. It is also certain that they all knew the implications. The same thing that happened to the ship that President Buchannan sent a few months earlier might also occur with their ship of food being fired upon with cannon shots across the bow of the ship and forcing it to turn away. But if they did, they would be firing upon food—a very minor threat from the government, which was exactly what Lincoln wanted to portray.

They also knew that the new Confederacy might not be as reasonable this time and possibly fire directly at the ship and its crew. They knew that resupplying Fort Sumter had the potential to push the South into a declaration of war against the Union. Their hope was that the South would yield and allow Fort Sumter to remain as a rightful possession of the Union and then open negotiations to take repossession of the other forts and military installations in the southern states. Ultimately, their hope was that the rebels would come back into the Union where their differences might be resolved peacefully.

The eyes of the nation were fixed on Charleston harbor. At the height of the tension, Robert Toombs, the new Confederate Secretary of State, wrote prophetically in a letter to the new President of the Confederate States, Jefferson Davis:

> The firing on that fort will inaugurate a civil war greater than any the world has yet seen…you will lose us every friend at the North. You will wantonly strike a hornet's nest, which extends from mountain to ocean. Legions now quiet will swarm out and sting us to death. It is unnecessary. It puts us in the wrong. It is fatal.[22]

Davis would not listen to Toombs; he ordered Governor Pickens to surround Fort Sumter with some 3,000 South Carolina militiamen and cannons to await orders to fire.

Abraham Lincoln was not surprised with the new Confederacy's response. If there was to be armed conflict, Lincoln was determined that it would not be the North who would initiate the bloodshed. The secession radicals of South Carolina, in their shortsightedness, were quick to oblige. They fired upon Lincoln's supply ship as it approached Charleston harbor, forcing its retreat. Then at 4:30 am on April 12, 1861, the order was given to fire upon Ft. Sumter. The extremely thick walls of the fort repelled most of the exploding shock but hot shot from the explosions caused numerous fires inside the fort. More than 3,000 rounds of shot and shell were fired at the fort and yet remarkably no one was killed on either side. On April 14th, after a constant barrage for 33 hours, Major Anderson ordered the lowering of the American flag and surrendered the fort. Anderson's men were allowed to vacate the fort, peacefully board their vessels, and proceed northward toward their homes.

---

22. The Civil War at Charleston, p 5

The southern radicals would promptly place the blame for war on Lincoln. According to them, he should have done as Buchanan and the United States Congress had done: simply allow them to leave the Union, and with them take the Government's military installations, arsenals and other possessions within their boundaries. But the Southern States' actions made it clear to the world and to God, that the South was clearly the instigator of the war.

With the now perceived "foreigners" expelled, the new Confederate flag was raised over Fort Sumter in a hail of cheers and jubilation. The proud citizens of Charleston, South Carolina were jubilant at their affront to the United States government. The celebrations in Charleston were repeated throughout the South. What a remarkable victory they had gained against their hapless and stunned foreign neighbors to the North.

"A House Divided Against Itself Cannot Stand"

Lincoln described his awareness of the impending danger when he used a Biblical phrase to describe the tenuous situation in America: "a house divided against itself shall not stand."[23] He believed that the divisive nature of the slavery issue threatened the very existence of this nation. Sensing "something more than common"[24] for which our Founding Fathers strove, Lincoln carried the deepest conviction that this nation was formed for a wise purpose known to God and he believed that its preservation was of the utmost importance not just to the nation, but to the world and future generations of the world.

23. *Holy Bible*, Matthew 12:25
24. *Collected Works of Abraham Lincoln , IV*, Roy Basler, p 23

The Southern minority of slave owners succeeded in exposing the Constitution to aberrations that, over time, could likely have led to its eventual demise. In 1861, the U.S. Constitution was in grave danger. President Lincoln was determined to stand resolute in preserving the Union of states, believing and frequently expressing his conviction that God willed that this nation remain whole, that the civil and religious freedoms proffered in the Constitution be preserved, and that the slaves be by some means set free. The eventual abolishment of slavery and the preservation of both the Union and Constitution came at a ghastly price of death and destruction that would be unleashed upon the citizens of the United States in the form of civil war; a maelstrom that was never imagined by the promoters of secession and slavery—all of which was prophesied through Joseph Smith and recorded in Doctrine and Covenants, section 87 with remarkable detail and accuracy.

In the closing months of the war, even the southern states of Georgia, North Carolina and East Tennessee had taken formal steps to secede from the Confederacy over disagreements with their inept new government. More division was inevitable. As president, Lincoln clearly saw this danger, which explains his unbending determination to preserve the Union. Once divided and weakened, Blacks, Mormons, Catholics, the Irish (and who knows whom else) would no longer have the power of the original Constitution to protect them.

"Wo to the Rebel Hordes"

South Carolina's open aggression and violent attack of Ft. Sumter brought everything into focus. Lincoln believed that if the South Carolinians made the fatal mistake of attacking Ft. Sumter that it would reap global disdain for the South, and galvanize the Northern populace to action; he was right. To the horror of the Southern citizens, and the surprise of the instigators of rebellion, the day after the hostile taking of Ft. Sumter, Lincoln issued a proclamation declaring that the obstruction of the laws in the Southern States was the work of "combinations too powerful to be suppressed by ordinary course of judicial proceedings," and called for 75,000 volunteers to, "suppress said combinations, and to cause the laws to be duly executed."[25]

At this same time, Lincoln summoned a special session of Congress, to meet on July 4th where both of these appeals were received with euphoric enthusiasm in the Northern States. Democrats united with Republicans in their indignation over South Carolina's affront to their government by attacking Ft. Sumter and they rallied behind their new President.

Upon taking office, Lincoln discovered some additional startling and powerful combinations that included members of President Buchanan's Cabinet. Lincoln found, for example, that former Secretary of the Treasury, Phillip Thomas had all but emptied the Federal treasury with no explanation of where the millions of dollars had gone. And that Buchannan's Secretary of War John B. Floyd, a Southerner, had depleted the U.S. Army down to a paltry 17,000 active duty soldiers and that most of these had been dispersed far out west. The largest contingent of the U. S. Army was stationed in Utah, at Camp Floyd (named after Secretary Floyd) to keep an eye on the Mormons, but it also appeared that they were held in Utah to keep them inaccessible to the new Republican administration. The Navy was similarly reduced and dispersed. It is hard to imagine that President Buchanan was not aware of these treasonous acts by his administration.

25. Lincoln, David Herbert Donald, p 296

Lincoln's Northern supporters were confident that they were significantly stronger than the South. There were some 20,000,000 people in the North compared to the South's 9,000,000. The North was enormously superior to the South in manufacturing and railroad miles. Many were certain that this uprising would be over in short order. This bluster was sounded in many newspapers. The *Chicago Tribune* predicted success "within two to three months at the furthest," because, "Illinois can whip the South by herself."[26] The *New York Tribune* boasted "that Jeff. Davis & Co. will be swinging from the battlements at Washington...by the 4th of July,"[27] and the *New York Times* also predicted victory in thirty days.

President Lincoln was solemn at hearing these reports and he warned them against overconfidence. He said, "The boastful contrasts of Northern enterprise and endurance, with Southern laziness and high mindedness" were rash miscalculations. He reminded them that the Northerners and Southerners all came from the same stock and had "essentially the same characteristics and powers. Man for man the soldier from the South will be a match for the soldier from the North and vice versa. "[28]

The Northern States leaders promptly appealed for volunteers, and young men eagerly stepped forward, anxious for the excitement of soldiering and reclaiming their broken Union. In a letter to President Lincoln, Renewick Dickerson of New Hampshire wrote, "I have but one son of seventeen Summers [sic], he is our only child, a man of stature— We are ready to volunteer, to fight for the integrity of the Union."[29] Another young volunteer wrote, "Woe to the rebel hordes that meets

---

26. David Herbert Donald Lincoln, Touchstone, New York, 1995, p 295

27. Ibid., p 295

28. David Herbert Donald Lincoln, Touchstone, New York, 1995, p 295

29. Ibid., p 297

them in battle array. We are wound up to the very pinnacle of patriotic ardor."[30] From the West, Governor O.P. Morgan, of Indiana, pledged 10,000 men "for the defense of the Nation and to uphold the authority of the Government."[31]

It was a different story in the upper Southern States as they showed little support, even though they were still part of the Union. The governor of North Carolina wrote the President: "I can be no party to this wicked violation of the laws of the country, and to this war upon the liberties of a free people. You can get no troops from North Carolina!"[32] The governors of Virginia, Tennessee, and Arkansas shared the same sentiment and all four promptly withdrew from the Union. Within a couple of weeks they joined the rebellion.

---

30. Ibid., p 297
31. Ibid., p 297
32. Ibid., p 297

3

Flee to the West

B EFORE THE RESTORED Church had even reached its one-year mark since its April 6, 1830 organization, God revealed to Joseph Smith that dangers lay ahead for the faithful new converts. On February 9, 1831 the Lord revealed that events unnamed in their future would necessitate their flight to the west for their safety.

> And even now, let him that goeth to the east teach them that shall be converted to flee to the west, and this in consequence of that which is coming to the earth, and of secret combinations.[1]

Secret combinations is a phrase that God has used throughout scriptures, Pearl of Great Price, the Book of Mormon and now in the Latter-days, in the Doctrine and Covenants. Secret combinations, or clandestine organizations with evil designs, all the work of the Adversary, have always been present to fight against God's holy works here on the earth.

> And whatsoever nation shall uphold such secret combinations, to get power and gain, until they shall spread over the nation, behold, they shall be destroyed...[2]

---

1. Doctrine and Covenants 42:64
2. Book of Mormon, Ether 8:22

Combinations

It is interesting that President Lincoln, in his first address to Congress in July of 1861, also referred to the evil designs of the Southern slave holders of South Carolina as *combinations.*

The following month, the Lord again issued a warning and a renewed call to flee to the west, revealing the danger that he had been foretelling. On March 7, 1831 the Prophet Joseph Smith received this disquieting revelation:

> For verily I say unto you, great things await you;
>
> Ye hear of wars in foreign lands; but, behold, I say unto you, they are nigh, even at your doors, and not many years hence ye shall hear of wars in your own land.
>
> Wherefore I, the Lord, have said, gather ye out from the eastern lands, assemble ye yourselves together ye elders of my church; go ye forth into the western countries...[3]

A third warning to flee was issued by the Lord three months later. In D&C 54:7 the Lord, through Joseph Smith said, "Wherefore, go to now and flee the land, lest your enemies come upon you..." Eighteen months later the prophet learned in revelation on Christmas day of 1832, that war would come to this favored land beginning with the rebellion of South Carolina. The other southern states would also separate from the Union in rebellion to the Constitutional government that God had gifted to this nation.

---

3. Doctrine and Covenants 45:62

Gather to the West

Through subsequent revelations Joseph Smith announced that God had revealed the new gathering place for his growing flock of believers to be in the western boundary of the United States, at that time near Independence, Missouri. In the summer of 1831, by commandment from God, Joseph led a group of twenty-eight Latter-day Saints from Kirtland, Ohio to Jackson County, Missouri. At Independence, after surveying the area and selecting a parcel of land upon which to build their temple, Joseph Smith held a public meeting that was attended by local settlers, some Indians and a few free Negroes. The local settlers were curious as to why the notorious Mormon Prophet would be in their remote location of the frontier and they came from miles around to see and hear him. In his address, he shared the gospel message, their plans to settle the area and their hope that they could live in peace with the Missouri settlers.

Before returning to Ohio, Joseph appointed a few from his travel-ing party to remain, one to open a store and serve as an agent for the Church to receive funds for land purchases in preparation for arrival of more saints. Another was appointed to establish a printing office. The Mormons had already encountered trouble with the local residents in New York and Ohio and Joseph hoped that a newspaper would help in the transition for the old settlers (as the locals would soon refer to themselves to distinguish them from the Mormon settlers) in Missouri. Although some locals in the area were not troubled at the arrival of the Mormons; others were suspicious of their religion and intentions.

While mostly peaceable, the Mormons were immediately different from the locals in Missouri. Mormon historian, B.H. Roberts wrote,

> The Saints could not join the Missourians in their way of life—in Sabbath-breaking, profanity, horse-racing, idleness, drunkenness, and debauchery... The local pro-slavery settlers were more than alarmed to know that these saints were coming ...from the Northern and New England States, and the hatred that existed at that time between the people of the slave-holding and free states, was manifested toward the saints by their "southern" neighbors.[4]

Neither is it surprising that the Mormons' assertion that God had led them to Jackson County, a place of inheritance for them, which did not set well with the old settlers. Trouble was imminent. The mushrooming number of new Mormon converts and the phenomena of their willingness to leave their homes and farms in the eastern states to unite with the other saints in Missouri created an unprecedented sociological, political and religious dilemma between the Mormons and Missourians. Within a year, some 800 faithful saints arrived in and around Independence, overwhelming most of the old settlers. Another 400 came the following year.

Persecution

By the spring of 1832, signs of the approaching storm appeared with rocks being thrown at few Mormon homes, frightening the families inside. In the fall of that same year a number of Mormon-owned haystacks were burned and bullets fired at some of their homes. About this same time, the Reverend Finis Ewing, head of the Independence Presby-

4. B. H. Roberts, *The Missouri Persecutions,* Bookcraft, Salt Lake City, 1965, p. 72

terian church, published the following statement: "The 'Mormons' are the common enemies of mankind and ought to be destroyed."[5] One of the local ministers, Reverend Pixley went house to house encouraging a general uprising against the alarming numbers of Mormons in the area.

In April 1833, some four hundred old settlers assembled in Independence, Missouri, to address the Mormon problem but they could not agree on a plan of action. Later in July yet another secret combination circulated, which the old settlers called their "Secret Constitution,"[6] delineating the grievances against the Mormons and "binding all who signed it to assist in 'removing the Mormons.'"[7] The document declared that the Mormons were idle, lazy, and vicious, and that they claim to receive revelations directly from God—to heal the sick by the laying on of hands, to speak in unknown tongues and perform all "the wonder-working miracles wrought by the inspired apostles and prophets of God."[8]

Their Secret Constitution went on to say that these practices were "derogatory of God and religion, and subversive of human reason."[9] Their anti-slavery sentiments and their affinity toward the Indians were also cited as reasons to remove them from Missouri. In their resolution they pledged to rid their country of the Mormons "peaceably if they could, forcibly if they must."[10] Their eradication efforts would take on the tenor of a holy crusade to clear their communities of the religious practices of these newcomers. This animosity and threats, real and imagined, all ran contrary to the sacred United States Constitution, which

---

5. B. H. Roberts, *The Missouri Persecutions,* Bookcraft, Salt Lake City, 1965, p. 73

6. Ibid., p. 74

7. Ibid., p. 74

8. B. H. Roberts, *The Missouri Persecutions,* Bookcraft, Salt Lake City, 1965, p. 72

9. Ibid., p. 74

10. Ibid., p. 74

was supposed to protect these Latter-day Saints and their civil and religious rights as citizens.

In early November, some five hundred armed and angry men began systematic attacks on the Missouri Mormon settlements and in the process, expelled more than 1,200 Mormon men, women, and children from their homes, sending them scattering into the cold winter elements. Desperate to defend their homes and families, a group of armed Mormon men banded together and skirmishes ensued in which two old settlers and one Mormon were killed, with one other Mormon seriously wounded.

The mob destroyed the printing press and home of W.W. Phelps and the Mormon mercantile establishment of Whitney & Gilbert. Terrified women and children were seen everywhere running to the woods for safety, some returning to find home and possessions burned to the ground. When news of the cruel and unlawful expulsion of the Mormons reached neighboring states, some sided with the old settlers. Lincoln's local newspaper in Springfield, Illinois had this to say about their violent expulsion.

Sangamo Journal.

Vol. II.   Springfield, Illinois, Sat., Dec 7, 1833   No. 106.

Straightway came the Mormons, headed by a fanatic, who is a disgrace to the creation of God. In their doctrine, they [claimed] as an inheritance the whole of Jackson County. By fraudulent and false statements, they were gathering together the scum of the earth—were offering inducements to the free negroes, everywhere to come up and join them, and had succeeded in alienating many of the Indians who surrounded them. That the people, among whom they had settled, should feel disposed to rid themselves of such a pest, we think is extremely natural; and that they would have fared better, in any other country, we are very much disposed to doubt.

The homeless Mormons who wandered south into Van Buren (later named Cass County) were quickly run off. The bulk of the Mormons were literally driven north. "Keziah Higbee, in the most delicate condition, lay on the banks of the river all night, while the rain descended in torrents, and under these circumstances was delivered of a male child; but the mother died a premature death through the exposure."[11] B. H. Roberts, in his book *The Missouri Persecutions*, wrote of the extreme conditions of the saints:

> All through this day and the day following (the 6th and 7th of November,) women and children were fleeing in every direction from the presence of the merciless mob. One company of one hundred and ninety—all women and children, except three decrepit old men—were driven thirty miles across a burnt prairie. The ground was thinly crusted with sleet, and the trail of these exiles was easily followed by the blood which flowed from their lacerated feet! This company and others who joined them erected some log cabins for temporary shelter and not knowing the limits of Jackson County, built them within the borders thereof. Subsequently in the month of January 1834, parties of the mob again drove these people into Clay County, and burned their wretched cabins, leaving them to wander without shelter in the most severe winter months. Many of them were taken suddenly ill and died.[12]

---

11. B. H. Roberts, *The Missouri Persecutions*, Bookcraft, Salt Lake City, 1965, p. 108

12. B.H. Roberts, *The Missouri Persecutions*, (Salt Lake City, UT: Bookcraft, 1965), p. 107.

God calls for Justice

When word of the suffering of the Jackson County saints reached Joseph Smith in Kirtland, Ohio, it was reported that he was overcome with grief and burst into tears. In response to this unjust and unlawful religious persecution, God commanded Joseph in D&C Section 101, to appeal to the judge for justice and redress of their losses in farms homes and livestock.

> And if he heed them not, let them importune at the feet of the governor;
>
> And if the governor heed them not, let them importune at the feet of the president;
>
> And if the president heed them not, then will the Lord arise and come forth out of his hiding place, and in his fury vex the nation;
>
> And in his hot displeasure, and in his fierce anger, and in his time, will cut off those wicked, unfaithful, and unjust stewards, and appoint them their portion among hypocrites, and unbelievers.
>
> Even in outer darkness...[13]

Joseph obeyed this commandment immediately and completely. He prepared a petition to Governor Daniel Dunklin of Missouri asking that he authorize a state militia to protect and aid the 1,200 freezing, and homeless Latter-day Saints in their return to their homes. The exiled Mormon leaders living in Missouri did the same, but their petition in-

---

13. Doctrine and Covenants 101: 84-90

cluded specifics of the forced illegal eviction from their homes and property, detailing their losses and the names of many of the perpetrators.

Governor Dunklin responded that without permission from Washington, the laws of his state did not authorize him to form a military force to protect them and that he could do nothing for them. He also expressed fear that the presence of a Mormon-protecting militia in Jackson County would incite a war. At this news, Joseph Smith, following God's commandment, petitioned the President of the United States, Andrew Jackson. His administration responded by saying that the President could not call out a military force to aid in the execution of the State laws, unless requested by constituted state authorities, implying a possible willingness to respond.

With this new information from President Jackson, the Mormons pled again with Governor Dunklin to make the requisition to Washington. But no appeal for federal help was ever issued by the state of Missouri. Instead Dunklin passed the problem to his legislature, ordering that a special committee be organized to investigate the matter. At this, the Mormons submitted their detailed petition to the state legislature, again imploring them for help in returning safely to their homes and to end their winter homelessness and suffering in Clay County. Remarkably, neither the judges, or the governor, nor the president did anything to help. While the homeless saints languished the remaining winter months in temporary shelters, God's promise to vex this nation "in his hot displeasure, and in his fierce anger, and in his time,"[14] loomed ominously over the United States.

14. Doctrine and Covenants 101: 89, 90

Rescue Mission

Soon after, the Prophet Joseph received a revelation that a body of at least 100 men was to be assembled to go to Jackson County to sue for relief of the oppressed saints there and do all that was peaceably possible to return them to their homes in Jackson County. This he did also. He sent envoys to Governor Daniel Dunklin to inform him of the impending arrival of the 200–strong Zion's Camp, into his state and of their peaceful intentions to succor their struggling fellow saints. Again he asked the governor if he and his government intended to help restore Mormon citizens to their deeded properties. They had pinned their hopes on Governor Dunklin's intercession and in this they were deeply disappointed. After receiving Governor Dunklin's reply and in complete obedience to God's command, they continued a cautious march toward Jackson County.

As they neared their destination and while camped at Fishing River, Joseph expressed to some that he had a premonition of danger. Shortly thereafter, five men rode into the camp cursing and exclaiming that the Mormons would see hell by morning, because at that moment some 200 men from several counties were in the process of crossing the Missouri to destroy them.[15]

As this was happening, a large black cloud formed in the west and quickly moved eastward soon becoming a violent storm that nearly prevented the return of the ferry that had just carried its first group of Missouri militiamen across the river. The storm's intensity caused Zion's Camp to abandon their tents and run for shelter in a nearby Baptist church. Wilford Woodruff recorded this incident in his journal where he noted that once inside the church Joseph Smith exclaimed, "Boys,

15. B. H. Roberts, *The Missouri Persecutions*, Bookcraft, Salt Lake City, 1965, p. 140

there is some meaning to this. God is in this storm."[16] Fierce winds and terrifying claps of thunder filled the night making it impossible for anyone to sleep, so the group sang hymns and waited out the storm on the church pews. For the Missourians, the storm thwarted their river crossing, soaked their ammunition and scattered their horses as the men ran for shelter.

In the end there was no battle, no killing, and no resolution for the saints. Bewildered by the burned out Mormon homes, Joseph and his Zion's Camp members met and worshipped in somber disillusionment with the displaced saints in Clay County, and then resolved to return to Ohio. Aside from the strong message of support for their oppressed brethren in Missouri and a strengthened solidarity among most of the Zion's Camp members, the endeavor ended in disappointment for the Mormons, a triumph for the Missouri persecutors.

Mercy in Clay County

The citizens of Clay County Missouri were magnanimous in their newfound role of receiving the 1,200 cold, homeless Mormons who fled north to their county from neighboring Jackson County. They did what they could to provide sustenance and shelter during the winter months for the destitute Mormon families. But as the months rolled on they too, began to worry over the Mormons' vast numbers and the social, religious and political challenges they brought with them.

Eventually, the locals began to speak against the Mormons settling in their county. A meeting was held in which tempers flared as a Jackson County representative, Samuel Owens, warned the assembly against sending them back to his county, swearing that he and his fellow In-

---

16. B. H. Roberts, History of the Church, (Salt Lake City, UT: Deseret News, 1968), vol. 2, p.104.

dependence residents were willing to fight to retain every inch of the Mormons' Jackson County property. At the same meeting, a Baptist minister declared that the Mormons had been in Clay County long enough and they must clear out or be cleared out. The moderator of the meeting, Mr. Turnham responded by saying, "Let us be republicans; let us honor our country, and not disgrace it like Jackson County. For God's sake don't disfranchise or drive away the Mormons. They are better citizens than many of the old inhabitants."[17]

After the Mormon hot potato was tossed from Governor Dunklin back to the local courts, Joseph Smith and other Mormon leaders called again upon a fair-minded Jackson County lawyer to represent them again in the local courts. Young Alexander Doniphan accepted their case. He was incensed over the actions of his Jackson County neighbors toward the Mormons and was one of the few unafraid to express it. Some months later, Doniphan, who served in the Missouri General Assembly, proposed a plan for a peaceful solution to the Mormon problem in Clay County. He sponsored a bill that called for the creation of two new Missouri counties, Daviess and Caldwell in the northern, sparsely populated part of the state, one of which he proposed to be a settlement location for the Mormons.

The General Assembly recognized the advisability of Doniphan's solution and passed the bill designating Caldwell County for exclusive occupation by the Mormons and as a general recompense for their losses in Jackson County. The Mormons were pleased with the General Assembly's reasonable location to settle, but disappointed that once again, they would have to relocate and start over. Heartened by finally having a sanctioned settlement where they might finally feel included as citizens,

17. B. H. Roberts, *The Missouri Persecutions,* Bookcraft, Salt Lake City, 1965, pp. 97–98.

they accepted the solution. Within a year the new Mormon town of Far West became one of the largest communities in the state. Within two years the open prairie of Caldwell County became a bustling Mormon city of some 5,000 residents with two hotels, a printing office, blacksmith shops, stores and some 150 hastily constructed homes.

During the next five years, Joseph Smith attended to the many matters that that fell upon the Lord's Prophet of the Restoration—the completion of the Kirtland Temple, the calling of missionaries, the continual arrival of new converts and their resettlement in the Kirtland and Missouri areas, the translation of the Bible and the Pearl of Great Price, responding to the continual stream of divine instruction from the Lord in establishing his Church, the Law of Consecration, the forced exodus from Kirtland to Missouri, his false imprisonment in Liberty jail, and the much greater expulsion of some 15,000 Latter-day Saints from Far West, Missouri, to Commerce, Illinois. Yet through all of this Joseph did not forget the 1833 commandment to appeal for redress up to the highest levels of this government for injustices against faithful Mormons.

The Prophet Now in Missouri

In 1838, apostate Mormons, angry with Joseph Smith for the financial collapse, (resulting mostly from the nationwide panic of 1837 which brought economic reversals throughout the entire country), along with anti-Mormon Ohioans, forced Joseph Smith, the general church leadership and the rest of the Mormon faithful to flee Ohio for their lives. Hoping to find a safer environment in Caldwell County, Missouri, they were sorely disappointed. The arrival of the infamous Mormon Church President and hundreds more of his followers only heightened the alarm of the Missourians. And when the Ohio Mormons joined up with the saints in Far West, the new headquarters for the church, it only aggravated the sentiments of the local inhabitants. Joseph Smith lamented on 12 March 1839:

> With my family I arrived at Far West, Caldwell County, after a journey of one thousand miles…enduring great affliction. Soon after my arrival at this place, I was informed that a number of men living in Daviess county had offered the sum of one thousand dollars for my scalp; persons to whom I was an entire stranger, and of whom I had no knowledge. In order to attain their end, the roads were frequently waylaid for me. At one time in particular, when watering my horse on Shoal Creek, I distinctly heard three or four guns snap at me. In consequence of such threats and abuse…my family were kept in a constant state of alarm, not knowing any morning what would befall me from day to day…[18]

On July 4th, 1838, the local militia made up of Caldwell County Mormons and a small group of Latter-day Saints marched around the Liberty pole in Far West for an Independence Day celebration. Sidney Rigdon, Joseph Smith's first counselor, gave a speech recounting the persecutions they had endured to that point. Then, apparently emboldened by the presence of the Church leadership now in Missouri and with the flight from Ohio fresh on their memories, he passionately declared that

18. B.H. Roberts, *History of the Church*, (Salt Lake City: Deseret Book, 1974). vol. 3, pp. 368-369.

the Latter-day Saints would no longer be driven from their homes by persecution from without or dissension from within. He exclaimed,

> And that mob that comes on us to disturb us, it shall be be-
> tween us and them a war of extermination; for we will follow
> them until the last drop of their blood is spilled; or else they
> will have to exterminate us, for we will carry the seat of war to
> their own houses and their own families, and one party or the
> other shall be utterly destroyed...[19]

Rigdon's defiance was published in a pamphlet that gave heart to the Mormons. But his warning of a war of extermination served to further inflame the resolve of the old settlers that the Mormons, in their large numbers, were now a dangerous element and needed to be driven out once again.

As the year went on, conditions worsened. In September, upon hear-ing that the saints in DeWitt County were being harassed by a mob, President Smith rushed to their aid. He wrote,

> I arrived there...and found the account which I heard was
> correct. Our people were surrounded by a mob, and their pro-
> visions nearly exhausted.

> Being now almost destitute of provisions, and having suffered
> great distress, and some of the brethren having died in conse-
> quence of their privations and suffering—I had then the pain
> of beholding some of my fellow-creatures perish in a strange
> land, from the cruelty of a mob—and seeing no prospect of
> relief, the brethren agreed to leave that place and seek shelter

19. "Oration Delivered by Mr. S. Rigdon on the 4th of July, 1838," (Far West, Caldwell County, MO: Printed at the Journal Office, 1838), www.sidneyrigdon.com/rigd1838.htm.

elsewhere, after having their homes burnt down, their cattle driven away, and much of their property destroyed. In our journey several of our friends died and had to be interred without a coffin, and under such circumstances, this was extremely distressing.[20]

Importune to Judges and Governors

Joseph Smith appealed to Governor Boggs for protection to which the governor replied that the quarrel was between the Mormons and the mob and that they might fight it out. It will be remembered that in 1834, Lilburn W. Boggs was the Lieutenant governor of Missouri who was reported to have been present, condoning the original expulsion of the Mormons from Jackson County Missouri. He was elected governor of Missouri of 1836 and found that his temporary solution of removing the Mormons from Jackson County would only grow to much larger proportions in the more northern counties of his state. But again, as their numbers multiplied, so did non-Mormon settlers in Caldwell and surrounding counties, resulting in mounting tension between the groups.

Again it was clear that the Mormons could appeal to no one for intervention and safety. With winter approaching, another forced expulsion was becoming more and more imminent. After passively leaving Jackson County, Clay County, Ohio and New York, with only minimal resistance, Joseph Smith alerted his followers that this time they would need to defend themselves and their homes. Soon after, the Caldwell County militia led by Col. George Hinkle, a trusted Mormon and the militiamen made up of mostly Mormon residents, sallied out to con-

---

20. B.H. Roberts, *History of the Church*, (Salt Lake City, UT: Deseret Book, 1967), vol. 3, p. 369.

front the growing number of threatening bands of Missourians. The Missourians eluded the Caldwell County militia and no battle took place but the Mormons responded by burning some buildings in the Gallatin area hoping it would discourage any further oppression. It didn't. Word of the burnings served as justification for more dramatic action by Governor Boggs.

The Northern Missouri troubles escalated to such a degree that the Governor ordered militias to be mustered to the area from neighboring counties. Many of these militia members had only expulsion and violence on their minds, which increased the fear of more aggression for the Latter-day Saints. When word that three Mormon men were taken from their home as prisoners, Col. Hinkle was ordered by Judge Elias Higbee to pursue and recover the prisoners.

The next morning, October 25th, a battle commenced in which three Mormons were killed, including the highly respected Apostle David W. Patton. One Missouri militiaman was also killed with some others on both sides wounded. A frantic and exaggerated message was rushed to Governor Boggs that some sixty Missouri militiamen had been slaughtered in the battle and dozens others taken prisoner along with a report the Mormons were on their way to the town of Richmond with the intent to sack and burn it. The casualty report was greatly exaggerated; no prisoners were taken and no Mormon assault on Richmond took place.

Extermination

Shortly after this report was made to Governor Boggs, he issued an executive order calling for the removal or extermination of the Mormons from Missouri. Issued on October 27, 1838, his order stated that due to,

> Open and avowed defiance of the law, and of having made war upon the people of this State...the Mormons must be treated as enemies, and must be exterminated or driven from the State if necessary for the public peace—their outrages are beyond all description.[21]

It is difficult to imagine such a scene on American soil. Having already been thrice (including the Ohio expulsion) driven from their homes, the Mormons keenly felt the danger of yet another forced eviction. Those assembling at Far West were soon confronted with an estimated 2,000 militia men ordered to Northern Missouri by Governor Boggs, many of them incited with his executive order to drive them out or exterminate them. It was a condition that is nearly beyond comprehension today and one that shocked Americans throughout the country.

Col. Hinkle secretly negotiated a peace settlement with Colonel Lucas of the Missouri Militia, which included the surrender of church leaders to the custody of Colonel Lucas. Hinkle believed he was following instructions and saving the Latter-day Saints from being massacred but most Mormons viewed Hinkle's action as treacherous and deceitful and they excommunicated him from the Church the following spring.

Joseph Smith and four of his trusted associates, including his brother Hyrum, were unwittingly enticed to participate in the negotiation meeting with the Colonel Lucas. Upon their arrival, they were promptly arrested and taken into custody. That night Colonel Lucas held an illegal court martial of Joseph Smith and his captured companions (military leaders cannot legally try citizens) and ordered their execution in the

---

21. "Missouri Executive Order Number 44," www.quaqua.org/extermination.htm.

town square of Far West for the following day. Fortunately for Joseph and his friends, Lucas gave the execution order to Alexander Doniphan who led a militia group under his command.

Again Colonel Doniphan would come to the aid of the Mormons by flatly refusing to obey the order and decrying its illegal nature, exclaiming that he would defend the prisoners with his own life until proper legal proceedings could take place. Doniphan's resistance must have weakened Col. Lucas' resolve because he rescinded the execution order and ordered their incarceration in Richmond to await a hearing. Joseph and his fellow prisoners identified forty men in Far West to testify in their behalf. A local minister and ardent persecutor of the saints rode to Far West with fifty men and escorted the witnesses to Richmond, then promptly had them all arrested, preventing them from testifying. Doniphan was so enraged that he stood and exclaimed:

> It is a dammed shame to treat these defendants in this manner.
> They are not allowed to put one witness on the stand; while
> the witnesses they have sent for have been captured by force
> of arms and thrust in the 'bull pen' to prevent their testifying.[22]

A month later after an irregular court of inquiry in Richmond, Joseph Smith and his group were imprisoned in the jail at Liberty, Missouri, where they languished in cold and unsanitary conditions for four months while prosecutors searched unsuccessfully for evidence to try them on charges of treason and murder. Fully aware that many in Missouri sought to take his life he wrote to his wife Emma saying, "If I do not meet you again in this life may God grant that we may meet in

---

22. B.H. Roberts, *The Missouri Persecutions*, (Salt Lake City, UT: Bookcraft, 1965), p. 259.

heaven, I cannot express my feelings, my heart is full, Farewell Oh my kind and affectionate Emma. I am yours forever."[23]

With the Mormon leaders' capture, and on the strength of Governor Boggs' order to drive them from the state, militiamen laid the town of Far West to ruin and routed the Mormons once again from their homes, farms and businesses, some ten thousand of them living in a four county area in the dead of winter—homes burned, livestock shot, men murdered, and a number of young Mormon women raped, some to the point of death, and again, not one man prosecuted for the crimes.

It was a condition that is nearly beyond comprehension today and one that shocked Americans throughout the country as these events in Missouri were chronicled in local newspaper accounts across the nation.

---

23. Carol Cornwall Madsen, "My Dear and Beloved Companion: The Letters of Joseph and Emma Smith," *Ensign*, Sept. 2008.

4

The Broken Constitution

W ITH THEIR PROPHET incarcerated in Liberty jail, the beleaguered saints made their way east, crossing the frozen Mississippi River into Illinois. Again it was the remarkable citizens of Quincy,
Illinois, like the people of Clay County, Missouri, who opened their
arms to them, offering shelter, food and clothing through the winter of
1839. Their compassion was an epic example of human goodness. Early
that winter the Quincy residents looked across the wide Mississippi at
a mass of people assembling on the other side and wondered why they
were out in the cold at the river's edge.

When Mayor John Wood learned these families had been driven
from their homes and had no recourse than to cross in to Illinois, he rallied his remarkable citizens to come to their rescue. In the coming days
some 10,000 homeless, cold and hungry Latter-day Saints converged
upon the town of 1,600 in Quincy. Nearly every home in Quincy was
opened to the desperate Latter-day Saints; some Quincy families vacated their own homes and turned them over to the Mormons. That

winter the refugees were fed, sheltered and warmed by the extraordinary people of Quincy.[1]

Later that spring, Joseph and the other Liberty jail prisoners were allowed to escape since the state of Missouri was unsuccessful in conjuring up charges against them. He was joyfully received by the saints in Quincy and immediately set about finding a new settlement location. They selected the village of Commerce, 47 miles north of Quincy on the Mississippi River. That summer was a flurry of activity, draining the swamp near the water's edge, planting crops, building homes, receiving an ever increasing number of new converts and building a Temple. With all of these critical tasks before him, Joseph knew that he had other unfinished business that required his attention.

Importune at the Feet of the President

The commandment of the Lord regarding retribution for the persecution of his saints had to again be addressed. Joseph could appeal no further to any judges or governors that would offer justice for the murders, rapes, plunder, and massive property losses in Missouri. The denial of their Constitutional right to worship as they chose was also an injustice that could not be ignored. In this, the fourth major Mormon expulsion in just a seven-year span, Joseph was constrained with impressions that he must make yet another appeal for redress to the President of the United States; this time he would do it in person. So in late October 1839, delegating a myriad of duties in Nauvoo to his Apostles, he, along with Orrin Porter Rockwell, Dr. Robert Foster and Elias Higbee,

---

1. Susan Easton Black, General Editor, *The Quincy Miracle, A Rescue Never to Be Forgotten,* History of the Saints Inc., Sandy, Utah, 2016, pp. 93-99

struck for Washington City in a two-horse buggy "to importune at the feet"[2] of President Martin Van Buren.

Their journey from Nauvoo took them through Springfield, Illinois, placing the future American President Lincoln and the Mormon Prophet in the same small town for four days. Joseph's journal indicates he "preached several times while there."[3] The infamous Prophet's four days in Springfield and the nearly 150 members of the Springfield LDS Branch who gathered to see him, could not have gone unnoticed by the locals. Did Lincoln have enough curiosity to listen to any of Joseph Smith's Springfield sermons? This would have been a unique opportunity for Lincoln, the Whig party floor leader in the Illinois State legislature to better understand the Mormon leader from both a religious and political view.

Just a few months earlier, Lincoln would probably have read the *Sangomo Journal's* account of Joseph Smith's escape from Missouri and his arrival in his state. A number of other newspaper articles that followed had chronicled his actions and those of the newly arrived Illinois Mormons. The Springfield sermons would have interested the serious searchers and the curious. Surely the political and religious issues of the Mormons would have been a topic of conversation by the soon to be engaged Abraham and Mary Todd. There is no record of Lincoln meeting Joseph Smith or of attending his sermons and conversely, there is no record that he did not attend; we are left to wonder.[4]

---

2. Doctrine and Covenants 101:88

3. B.H. Roberts, *History of the Church*, (Salt Lake City, UT: Deseret Book, 1974), vol. 4, p. 20.

4. Ron L. Andersen, *Abraham Lincoln and Joseph Smith, How Two Contemporaries Changed the Face of American History*, Plain Sight Publishing, an imprint of Cedar Fort Publishing Inc., Springville, Utah, 2014, p.145

Records do show that in the days just prior to Joseph Smith's arrival, Lincoln was out of Springfield tending to legal matters in the towns of Clinton and Decatur but that he returned on November 2nd to see his law partner, John Todd Stuart off for Washington City to begin his newly elected term as an Illinois Congressman. Stuart's cousin, Mary Todd, would certainly have been at his Washington sendoff as well. On that date, noting his partner's departure for Washington, Lincoln good naturedly made the following entry in the Stuart & Lincoln fee book, "Commencement of Lincoln's Administration."[5]

During Joseph Smith's days in Springfield, court records show that Lincoln was very busy in legal and political matters in his first days as a law firm of one, and this likely consumed much of his attention. Lincoln, who was now in his third term in the Illinois legislature, was certainly aware of the dramatic political implications that the Mormons brought with them. The Mormon immigration was debated in the Illinois statehouse with a generally compassionate slant from both sides of the aisle. They, like most in America were appalled by the harsh violation of the civil and religious rights of the Mormons while in Missouri, now refugees in their state.

With Joseph Smith arriving in Springfield on November 4th, this meant that again, Lincoln missed an almost certain opportunity to meet the Mormon Prophet; this time by just two days. Joseph would have been aware of John Todd Stuart's successful election to Congress just a few weeks earlier. His purpose for remaining in Springfield for those four days was to personally consult with political leaders in the State Capital. He undoubtedly would have sought out the Stuart & Lincoln Law office to plead his case with the new Congressman had Stuart still

5. Ibid p.145

been in town. Joseph was probably disappointed to hear that the new Congressman was just two days ahead of him in their joint yet separate journeys to Washington City.

Joseph Smith and Elias Higbee arrived in Washington on November 28, 1839, the other two having to abandon the trek due to illness. It was an arduous month-long journey through cold and inclement weather. In obedience to God's command to importune for justice, they carried 491 personal claims for redress; itemized accounts of Missouri losses by members of the Church and a petition to the Senate and House of Representatives detailing the events that led to their expulsion from Missouri. In it he concludes, "For ourselves we see no redress, unless it is awarded by the Congress of the United States. And here we make our appeal as American Citizens, as Christians, and as Men."[6] The following day Joseph recorded that,

> We proceeded to the house of the President [The White House]. We found a very large and splendid palace, surrounded with a splendid enclosure, decorated with all the fineries and elegancies of the world. We went to the door and requested to see the President, when we were immediately introduced into an upper apartment, where we met the President, and were introduced into his parlor, where we presented him our letters of introduction. As soon as he read one of them, he looked upon us with a kind of half frown, and said,

---

6. Ibid p.147

"What can I do? I can do nothing for you! If I do anything, I shall come in contact with the whole state of Missouri."[7]

But we were not to be intimidated; and demanded a hearing, and constitutional rights. Before we left him he promised to reconsider what he said, and [we] observed that he felt to sympathize with us, on account of our suffering. [8]

In their discussion, President Van Buren enquired into how their religion differed from other religions of the day. To which "Brother Joseph said we differed in the mode of baptism and the Gift of the Holy Ghost by the laying on of hands."[9]

The following days were spent in "hunting up the Representatives in order to get our case brought before the House..."[10] They succeeded in holding a meeting with the Illinois delegation, which included Lincoln's law partner, John Todd Stuart. In a letter to his brother, Hyrum, Joseph wrote that, "The gentlemen from Illinois are worthy men, and have treated us with great kindness, and are ready to do all in their power..."[11] This Illinois delegation agreed to take their petition forward to the Senate for referral to a proper committee.

While in Washington, Joseph took opportunity to preach his gospel message; one such discourse was described by Matthew Davis in a letter to his wife Mary:

I went last evening to hear "Joe Smith," the celebrated Mormon, expound his doctrine... Everything he says, is said in a

7. Ibid p 148
8. Ibid p.148
9. Ibid p.148
10. Ibid p.148
11. Ibid p.148

manner to leave that impression that he is sincere... Throughout his whole address he displayed strongly a spirit of charity
and forbearance... I have changed my opinion of the Mormons... They are an injured and much-abused people.[12]

Joseph Smith continued to importune through letters to the State
legislature back in Illinois to which State Senator Adams responded by
saying,

I had the gratification of the receipt of yours of the 16th of
December... I also saw yours of the 19th December to Mr.
Weber. We are now consulting and feeling the pulsations relative to your case being brought before the legislature, now in
session, by a series of resolutions, instructing our senators, and
requesting our representatives to argue relief in your case.[13]

Never before had the Mormon Prophet received such fair-minded
political support as that which he was receiving from the Illinois delegation in Washington and from the Illinois State Legislature of which
Lincoln was a part. Joseph was heartened by their sincere and fair
representation.

However as time went by, the alarm heightened with the ever-in-
creasing number of Mormons arriving in Illinois, caused the initial tide
of compassion to wane as witnessed by Illinois State legislator John
B. Weber, who upon receiving Smith's appeal, responded that he had,
"called upon many prominent members of the Democratic party all
of whom expressed a willingness to aid in bringing about justice. But

---

12. Ibid p.148,49
13. Ibid p.149

I regret to inform you that but few have exhibited the energy…which might reasonably be expected from all lovers of liberty…"[14]

While in Washington, Joseph also met with the pro-slavery champion and former vice president, Senator John C. Calhoun from South Carolina. His response towards him was sympathetic yet hollow as well. After several discouraging weeks in Washington, Joseph Smith was successful in gaining one final audience with President Van Buren, "who treated me very insolently, and it was with great reluctance he listened to our message, which, when he had heard, he said, 'Gentlemen your cause is just, but I can do nothing for you;' and 'If I take up for you I shall lose the vote of Missouri.'"[15] It was a fateful moment in the eternities when the Prophet of the Restoration, like Abinadi, stood before the President, the principle steward of the sacred Constitution, and in the name of God, importuned that the "just and holy principles"[16] of God's Constitution be honored and that His saints be recompensed of the wrongs committed against them. The President of the United States rejected the Prophet, and now the vexing judgments of God awaited this condemned nation.

After these interviews Joseph recorded, "I became satisfied there was little use for me to tarry, to press the just claims of the Saints on the consideration of the President or Congress…"[17] Soon after this he left for Illinois, leaving Elias Higbee in Washington to continue their pursuit of justice with the president and Congress. A few sparsely attended committee hearings followed in which the Mormon's plight was heard. Missouri's position was skillfully defended by the powerful Missouri

---

14. B. H. Roberts, *History of the Church*, Salt Lake City, 1976, vol. 4 p. 78

15. Ibid p. 80.

16. .Doctrine and Covenants 101:77

17. B. H. Roberts, *History of the Church*, Salt Lake City, 1976, vol. 4 p. 80

Senator Thomas Hart Benton. Joseph Smith would later condemn him for arguments against the Mormons' appeal for justice. On February 26th, 1840, Higbee wrote Joseph saying, "I am just informed…that the decision is against us…that they believe redress can only be had in Missouri, the courts and the legislature. We now have a right…of asking God for redress and redemption, as they have been refused us by man."[18]

The Prophet of God had fulfilled the Lord's commandment and had been rejected by judges, governors and presidents in this nation of freedoms and rights established by the hand of God himself.

> And if the president heed them not, then will the Lord arise and come forth out of his hiding place, and vex the nation;
>
> And in his hot displeasure, and in his fierce anger, in his time, will cut off the wicked, unfaithful, and unjust stewards, and appoint them their portion among hypocrites, and unbelievers;
>
> Even in outer darkness where there is weeping, and wailing, and gnashing of teeth.[19]

Now there is a question of great importance to be asked here. Did the Constitution justify the inaction of Presidents Jackson and Van Buren? Remarkably, the United States Constitution was, at that time, unclear as to whether Presidents Andrew Jackson in 1833 and Martin Van Buren in 1838, and the two Missouri Governors, Dunklin and Boggs, were actually responsible for the protection of the Mormons from the

---

18. Ron L. Andersen, *Abraham Lincoln and Joseph Smith, How Two Contemporaries Changed the Face of American History,* Plain Sight Publishing, an imprint of Cedar Fort Publishing Inc., Springville, Utah, 2014, p.150

19. Doctrine and Covenants 101:89-91

intense religious persecutions which they had endured. Article IV Section 4 of the Constitution states:

> The United States shall guarantee to every State in this Union
> a Republican Form of Government, and shall protect each of
> them against Invasion; *and* on Application of the Legislature,
> or of the Executive against domestic Violence.

In 1834, Joseph Smith importuned President Andrew Jackson for federal assistance in the unlawful and reprehensible expulsion of some 1,200 Latter-days Saints from Jackson County Missouri over their religious convictions. President Jackson's response was sympathetic of their plight. But he informed the Prophet that the Federal Government could not intervene without Missouri Governor Daniel Dunklin's formal appeal for their intervention. President Jackson's message was that, since there was no "Application of the Legislature, or of the Executive" against this domestic violence, the President of the United States could not offer the assistance that Joseph pled of him.

With this news, the heartened Prophet rushed a new appeal to Governor Dunklin, communicating President Jackson's apparent willingness to intervene, upon receiving Governor Dunklin's request of help. That appeal from Dunklin to Andrew Jackson never took place. The result was that no judge, no governor nor even the President would intercede to re-establish their rights.

The U.S. Constitution was broken from the moment it was ratified. It contained two significant and costly flaws, which literally brought the condemnation of God to this country in the form of the Civil War, "beginning at the rebellion of South Carolina."[20] We know that God raised up men for the very purpose of establishing the extraordinary

---

20. Doctrine and Covenants 87:1

government for the people and by the people. But a careful study of the actual proceedings of the Constitutional Convention reveals that some of the men in that convention of 1787, may not have been among those whom God raised up. Most, but not all of the convention delegates knew that provisions had to be in place to enforce adherence to the principles of the national government prescribed in the Constitution. They knew that success hinged upon all states in the Union embracing these "just and holy principles."[21]

But some of these delegates were wary of a strong federal government and preferred that the states not be obligated to follow certain things follow the Constitution, but rather follow it when they thought it expedient, and disregard it when they felt it to be contrary to their other motives. The opposing Constitutional Convention delegates Elbridge Gerry from Massachusetts, Alexander Martin from North Carolina and Maryland delegates John F. Mercer and Luther Martin prevailed, resulting in a compromise: in times of domestic violence in a state, the United States government would not intervene unless requested to do so.

This was the first of two major flaws in the original Constitution. It would take the Fourteenth Amendment to the Constitution to repair the damage, ratified in 1868, eighty-one years later. This amendment mitigated the damage done by these four delegates, but not in time to save the Latter-day Saints untold harm, terror and injustice. The Fourteenth Amendment states, "nor shall any State deprive any person of life, liberty, or property, without due process of law."

This meant that when the lawless mobs in Jackson and Caldwell Counties of Missouri, twice drove the Mormon citizens from their homes, then burned and stole their property, the Federal Government

---

21. Doctrine and Covenants 101:77

was powerless to require that the State of Missouri be brought to justice for not abiding by the "just and holy principles"[22] of the Constitution.

The Constitution's preamble states:

> We the People of the United States, in Order to form a more perfect Union, establish Justice, insure domestic Tranquility, provide for the common defense, promote the general Welfare, and secure the Blessing of Liberty to ourselves and our Posterity, do ordain and establish this Constitution for the United States of America.[23]

It appears that the Adversary had infiltrated the Constitutional Convention and succeeded in ensuring that the believers in the restored gospel in Missouri would not receive the blessing of a more perfect Union. They would be denied the justice, tranquility, common defense, general welfare, and blessings of liberty guaranteed in the United States Constitution. And the Father of Lies did it with a seeming harmless provision of not holding States accountable for unlawful violence.

Consider again Doctrine and Covenants 101:76, 77 given to Joseph Smith on December 16, 1833, approximately five weeks following the saints' expulsion from Jackson County.

> And again I say unto you, those who have been scattered by their enemies, it is my will that they should continue to importune for redress, and redemption by the hands of those who are placed as rulers and are in authority over you.

> According to the laws and the constitution of the people, which I have suffered to be established, and should be main-

---

22. Doctrine and Covenants 101:77
23. The United States Constitution

tained for the rights and protection of all flesh, according to just and holy principles.[24]

These eloquent and inspired "just and holy principles"[25] were denied the members of The Church of Jesus Christ of Latter-day Saints in New York in 1829, Ohio in 1837, in Missouri in 1834 and 1838 and in Illinois in 1846, and the Federal government was impotent and disinclined to "maintain their rights and protection."[26] It must be remembered that the divine proclamation of the Divine gift of a constitution, one that would bless people throughout the entire world, came through Joseph Smith, the Prophet of God in this last dispensation. It was granted as a means to create an environment across the globe, where the freedom of religious expression would be honored and cherished. With this powerful protection, the restored gospel has been allowed to be preached to "all nations, kindreds, tongues and people."[27]

This message of redemption from our sins through the Lord Jesus Christ has gone to the nations that have embraced the civil and religious freedoms inspired by the U.S. Constitution. Those nations which have not allowed missionaries into their borders are nations that have not patterned their governments after the U.S. Constitution and they forbid the free expression of religious practice. It must be remembered that the very people for whom the Constitution was given, those who would in these latter days, believe in the restored gospel of Jesus Christ, were the very ones who were denied these sacred privileges in New York, Ohio, Missouri and Illinois. Divine retribution awaited this nation for its slothfulness and oppressions of the people of God.

24. Doctrine and Covenants 101:76, 77

25. Doctrine and Covenants 101:77

26. ibid.

27. Doctrine and Covenants 42:58

So here was the problem. With the original Constitution as it was, it could be argued that indeed, President Andrew Jackson had no business interfering in unlawful violence in any state, including Missouri's oppression of the Mormons. Four years later when again the Saints were driven from Far West to Illinois, Joseph Smith personally appealed to President Martin Van Buren for protection and redress. Van Buren's reply that, "Your cause is just, but I can do nothing for you,"[28] could be argued to be constitutionally justified. And John C. Calhoun's reply of empty sympathy was arguably accurate according to the flawed Constitution, holding no provisions that could bind a state to uphold for all citizens the right of a peaceful existence.

On the other hand, had Presidents Jackson and Van Buren, the desire to protect the religious rights of the Mormons from the gross injustices inflicted upon them, they too could probably have justified measures for the protection of the saints such as calling up militias to act under federal orders to aid in the resettlement of the Mormons back into their legally deeded homes, farms and businesses. Neither President appeared to have had that inclination.

The other flaw in the original Constitution was over the catastrophic issue of slavery in America. There were six Constitutional delegates who bristled when the majority of the convention delegates agreed that the time had come to put an end to slavery in America. These six, John Rutledge, Charles Pinckney, Charles Cotesworth Pinckney and Pierce Butler of South Carolina, William R. Davie from North Carolina and Oliver Ellsworth of Connecticut, declared that they would abandon the convention should any threat be made to slavery. Slavery had become the cornerstone of the southern states' economy and they would not tol-

---

28. B.H. Roberts, *History of the Church*, (Salt Lake City, UT: Deseret Book, 1974), vol. 4, p. 80.

erate any interference of the institution, as they called it. Had any one of those states' delegations forsaken the convention, the required minimum number for a quorum would have been lost and the entire process of Constitution-building would have come to a halt. Our founding fathers were *forced to compromise* in order to avoid a complete loss of the process.

Not only did these pro-slavery delegates force a retreat from actions to end slavery in America, they insisted that a compromise be included in the sacred document in exchange for them remaining through to completion and signing of the Constitution. This compromise that was delineated in Article 1, Section 1, Clause 3 became known as the three-fifths ratio. This became the formula for allocating seats in the House of Representatives, which was based on population. The compromise allowed that all slaves would count as three-fifths of a person even though they would remain ineligible to vote or exert any influence for their own civil and religious rights in America.

This unfortunate travesty not only turned a blind eye to the evils of slavery, it created a decades-long imbalance in the halls of Congress. Pro-slavery Congressmen dominated the legislature of the government because these poor slaves who could not vote for their freedom, added dramatic numbers to the population counts for the candidates for Congress whose intent was to prolong their captivity, oppression and torture.

And there it was. These six delegates succeeded in polluting the sacred Constitution by forcing another dangerous compromise legitimizing slavery. Lucifer had scored another horrific affliction and slave masters in the south, with their political representatives in Congress could now enhance the oppressive power of the pro-slavery movement by inflating the number of pro-slavery representatives in the House of

Representatives. This flaw in the Constitution legitimized further erosion of freedoms in this Promised Land. As sacred and inspired that the final product was, apparently Satan's influence was also represented in the U.S. Constitution. This sacred gift of liberties would someday in the future, need to be saved, corrected, with these impurities purged. That lot would fall to Joseph Smith the Prophet and Abraham Lincoln the President.

Years later, Lincoln would lament this three-fifths ratio and the unfortunate imbalance and damage that it brought upon America when he said,

> Maine and South Carolina have exactly the same number of senators, of House members and of electoral votes in choosing a president. Equal power. But Maine has more than twice as many white citizens as South Carolina; the 'equality' is brought about by adding three-fifths of South Carolina's slave population. The slaves do not vote; they are only counted and so used to swell the influence of the white people's vote. Equal power for the state with fewer than half the voters means each white man in South Carolina is more than double of any man in Maine... The South Carolinian is more than double of any one of us in this crowd.[29]

Even though Joseph returned from Washington City back in early 1840, deeply disappointed with President Martin Van Buren's unwillingness to come to the aid of the Mormons, he remained intent on pursuing compensation and justice for the extensive losses, both of life and property from the Missouri expulsion. Three years later, with the approaching presidential election in late 1843, Joseph Smith wrote a let-

29. William Lee Miller, *Lincoln's Virtues,* (New York: Vintage Books, 2002), p.259.

ter to the four leading candidates for the Executive office: Henry Clay, John C. Calhoun, Lewis Cass and Martin Van Buren. Herein he stated his own views of the Constitutional rights that had been so blatantly denied the Latter-day Saints and asked their position should they be elected, in pursuing justice for these oppressed citizens.

Only Clay and Calhoun responded, and both cordially declined to intervene, Clay saying that if elected, he could not enter the presidency encumbered with promises or pledges to any portion of the voters. Calhoun reminded Joseph Smith that his position had not changed since their conversations in Washington—redress for their losses remained a state and not a federal matter. Joseph's impassioned rejoinder to Calhoun warned him that by his and Congress's inaction toward the historic violation of Constitutional rights against the Mormons that, "God will come out of his hiding place, and vex this nation with a sore vexation: yea the consuming wrath of an offended God shall smoke through the nation..."[30] This is the same message the Lord gave to Joseph Smith in the revelation found in D&C 101:89 and noted earlier.

He then emphatically challenged Calhoun's positions by reminding him that, should a state like Missouri be guilty of insurrection or rebellion, "The President has as much power to repel it as Washington had to march against the whiskey boys of Pittsburg, or General Jackson had to send an armed force to suppress the rebellion of South Carolina"[31] twelve years earlier in 1832. Here Joseph Smith cited the actions of President George Washington when in 1794, he personally led an army of 13,000 militiamen to western Pennsylvania to quell an uprising against the first federal tax, which happened to be on whiskey and other spirits.

---

30. Joseph Smith's Views on Government, Jos. Hyrum Parry & Co., Salt Lake City, 1886, p. 31

31. Ibid p. 33

George Washington was present and presided over the Constitutional Convention and was well aware of the clause requiring a request to intervene in the Constitution and yet he felt justified to ensure complete compliance to national law. He demonstrated the strength of his conviction by personally leading the military force to the Pittsburg area to subdue the defiance. He was successful without any bloodshed.

Joseph's second case-in-point was his reference to President Andrew Jackson's own actions in 1832 when he threatened to send 40,000 troops to South Carolina to quell the nullification movement by the state in defiance of tariff laws passed by the federal government. Calhoun, of South Carolina, was intimately aware of the crisis because he was a strong proponent of the secession of South Carolina from the Union in that early date of 1832. This was same incident that caused Joseph Smith to ponder on the slave question that Christmas day in 1832, resulting in his D&C 87 revelation on war, "beginning at the rebellion of South Carolina." Both of these presidential actions were taken to ensure compliance to federal law as prescribed in the Constitution. Presidents Jackson and Van Buren could have taken action to redeem and redress the oppressed Missouri Mormons. But they did not, and by so doing they implicated themselves as being among the "wicked, unfaithful, unjust stewards" of the Constitution spoken of by God in D&C 101:90.

Twelve years had passed since Joseph Smith's dramatic prophecy, warning of an impending civil war. In it God proclaimed his wrath and indignation over the suffering of His saints and as His avenging chastisement for the nation's sins, very much like President Lincoln would later characterize the war. And even though it would be another seventeen years before the obscure lawyer of Springfield would be placed in the ill-fated Executive chair to preside over God's indignant outpouring of righteous judgment, Joseph and his followers never wavered in their faith that the day would come as promised, when they would be avenged by the hand of God because no hand of man or this government would step forward to protect a religious class of innocent and oppressed citizens—the very believers in the restored gospel.

The Prophet's response to Lincoln's political idol, Henry Clay was no less fervent. Joseph exclaimed, "O frail man, what have you done that will exalt you? Can anything be drawn from your *life character or conduct* that is worthy of being held up to the gaze of this nation as a model of virtue, charity and wisdom?"[32] Then implicating both Henry Clay and John C. Calhoun before God as being included in the group of "wicked, unfaithful, unjust stewards" of the Constitution he denounced them further.

> ...when fifteen thousand free citizens were exiled from their own homes, lands and property...and you then, upon your oath and honor occupying the exalted station of a Senator of Congress from the noble-hearted State of Kentucky, why did you not show the world your loyalty to law and order, by using all means to restore the innocent to their rights and property?[33]

> ...God will set a flaming sword to guard the tree of liberty while such mint-tithing Herods as Van Buren, Boggs, Benton, Calhoun and Clay are thrust out of the realms of virtue as fit subjects for the kingdom of fallen greatness.[34]

---

32. B.H. Roberts, *The Rise and Fall of Nauvoo*, Provo, UT: Maasai Publishing, 2001, p. 387.

33. Joseph Smith's Views on Government, Jos. Hyrum Parry & Co., Salt Lake City, 1886, p. 38

34. Ibid p. 40

Here Joseph is declaring the fate of the "unjust stewards" of this government referred to in God's revelation in D&C 101:90.

> And in his hot displeasure, and in his fierce anger, in his time, will cut off those wicked, unfaithful, and unjust stewards and appoint them their portion among hypocrites, and unbelievers.

In spite of the Prophet's severe rebuke of Henry Clay's position, he later commented that of the pool of presidential candidates, his respect for Clay remained intact.

5

Something of Ill-Omen Amongst Us

On January 27, 1838, Abraham Lincoln had been invited to address the Young Men's Lyceum of Springfield. The young lawyer had been serving in the Illinois State Legislature and gaining some notoriety amongst his Springfield acquaintances. Some eighteen months earlier he had his stunning experience with Dr. Peter Akers where he was left with the fearful premonition that a civil war lay ahead and that he would play a key role in that dreaded crisis.

In the eighteen months that followed, 28 year-old Abraham Lincoln, came to the very same realizations about America that Joseph Smith had through his Divine revelations. The fearful danger that these young men came to perceive is that, not only would freedom for the slaves be a primary issue of the Civil War, but the near loss of an even greater treasure loomed in those dreadful battlefields: the literal survival of this government through the U. S. Constitution. The very Constitution that God established through "wise men raised up" for that very purpose. We know from whence Joseph Smith received this crucial enlightenment; but where would Lincoln have come to such dramatic and accurate conclusions? Again, we are left to wonder.

This speech reflected those premonitions. Lincoln, still more than 20 years from the White House, made some truly remarkable, even prophetic utterances in that cold January meeting in Springfield. It's evident from his message that this young man had been unusually observant of national trends and was troubled by what he saw in America. This frontier bachelor, far from the Ivy League universities and centers of government in the East, displayed an insight that was beyond his years and circumstances. With it he described astute observations and warnings of future entrapments that lay ahead of unwary America—and amazingly, history that he helped to shape, proved him right. His speech, entitled The Perpetuation of Our Political Institutions was a bold and lucid warning to the audience that grave dangers lay ahead for them and all Americans for the gross violations of the guaranteed freedoms in this country.

In his message he referred to the atrocities that, four years earlier he had read of in numerous newspaper accounts of the Mormons' dramatic persecutions in Jackson County and their eventual resettlement to Far West in his neighboring state. What Lincoln did not know at the time of this speech, was that later that same year, the most egregious violation of civil and religious rights in America (outside of slavery) was about to take place when again, the Mormons would be driven by state authorized mobs from their homes in Far West.

This time the atrocities would be ten times the scale of the 1,200 driven from Jackson County Missouri in 1833. These Mormons were driven east, again in wintery conditions; across the frozen Mississippi River into his state of Illinois—some 12,000 homeless American citizens. An even greater barbarity was yet to come and this time, it would be again, against the members of The Church of Jesus Christ of Latter-day Saints. It would take place in 1846 when some of Lincoln's fellow Illinois citizens would drive some 20,000 Mormons out of the United States. And why? Because their religion was considered unsavory to an increasing number of American Christians.

Lincoln was troubled by what he had been observing in other parts of the country as well. He perceived a dangerous disregard for the constitutional privileges that this government acclaimed and he boldly shared his conviction that the American government, or more precisely the Constitution, was endangered. He began by reminding his audience of the uniquely favored circumstances of the American people who had prospered immensely under a government that offered them more "civil and religious liberty"[1] than did any other nation in history. He then described his mounting concern for what he viewed as an imperiled America by saying with an intriguing degree of accuracy,

> At what point then is the approach of danger to be expected? I answer, if it ever reach us, it must spring up amongst us. It cannot come from abroad. If destruction be our lot, we must ourselves be its author and finisher. As a nation of freemen, we must live through all time, or die by suicide.

> I hope I am over wary; but if I am not, there is, even now, something of ill omen, amongst us. I mean the increasing disregard for law which pervades the country; the growing disposition to substitute the wild and furious passions, in lieu of the sober judgment of Courts; and the worse than savage mobs, for the executive ministers of justice. Accounts of outrages committed by mobs, form the every-day news of the

---

1. Sangamo Journal, *Lincoln's Lyceum Speech*, February 3, 1838

times. They have pervaded the country, from New England to Louisiana… Alike, they spring up among the pleasure hunting masters of Southern slaves, and the order loving citizens of the land of steady habits. Whatever, then, their cause may be, it is common to the whole country.[2]

Then he referred to recent events of unlawful lynchings that had occurred to gamblers in Mississippi, the burning alive of an innocent Black man in St. Louis, and the recent murder of an abolitionist newspaperman in nearby Alton, Illinois; all done by lawless mobs. Lincoln continued, "Such are the effects of mob law…becoming more and more frequent in this land so lately famed for love of law and order…"[3]

But all this even, is not the full extent of the evil. By such examples, by instances of the perpetrators of such acts going unpunished, the lawless in spirit, are encouraged to become lawless in practice; and having been used to no restraint… they thus become, absolutely unrestrained.[4]

Lincoln's denunciation of "the ravages of mob law," and "the increasing disregard for law which pervades the country"[5] were almost prophetic in their certainty and most assuredly, by their accuracy. It is unlikely that Lincoln and Joseph Smith ever collaborated on their early prophetic warnings for this nation, but they are remarkably parallel in their descriptions, accuracy and in their fear of and reverence for the

---

2. Ibid.
3. Ibid.
4. Ibid.
5. Sangamo Journal, *Lincoln's Lyceum Speech*, February 3, 1838

judgments of God. With the conviction of a prophet, twenty-eight year old Abraham Lincoln courageously continued his warning,

> Whenever the vicious portion of the population shall be permitted to gather in bands of hundreds and thousands, and burn churches, ravage and rob provision-stores, throw printing presses into rivers, shoot editors, and hang and burn obnoxious persons at pleasure and with impunity, depend upon it, THIS GOVERNMENT CANNOT LAST![6]

Through the newspapers, Lincoln the lawyer would be aware that none of Missouri persecutors of 1833 had been brought to justice, and that the Mormons were never permitted to return to their homes in Jackson County. He then continued and wisely described the Latter-day Saints' frame of mind following the repeated crimes committed against them for their religion.

> "While, on the other hand, good men, men who love tranquility, who desire to abide by the laws, and enjoy their benefits, who would gladly spill their blood in the defense of their country; seeing their property destroyed; their families insulted, and their lives endangered; their persons injured; and seeing nothing in prospect that forebodes a change for the better; become tired of, and disgusted with, a Government that offers them no protection... Thus, then, by the operation of this mobocratic spirit, which all must admit, is now abroad in the land, the strongest bulwark of any Government, and particularly of those constituted like ours, may effectually be broken down and destroyed..."[7]

6. Ibid.
7. Ibid.

This prophetic observation by young Lincoln was certainly confirmed in later years by the Mormons themselves. Even though driven by force by the Illinois mobs in 1846, the Saints remembered God's warning to flee to the west for their protection and freedom. They had indeed, lost confidence in this government or more accurately, in the unwise stewards (elected politicians) of the sacred Constitution. After consultation with the Prophet Joseph before his martyrdom, Brigham Young knew that their only peace would be outside of the United States and the location designated by Joseph Smith before his death was the valley of the Great Salt Lake, in the then Mexican territory in 1847. These offenses occurred because unscrupulous elected officials hid behind a loophole in the Constitution, justifying their unwillingness to abide in all instances within the Constitution's just and holy principles.

Young Lincoln concluded his message by referring to a Biblical utterance, this one by Jesus, something Lincoln would do more than four hundred times during his Presidency. "Upon these let the proud fabric of freedom rest, as the rock of its basis; and as truly as has been said of the only greater institution, *the gates of hell shall not prevail against it.*"[8]

His placing of this government and nation just below the "only greater institution," or God's kingdom, reflects his oft-stated belief that the U.S. Constitution was a gift from the Almighty. And his plea that the gates of hell should not prevail against this new government reveals his belief in the ubiquitous opposing powers of darkness, which have warred against God's goodness since the beginning of time. In the coming years, Lincoln would make many more references to the concept of good versus evil, and right against wrong, in fact they are a common thread through many of his speeches and conversations.

---

8. Holy Bible, Matthew 16:18

In just a few years, Lincoln would watch as his fellow Illinoisan, Joseph Smith, who used this gates of hell reference at least six times in sermons and letters, placed himself as a candidate for the President of the United States in the 1844 election in his effort to ensure that the gates of hell not prevail against God's work in this chosen land. He too was certain that a national war was on the horizon and he, like Lincoln, believed that the only hope of evading this calamity was a righteous people, who remembered their God as the author of their liberty through the inspired Constitution. Again and again, these two presidential prophets expressed their deep foreboding that formidable forces of lawlessness were combining to thwart the works of God and extinguish the fragile experiment of government by the people, for the people and of the people.

It is a safe assumption that Lincoln's warning regarding their imperiled government left few, if any of his audience that night, disconcerted at the end of his speech. Rare was the American in 1838 that had doubts about the stability of their nation's government. But two elements about this notion are worthy of serious consideration. This theme of an endangered republic and government given 23 years before his presidency and the Civil War, is a theme that Lincoln never left off addressing throughout those 23 years, knowing full well that many regarded such rhetoric as being unfounded and provocative.

Two years into the war, in mid-November 1863, President Lincoln was somber as he and his party traveled to the village of Gettysburg, Pennsylvania. A massive battle had been fought there earlier in July. He had been invited to dedicate the new national cemetery there, necessitated by the nearly 4,000 young men whose lives ended on that battlefield. The President had many years to contemplate the unfortunate accuracy of his prophetic Lyceum speech 25 years earlier. The disregard for the laws that protected civil and religious rights had, in his mind brought on this judgment of God in the specter of a Civil War.

In the opening of his immortal Gettysburg address, he stated emphatically that secession and the war was "testing whether that nation or any nation so conceived *can long endure.*"[9] And he closed with a challenge to all Americans that they "highly resolve that these dead shall not have died in vain—that this nation, under God, shall have a new birth of freedom—and that government of the people, by the people, for the people, *shall not perish from the earth.*"[10] Five years before this celebrated speech, in his storied debates with Stephen A. Douglas for the Illinois Senate seat, Lincoln repeatedly admonished the people using a New Testament scripture that "a house divided against itself *cannot stand,*"[11] that "this government cannot endure permanently half *slave* and half *free.*"[12] There were numerous other such warnings uttered by Lincoln in the years between this Lyceum speech and his assassination.

The other significant consideration is the fact that Lincoln was not the only other notable American figure that shared the same foreboding for this nation's future.

The American Prophet, Joseph Smith had these words on the subject of our endangered Constitutional freedoms:

> I prophesy in the name of the Lord of Israel, unless the United
> States redress the wrongs committed upon the Saints in the
> state of Missouri and punish the crimes committed by her

9. Abraham Lincoln, *The Gettysburg Address*, November 19, 1863

10. Ibid.

11. The Holy Bible, Matthew 12:25

12. Ron L Andersen, A. Lincoln - God's Humble Instrument, (Salt Lake City, UT: Millennial Mind Publishing, 2010), p. 117.

officers that in a few years the government will be utterly overthrown and wasted, and there will be not so much as a potsherd left for their wickedness in permitting the murder of men, women, and children and the wholesale plunder and extermination of thousands of her citizens to go unpunished, thereby perpetuating a foul and corroding blot upon the fair fame of this great republic.[13]

Five years prior to Lincoln's impassioned Lyceum address, Joseph Smith sat pondering and praying on the subject of slavery, following which he recorded the revelation, cited earlier, given to him on Christmas day in 1832:

> Verily, thus saith the Lord concerning the wars that will shortly come to pass, beginning at the rebellion of South Carolina, which will eventually terminate in the death and misery of many souls; and the time will come that war will be poured out upon all nations, beginning at this place. (D&C 87:1-2).

Joseph Smith was strikingly specific in detail to the point of accurately pinpointing South Carolina as the flashpoint for the war. On December 10, 1832, just fifteen days before Joseph's revelation on war, President Andrew Jackson issued his proclamation to the people of South Carolina that disputed a state's right to nullify a federal law. Jackson's proclamation was written in response to an ordinance issued by a South Carolina convention that declared that the tariff acts of 1828 and 1832 were null, void and non-binding upon their State. They refused to obey the national law. They further stated that on February 1,

---

13. Joseph Smith, Jr. *History of the Church of Jesus Christ of Latter-day Saints,* 7 vols., Salt Lake City: Deseret Book, 1973, 5:394

1833 South Carolina would secede from the Union if the government attempted to enforce this new federal law in their state.

In response to this threat, Congress passed the Force Act that authorized the use of military force against any state that resisted the tariff acts, and with that Jackson threatened to send 40,000 U.S. troops to the Palmetto State to ensure compliance. South Carolina withdrew their defiance and begrudgingly remained in the Union. This 1832 precursor to the secession of 1860 likely precipitated Joseph Smith's meditations on slavery and the subsequent Civil War prophecies.

Certainly some of Lincoln's foreboding of an endangered republican government sprang as well from the attempted secession of South Carolina in 1832. This recalcitrance by South Carolina posed a dramatic dilemma for this still unstable nation. If one state could simply defy federal law and then go as far as to exit the Union, certainly other states could do the same over future disagreements. The end result would be a continent of separate nation-states that would be weaker than a grouping of united states. More importantly, each would form their own diluted and weakened version of the original Constitution, the inspired one. This was the very condition that Lincoln had feared for many years.

Joseph Smith's prophecy on war further declares:

> For behold, the Southern States shall be divided against the Northern States, and the Southern States will call on other nations, even the nation of Great Britain, as it is called...[14]

As prophesied, the Southern states did effect an illegal separation from the Union. This pronouncement by the President of The Church of Jesus Christ of Latter-day Saints that the South would appeal to Great Britain was again remarkably accurate. With Great Britain's voracious

14. Doctrine and Covenants 87:3

appetite for the South's affordable and abundant cotton that had fueled their burgeoning textile industry, the Confederacy pinned their hopes on British support of their cause. In November 1861, they secretly dispatched two emissaries to England to encourage their recognition and support. But to the relief of President Lincoln and the North, England chose to remain neutral, to avoid involvement and to smugly watch America defeat itself, something they had failed to do twice before.

> And it shall come to pass, after many days, slaves shall rise up
> against their masters, who shall be marshaled and disciplined
> for war.[15]

As bold as the Great Britain component of the revelation was, this next declaration was, at that time, equally unlikely to come to pass. As absurd as talk of civil war was in 1832, even more ludicrous was the notion that Black men would ever be successful in battle, let alone be viewed as capable of being called upon to represent a white American cause from either side of the slavery debate. Yet here the Mormon prophet boldly declares that after they would be marshaled and disciplined for war they would rise up against their masters.

President Lincoln's Emancipation Proclamation in September of 1863 brought slaves in droves to Union regiments operating in the southern states. They left their plantation owners and then as prophesied, picked up arms against them in the war that was fought to end the oppression of the Black race in America. It was an irony of epic proportions to witness Black men in Union uniform along with their white counterparts, patrolling the streets of the once grand pro-slavery city of Charleston, South Carolina, the cradle of the secession, after its fall into Union hands in early 1865. Lincoln explained that his decision to arm

---

15. Doctrine and Covenants 87:4

the Blacks was for the sake of preserving the cause that his Caucasian Army was losing. In his second annual message to Congress he declared, "In *giving* freedom to the *slave*, we *assure* freedom to the *free*—honorable alike in what we give, and what we preserve. We shall nobly save, or meanly lose, the last best hope of earth."[16]

What was the last best hope of earth? The God-given United States Constitution.

Whenever the topic arose, Lincoln was quick to defend his conviction that the Black soldier would be equal to any other. His decision to arm the Blacks was courageous and rife with controversy. For two hundred and fifty years Black men were considered incapable to bear arms; it was inconceivable to suggest that they could be called upon to defend white Americans in battle. There was no American precedence for Lincoln's faith in their character, bravery and resolve.

But the 180,000 former slaves who fought in the final years of the war to preserve the Union, were brave and able fighters who literally turned the tide of the war, finally to the Union's favor. Their valor on the battlefield also demolished the centuries old prejudice that the Black mans' nature was embodied in incompetence. Their valor on the Civil War battlefields was proof positive of this fallacy and with this they crushed the fundamental element of two and a half centuries of white America's oppression of their race that was founded on this miscalculation of inferiority.

It is a curious reality to see that Abraham Lincoln and his Illinois neighbor, Joseph Smith, would, for so long share this common vision of the nation's future. Both men would run for President with the intent

---

16. Ronald C. White, Jr., *The Eloquent President*, (New York: Random House, 2005), p. 170. Abraham Lincoln: Annual Message to Congress, Washington D.C., December 1, 1862.

to avoid the prophesied crisis, and to save and repair the broken Constitution by preserving the Union and freeing the slaves. Only the frontier lawyer would succeed in this high endeavor to exact the fulfillment of their common yet, uncollaborated prophecies.

The Mormon Prophet's revelation continues:

> And thus, with the sword and by bloodshed the inhabitants of the earth shall mourn; and…be made to feel the wrath, and indignation, and chastening hand of an Almighty God…[17]

Lincoln had a practice of turning ideas over and over in his mind and writing his conclusions and musings on the backs of envelopes and pieces of paper and then placing them in his tall stove pipe hat or in nooks and drawers in his desk. One such written meditation was not discovered until after his death. It is of singular significance in catching a glimpse of Lincoln's faith and conviction that God was the silent architect of the war that was ravaging the country. John Hay, Lincoln's private secretary, discovered this private notation among a number of other such notes and kept it. In 1872, Hay gave it a title: *Meditation on the Divine Will*. He included it in the biography of Lincoln that he and John Nicolay published in 1890, with the description, "This meditation was not meant to be seen of men."[18]

Meditation on the Divine Will

September 2(?) 1862, sixteen months into the war

> The will of God prevails. In great contests each party claims to act in accordance with the will of God. Both may be, and one must be wrong. God cannot be for, and against the same

---

17. Doctrine and Covenants 87:6

18. The Eloquent President, p 154

thing at the same time. In the present civil war it is quite possible that God's purpose is something different from the purpose of either party—and yet the human instrumentalities, working just as they do, are of the best adaptation to effect His purpose. I am almost ready to say this is probably true—that God wills this contest, and wills that it shall not end yet. By His mere quiet power, on the minds of the now contestants, He could have either saved or destroyed the Union without a human contest. Yet the contest began. And having begun He could give the final victory to either side any day. Yet the contest proceeds.[19]

This private musing by President Lincoln merits a close analysis. *The will of God prevails.*

Lincoln had expressed this belief dozens of times and in various ways. There can be no doubt of his sincerity in this solitary expression. He once told a friend:

That the Almighty does make use of human agencies and directly intervenes in human affairs is one of the plainest statements in the Bible. I've had so many evidences of His direction, so many instances when I have been controlled by some other power than my own will, that I cannot doubt that this power comes from above...All we have to do is trust the Almighty and keep on obeying His orders and executing His will. I frequently see my way clear to a decision when I am conscious that I have not sufficient facts upon which to found it. But I cannot recall one instance in which I have followed my own judgment founded upon such a decision, where the

19. The Eloquent President, p 153

results were unsatisfactory; whereas, in almost every instance where I have yielded to the views of others I have had occasion to regret it.[20]

In this present civil war it is quite possible that God's purpose is something different from the purpose of either party…

This conviction that God was at the helm of the war must have been at least some solace to Lincoln, who suffered greatly in mind and spirit at the massive number of war deaths, nearing 200,000 by the time of Lincoln' penning of this meditation, and at the terrible economic strain placed on the nation with the enormous costs of financing the war. Lincoln had come to believe what Joseph Smith knew by revelation, that wrath, indignation and the chastening hand of God was in play with the war amongst a people who had become complacent with the Constitution and oppressive of the Saints through whom God was establishing his kingdom in the latter days.

I am almost ready to say this is probably true—that God wills this contest, and wills that it shall not end yet. By His mere quiet power, on the minds of the now contestants, He could have either saved or destroyed the Union without a human contest. Yet the contest began. And having begun He could give the final victory to either side any day. Yet the contest proceeds.

It is safe to say that few mortals, if any, were closer to God, and looked to Him more intently than did Lincoln during this time. The public and the politicians were unaware of Lincoln's solemn Meditation, it appears to have been written only as his own contemplation; however, he would reflect these same sentiments in at least two conversations in the following days and in his Proclamation that established our time-honored tradition of Thanksgiving a year later.

20. In War and Peace, Stephen L. Richards

Just days following this *Meditation,* Lincoln stunned his Cabinet by revealing his vow to God that if the Union Army would be successful in driving out the Confederates from Maryland, which they did just days earlier at Antietam, he would interpret that as an indication from God that He approved of Lincoln's private and personal decision to free the slaves in the rebelling States by issuing the Emancipation Proclamation saying solemnly to his cabinet, "God had decided this question in favor of the slaves."[21]

The election of Abraham Lincoln brought a landslide of repercussions. He was the first president representing the new antislavery Republican Party. Within days, hundreds of U.S. Congressmen, judges and military officers from the southern states resigned their posts and aided in the formation of the new government of the Confederate States of America. Over the previous six years, Lincoln had spoken relentlessly on the evils of slavery. To the proslavery south he was a villain, a fiend, the Gorilla, the Black Republican.

Two years earlier the race for Illinois U.S. Senate captured the interest of America. Stephen A. Douglas, the most powerful Senator in America was receiving a formidable challenge from a tall awkward Illinois lawyer, Abraham Lincoln who had a clear and compelling message which captivated many with his moral stance against slavery. Lincoln's assault on slavery and the damage that it had brought upon this nation, had captivated the country with his calls for ending the horrible evil.

A portion of the radicals in the Republican Party members of Congress worked hard to get Lincoln and his antislavery position into the White House. But they too became dismayed with Lincoln when he dropped the bombshell in his Inaugural Address that he would not in-

---

21. The Eloquent President, p 168

terfere with slavery, that he felt that the President lacked the authority to do so. He was correct because of the unfortunate three-fifth clause in the Constitution which essentially legalized slavery in this country. Lincoln's continual rhetoric over the years regarding the need to abide by the law, caused him to push incessantly and legally against the spread of slavery in the new territories and states but not to end slavery where it was legitimized by the Constitution. The South did not believe him in this pledge to leave slavery alone and the Radical Republicans were up in arms over his perceived betrayal to their cause.

The change of any administration in this country always entails filling governmental positions vacated by appointees of the outgoing administration. Such was the case with Lincoln, but doubly so with the resignation of so many southern sympathizing officials. He and his Cabinet were buried with office seekers vying for the vacancies. Congress was in recess at the time, meaning that Lincoln with his new Cabinet and the Lieutenant General Winfield Scott had to address the multiple crises that were forced upon them by the rebellion of South Carolina and the states that followed them. After dealing with the Fort Sumter crisis, Lincoln called for a special session of Congress for July 4, 1862. His election was accompanied with a dramatic victory for numerous other Republican candidates who defeated their Democratic opponents. Absent the Senators and House Representatives from the eleven southern states, which had seceded, this Congress would have a heavy Republican majority, which included the much offended radical Republicans over Lincoln's refusal to interfere with slavery.

6

A Battle between Right and Wrong, Good and Evil

F OR MANY YEARS American history classes have taught that the Civil War was fought over the issues of slavery, secession, states' rights and for the preservation of the Union. But there is much more significance to this national tragedy. As noted earlier, Latter-day Saints are given to know through the revelations in D&C 87, 101 and 103, that it befell Americans as a punishment for the failure of the unwise stewards of the Constitution to protect the members of the Church of Jesus Christ of Latter-day Saints in the free exercise of their faith. For this, the war came so that the saints would "be avenged of their enemies."[1] Even Abraham Lincoln concurred that the Civil War should be seen as the "wrath and indignation and chastening hand of an Almighty God."[2] In his fifth of eleven proclamations to America, he admonished Americans with this wise yet harrowing counsel.

---

1. Doctrine and Covenants 87:7
2. Doctrine and Covenants 87:7

Proclamation for Thanksgiving

July 15, 1863

> It has pleased Almighty God to hearken to the supplications and prayers of an afflicted people, and to vouchsafe to the army and the navy of the United States victories on land and on sea… but these victories have been accorded not without sacrifices of life, limb, health, and liberty, incurred by brave, loyal, and patriotic citizens. It is meet and right to recognize and confess the presence of the Almighty Father, and the power of his hand equally in these triumphs and in these sorrows.[3]

Three months later he followed this with his sixth proclamation; with it he emphasized this point with a similar message of praise to God and a yet another charge to recognize His holy hand in this lamentable judgment of civil war.

Proclamation for Thanksgiving

October 1863

> The year that is drawing toward its close has been filled with the blessings of fruitful fields and healthful skies. To these bounties, which are so constantly enjoyed that we are prone to forget the source from which they come…

> No human counsel hath devised, nor hath any mortal hand worked out these great things. They are the gracious gifts of

---

3. *Life and Works of Abraham Lincoln*, Edited by Marion Mills Miller, Litt. D., p. 158

the most high God, who, while dealing with us in anger for our sins, hath nevertheless remembered mercy.

It has seemed to me fit and proper that they should be solemnly, reverently, and gratefully acknowledged as with one heart and one voice by the whole American People. I do, therefore, invite my fellow-citizens in every part of the United States…to set apart and observe the last Thursday of November next as a day of thanksgiving and praise to our beneficent Father who dwelleth in the heavens. And I recommend to them that…they do also, with humble penitence for our national perverseness and disobedience, commend to his tender care all those who have become widows, orphans, mourners, or sufferers in the lamentable civil strife in which we are unavoidably engaged…[4]

A. Lincoln

"The Almighty Has His Own Purposes"

The truth is, God had His own purposes from those of the opponents of both the North and the South. Lincoln declared it emphatically in his second inaugural address, just five weeks before his assassination and the culmination of his monumental accomplishments.

Both (North and South) read the same Bible and pray to the same God, and each invokes His aid against the other. It may seem strange that any men should dare to ask a just God's assistance in wringing their bread from the sweat of other men's faces, but let us judge not, that we be not judged. The prayers

---

4. *Life and Works of Abraham Lincoln*, Edited by Marion Mills Miller, Litt. D., p 159-161

of both could not be answered. That of neither has been answered fully.

The Almighty has His own purposes (emphasis added). 'Woe unto the world because of offenses; for it must needs be that offenses come, but woe to that man by whom the offense cometh'.[5]

As noted earlier, one such purpose was the promised avenging of the Latter-day Saints for the repeated persecutions that they were forced to endure for their religion. The Catholics also suffered at the hands of self-righteous and intolerant Protestants prior to the war; this too was contrary to their Constitutional rights. Religious freedom is the first freedom cited in the Bill of Rights. The First Amendment states,

Congress shall make no law respecting an establishment of religion, or prohibiting the free exercise thereof; or abridging the freedom of speech, or of the press; or the right of the people peaceably to assemble, and to petition the Government for a redress of grievances

The days of unrelenting persecutions done primarily by American Protestants toward the Mormons and Catholics were eventually curtailed with the sufferings caused by the war. For example, in the mid 1850s a new political party was formed. It was called the American Party, also referred to as the Know Nothing Party by those opposed to it. It grew by an estimated one million members in one year alone. Their primary political platform: Prohibit Catholics from being elected to public office and prevent them from being hired into public service employment. Lincoln emphatically opposed this party.

---

5. Abraham Lincoln, *Second Inaugural Address*, March 4, 1865

A New Birth of Freedom

There was yet another important outcome of the war and Lincoln seemed to have had glimpses of it. In his Gettysburg address he uttered the powerful declaration that, "this nation, under God, shall have a new birth of freedom."[6] The Civil War put an end to slavery, the soul cankering evil embraced by slave owners and their families for generations. Satan's weapon of slavery had the power to nearly topple the Constitution. The dramatic demise of slavery in America under Abraham Lincoln's leadership was one of the new births of freedom, but there were yet others.

The terrible war also tempered the destructive states rights zeal that led to the conflict. Slavery was always the goal of the southern insurgents, but it was disguised within the appeal that a state should be able to decide what is legal or not within their own boundaries. The carnage and destruction of the war was horrible for all, but especially so for the slave owners. The vast majority of these instigators of the rebellion lost nearly everything. With no more slaves, they were left only with themselves to plant and harvest their crops. There was no fight left in any of them to continue their sophistries and consequently states rights excesses were snuffed out because of the length and severity of the war.

Again, Lincoln's private conclusion as to the severity and protraction of the war:

> I am almost ready to say this is probably true—that God wills this contest, and wills that it shall not end yet. By His mere quiet power, on the minds of the now contestants, He could have either saved or destroyed the Union without a human

---

6. Ronald C. White, Jr., *The Eloquent President*, Random House, New York, 2005, p 223

contest. Yet the contest began. And having begun He could give the final victory to either side any day. Yet the contest proceeds.

Why, after some 18 months of war and more than two hundred thousand casualties would God want the war to continue? The war would go on for another three and a half years where the total casualty count reached a staggering estimate of 750,000.

April 6th

As described earlier, President Lincoln made his first move to save the Constitutional government by writing a simple and cordial letter to the governor of South Carolina. In it, he explained that he was sending food to the U.S. soldiers stationed at Fort Sumter. That letter was written on April 6, 1861, as was his order to have the ship of supplies ready to set sail for Charleston harbor by April 6th. It left port arriving and it arrived six days later, where it was fired upon and forced to retreat.

This appears to be merely coincidental to [many] Latter-day Saints. But it becomes interesting when coupled with the fact that it was exactly four years later on April 6, 1865, that the final decisive battle of the Civil War was begun. General Ulysses S. Grant launched his bloody attack on the stronghold of General Robert E. Lee near Petersburg, Virginia. This battle would rage on for three days, leading to the surrender of General Lee to General Grant—and the end of the war. It was a four-year war beginning on April 6, 1861 and ending on April 6, 1865.

Many important events in the working of the Almighty God through the history of the world had this same date for its commencement. Latter-day Saints hold this date as sacred in the "Rise of the Church of Christ in these last days, being one thousand eight hundred and thirty years since the coming of our Lord and Savior Jesus Christ in the flesh."[7] On Tuesday, April 6, 1830 Joseph Smith and five others established the restored church of God in Fayette, New York. On April 6, 1840, the Apostles set foot in England at Liverpool. In the Kirtland Temple at a conference held on April 3, 1836, Christ appeared to accept His Temple. The restoration of the Keys of the Priesthood by Moses, Elias, and Elijah followed.[8]

Jewish tradition places a number of important sacred events occurring on or near April 6th, the month of April being designated by Moses as the first day of Nisan, which in our present calendar would be in early April. This date is viewed as the beginning of each new year. Among their long-lived traditions is the belief that the creation of the universe took place on that day. On this day Adam and Eve partook of the forbidden fruit and consequently their separation from God's presence and the beginning of their new life. They see the beginning of April as the birthdates of Abraham and Jacob as well as the day of their deaths. Their tradition also designates the first of April as the day that God, through Moses parted the Red Sea to allow the freed Israelite slaves to walk to freedom on dry ground.

Knowing, as we do that God was behind the Civil War, it may not be inconsistent to consider that Lincoln's conclusion that God willed that the war continue, was accurate. It is possible that God had decreed that this monumental junction in the history of mankind might have a starting date and ending date of April 6th, emphasizing the pivotal accomplishments that the Civil War brought to not only America but to the world and to the process of the restoration of God's light and truth.

---

7. Doctrine and Covenants 20:1

8. Doctrine and Covenants 109

Saving the Constitution

In addition, it has rarely been suggested that the Civil War was fought to also preserve the beleaguered Constitution, again as President Lincoln incessantly affirmed while in the White House. In fact, as much as he distained slavery, the preservation of the government that was inspired by the U. S. Constitution became his primary objective upon entering the white House. Congress had been in recess, the Southern states congressmen abandoned their sacred oaths of office and deserted their seats in Congress during those critical opening months of Lincoln's administration.

He called a special session of both houses of Congress to report on the events that has taken place. In this July 4, 1861 message he did not make one reference to slavery, much to the dismay of many Republicans who had elected him, rather his concern was for the Constitution to which he referred and specifically named 23 times in the speech. His firm belief was that the Constitutional government of this Republic was facing imminent danger. So concerned was he of this fact that in this speech he made 25 references to the impending destruction of the government if strong measures were not employed to oppose the "formidable internal attempt to overthrow it."[9]

It is of importance to remember that some 30 years earlier in his Lyceum Speech Lincoln declared that should lawlessness and disregard for the Constitutional principles continue, "Count on it, THIS GOVERMNENT CANNOT LAST!"[10] As President, he must have marveled at the accuracy of his youthful impressions for this government and how the premonitions of his personal future involvement in the tragedy of

---

9. Abraham Lincoln, Lyceum Speech January, 1938

10. Abraham Lincoln, Lyceum Speech January, 1938

Civil War had come true, just as he feared they would. He now found himself before the United States Congress on this July 4th, three decades later, guiding them on how they together, must now save the Constitution. In this speech, he reiterated his warning multiple times. Here are just a few of his cautionary statements:

> "...to so abandon that position under the circumstances would be utterly ruinous."

> "...prevent...such attempts to destroy the Federal Union."

> "...in fact, it would be our national destruction consummated."

> "[The South] recognizes no fidelity to the Constitution, no obligation to maintain the Union."

This next statement portrays the fact that Lincoln still possessed an unusual understanding and foreknowledge of the global impact that this crisis carried with it.

> And this issue embraces more than the fate of these United States. It presents to the whole family of man the question whether a constitutional republic, or democracy—a government of the people by the same people—can or can not maintain its territorial integrity against its own domestic foes. It presents the question whether discontented individuals, too few in numbers to control administration..., can always, break up their government, and thus practically put an end to free government upon the earth. It forces us to ask, is there in all republics this inherent and fatal weakness? Must a gov-

ernment of necessity be too strong for the liberties of its own
people, or too weak to maintain its own existence?

He [the President] sincerely hopes that your views and your
action may so accord with his as to assure all faithful citizens who have been disturbed in their rights of a certain and
speedy restoration to them under the Constitution and the
laws.[11]

The intent of this book is to demonstrate that there were yet other
eternal and pivotal purposes for the American Civil War. It was a clash
of the forces of good and those of evil over the protected privilege of
free religious thought and expression for the entire world in this, the
last dispensation. Lucifer knew that he could not prevent God from
enlightening his children on the earth, but once done, Lucifer had at
his disposal, evil men whom he had filled with greed and hatred who
would become his servants in destroying the work of God. Throughout
history, whether by unjust laws, mobs or by conquest, the adversary has
successfully deteriorated faith and belief in God.

Satan was very aware of the much prophesied restoration of all
things that began in a sacred grove of trees in 1820; he was there when it
occurred. In his attempt to subdue young Joseph, he was driven away by
the power of the presence of God the Father and His son Jesus Christ. .
Much like Jehovah, his plan had been in the making for centuries before
the outbreak of the cataclysmic Civil War.

Unlike the previous dispensations of truth and light, in this the last
dispensation, Christ has affirmed that Satan will not be successful in removing the light and power of God. What would make this final resto-

---

11. Abraham Lincoln, Speech to the U.S. Congress, July 4,1861

ration different from the others? One of Jehovah's powerful instruments that would make this possible was and is, the United States Constitution. Satan's tool to destroy this Constitution was slavery in America. Never before had there been such a governmental guide to ensure the civil and religious freedoms of the people. It could only have been introduced in a nation with a specific set of circumstances—those possessed by the United States.

Elder McConkie's grasp and understanding of the importance of this creation is impressive. Here's just one quote from a series of articles serialized in the *Deseret News* in 1945. "The Constitution is the very foundation and substance of the freedom of all men of this nation, and it is as needful, or more needful that its precepts be kept alive today than at any other time in the history of man's struggle for freedom. Freedom is dearly bought, but easily sold." Also, in 1978 Bruce R. McConkie gave another masterful discourse that reminds us of the vision for a universal constitution. https://www.lds.org/general-conference/1978/04/the-morning-breaks-the-shadows-flee?lang=eng

Many who sought freedom to worship God according to the dictates of their conscience migrated to America. And in due course, by the power of the Father, a new nation was created, a nation "conceived in liberty, and dedicated to the proposition that all men are created equal." (Abraham Lincoln, Gettysburg Address.) The United States of America came into being. Beyond the mountains, now not many leagues away, a new day was gestating in the womb of nature. As the earth continued to turn slowly and steadily on its decreed course, as the dawn brightened and the morning light increased, as the Constitution of the United States guaranteed religious freedom, as men were tempered in their feelings and began to view each other with more equity and fairness, as the

Bible was published and read by more people, as darkness ebbed and light increased, the time for the rising of the gospel sun was at hand.

God has guided other peoples in the development of governmental systems where the voice of the people was the rule of law, such as the reign of the judges with the people of Nephi. This form of government was successful when righteous men ruled. But these ruling systems were eventually toppled by the adversary with the murder of the righteous chief judge. Satan accomplished the murder of Abraham Lincoln, but the Constitutional system with its bicameral structure of Congress and the Supreme Court remained intact following his assassination. The Constitution contained directives for the transfer of power to the pre-appointed successor in the Vice President, simply replacing him while the governmental system remained in force. This Constitutional government was unlike anything that the forces of evil had ever encountered. This system could only be overcome by a powerful military force or internal rebellion and Satan's strategy was to create an internal rebellion of such magnitude through the institution of slavery.

Prior to his presidency, Lincoln summarized the real issue in his seventh and last debate with Stephen A. Douglas in 1858, spoken in the midst of this American convergence of racial and religious intolerance that Satan had so adeptly instilled in the minds and hearts of so many Americans. Lincoln declared that the "real issue" in this contest, this "eternal struggle" rested between right and wrong, which "have stood face to face from the beginning of time..."[12] The American Civil War was a collision of colossal proportions of God's forces for good and Satan's forces for evil. Satan's primary focus at this juncture was to destroy the divine instrument that had the power to protect the free expression

12. William Lee Miller, *Lincoln's Virtues*, Vintage Books, New York, 2002, p. 338

of religious thoughts and feelings, not just in America, but throughout the world—the United States Constitution. And he so very nearly succeed in toppling it into oblivion using slavery as his weapon.

Did Lincoln believe in Satan? There is not much recorded about his belief in the Adversary directly but he spoke often about the influence of evil. We do know that he was an incessant reader of the Bible and could quote passages from it better than most ministers. There are more than 50 references to the devil and 30 to Satan in the Bible. Here are two instances where he did refer to the devil.

In an 1836 letter to a friend, he made a brief reference to "Satan's rage."[13] In another letter to Reverend Ide, J.R. Doolittle and A. Hubbell on May 30, 1864 he expressed his disdain for slavery and Southern ministers who with regularity preached from the pulpit about the righteousness of slavery and God's approval of it,

> To read in the Bible, and the word of God Himself, that 'in the sweat of thy face shalt thou eat bread, and to preach therefrom that, 'In the sweat of other men's faces shalt thou eat bread,' to my mind can scarcely be reconciled with honest sincerity. When a year or two ago, those professedly holy men of the South met in the semblance of prayer and devotion, and in the name of Him who said, 'As ye would all men should do to you do ye even so to them,' appealed to the Christian world to aid them in doing to a whole race of men as they would have no man do to themselves, to my thinking they condemned and insulted God and His church far more than did Satan when he tempted the Saviour with the kingdoms of the earth. The devil's attempt was no more false, and far

---

13. William J. Johnson, *Abraham Lincoln The Christian*, Mott Media, Milford Michigan. 1910, p 35

less hypocritical. But let me forbear, remembering it is also written, 'Judge not, lest ye be judged.'[14]

From this it is safe to conclude that Lincoln had no doubts about the Biblical references to Satan and that he believed in the Adversary's power to destroy that which is Godly and good.

The Dramatic Success of the Apostles

To comprehend this additional, and most important battle front of the Civil War we must go back several centuries before the Declaration of Independence was signed by our Founding Fathers. The Great Apostasy brought centuries of darkness, where the fullness of the gospel of Jesus Christ was snuffed out by the forces of Satan who martyred the Holy Apostles, with the consequent removal of the power and authority of the Holy Priesthood from the earth. Even then, in these centuries following Christ's time and teachings and atonement, the pure in heart were still able to receive the Light of Christ. They could pray and those prayers would be heard and answered as God willed. In addition, they could be guided by the influence of the Holy Ghost. But the fullness of the gospel, containing all of the saving ordinances, doctrines, authority and laws of Heaven had been lost.

It is important to acknowledge that the work of the Apostles following their receipt of the Gift of the Holy Ghost and Christ's charge to "go ye into all the world, and preach the gospel to every creature"[15] was a remarkable achievement. Their unequalled success in planting in the heart of the humble believers, the blessed name of Jesus Christ, the Son of God was accomplished in a vast portion of the old world. Apostles

14. Ibid., p 135
15. Holy Bible, Mark 16:15

Peter and Paul preached the gospel of Jesus Christ with remarkable success in Asia Minor and into Italy; both were martyred in Rome. Andrew introduced the gospel far into Russia and its southern borders. Thomas preached with success as far as India. Phillip and Bartholomew took the message to North Africa and Ethiopia.

By the spring of 1820, when God the Father and his Son Jesus Christ opened the great restoration of all things through Joseph Smith, the name of Christ, his sacrifice and teachings, in various forms was known and embraced by an estimated 200 million people in the world. This astonishing work of Christ's Apostles was a glorious labor of courage and devotion to their Redeemer. The hosts of Satan's angels opposed them at every turn until all except John were martyred. They laid a firm foundation for the fullness of the Lord's gospel to be restored in these latter days. The success of Christ's apostles was extraordinary; unmatched in all of history, with one possible exception: that of Christopher Columbus. More about him later.

When Jehovah deemed that the time had come to set the foundation for the restoration to begin, he worked through courageous men of faith to methodically bring forth His light upon the earth. One of the first religious reformers to emerge was John Wycliffe, when in the late 1300s he set about to translate the Bible from Latin into English. In those dark ages, few were able to read and very few books, particularly those of the Bible existed outside of the hands of the dominant Catholic Church. These church leaders saw themselves as the guardians of the Bible message and saw no good coming from individuals reading and searching to know the great God in Heaven for themselves.

The Catholic Church throughout Europe strongly opposed Wycliffe's translation and they conspired with kings and magistrates in

Europe to stop him. Church hierarchy of that day affirmed that the emerging English language was unsuitable to convey God's word. Some claimed that common people's access to the Bible would corrupt the doctrines; others candidly expressed fear that open access to the scriptures would reduce dependence upon the church, which could translate into a reduction in their accumulation of wealth from devout followers. Consequently, Wycliffe was denounced as a heretic and treated accordingly. After he died and was buried, his bones were dug up and burned to punctuate the authorities' disdain for his efforts.

While some were inspired to translate the Bible, others were moved to prepare the means to publish it. In 1455, Johannes Gutenberg's invention of a printing press with movable type, paved the way for books to be produced in large numbers. One of the first books he printed was the Bible. As the Light of Christ distilled upon the Gentiles of Europe (asserted by some scholars to be the remnant of the northern Kingdom of Israel[16]), many more yearned to understand the Bible's forbidden content for themselves. This Renaissance or "rebirth" spread throughout Europe. Although the printing of the translated Bible was deemed illegal, they were secretly produced and read by thousands of Europeans at the peril of their lives. Making the scriptures available and helping God's children learn to read them was a vital element in God's eventual restoration of the gospel.

In the early 1500s, William Tyndale was a brilliant young priest who had studied at Oxford. He could speak eight languages and had many opportunities for a distinguished career, but he would make it his life's work to translate the Bible into English from the Hebrew and Greek translations, and then illegally distribute it. This translation proved to

16. Stephen J. Spykerman, *A Game Changing Revelation Vol 1* (2014) p. 182

be more accurate than the Latin version by Wycliffe a century earlier. Tyndale's friends warned him that he would be captured and killed, for doing so, but he continued undaunted. Once, in a conversation with a learned man, he said: "If God spare my life, ere many years I will cause a boy that driveth a plough shall know more of the scripture than thou dost.'"[17] Young Joseph Smith and Abraham Lincoln would be among those thousands of young plowboys who would read the translated Bible as foreseen by Tyndale and would be influenced by its messages as they in turn would influence millions.

Tyndale lived his life as a fugitive, being pursued by church and civil authorities who had declared him a criminal for making and distributing his English Bible. Wherever he went, from county to country in Europe, he would find printers and other truth-seekers who would willingly risk their own lives to secretly print the English Bibles and then distribute them to anxious readers. Elder Robert D. Hales declared,

> Eventually Tyndale, like other reformers was captured and executed for his efforts—strangled and burned at the stake near Brussels. But the belief for which he gave his life was not lost. Millions have come to experience for themselves what Tyndale taught throughout his life: "The nature of God's word is, that whosoever read it…it will begin immediately to make him every day better and better, til he be grown into a perfect man."[18]

Satan was also preparing for centuries to oppose the restoration of all things during the final dispensation. He had many tools at his disposal. Using greed for the treasures of the earth, history is replete with ex-

---

17. Robert D. Hales, "Preparations for the Restoration and the Second Coming: My Hand Shall Be over Thee" quoted in S. Michael Wilcox, *Fire in the Bones: William Tyndale—Martyr, Father of the English Bible* (2004), p. 47.

18. Ibid.

amples of kings and governments being turned against God's believers. For over 300 years, the Roman Empire sought to extinguish the Christian faith and its believers. In later centuries, the Catholic Church's decreed inquisitions hunted down the seekers of God's true light and once found, they were tortured and killed for their faith. The Book of Mormon contains numerous accounts of peoples and governments who warred against believers and followers of Christ because of their faith in Him. In more recent American history, hatred and lies fabricated by Satan were ruthlessly employed in persecutions and expulsions of the Latter-day Saints for their faith.

Slavery can be added to Satan's arsenal of evil. Since early history, conquering armies made a practice of selling into slavery the men, women and children captured by their victories.

Although, with all his heart, Lincoln had always wanted to see the slaves freed, his reverence for the Constitution, broken as it was with the three-fifths clause that allowed for slavery, kept him from joining abolition groups to end it. Over the years, Southern majorities in local and national governments had also managed to pass various laws to fortify the institution of slavery. But as he admonished in his Lyceum speech, obedience to the law was a citizen's paramount duty; Lincoln was unbending in his determination to respect and obey the law—even bad law. William Lee Miller observed that, "As an emerging political leader and shaper of opinion in 1854-1860, and as President of a war-torn nation in 1861-1865, he always opposed slavery strongly—but *within* the law, *under* the Constitution, *affirming* the continuing bond of the Union."[19] To the great misfortune of millions, the Constitution possessed its two serious flaws, the one that recognized slavery and the

---

19. *Lincoln's Virtues,* William Lee Miller, p 236

other that prohibited the federal government from intervening when a state fomented or allowed violence upon its own citizens. In spite of that, Lincoln and the new Republican Party were unabashed in their determination to block the spread of slavery in the new territories and future states. In this way they could at least control its insidious spread, and do so within the law.

In 1850, many citizens in the North erupted were troubled with the passage of the Fugitive Slave Law. It was aimed directly at the abolitionists' successful campaigns to protect and extend freedom to escaped slaves from the South. This law eventually resulted in the unscrupulous capture of a number of free Black Americans who never had been slaves, tearing them from their families, never to be seen again. They would be "returned"[20] to live the rest of their lives, lost in Southern slavery.

Lincoln was deeply troubled by this new act but did not oppose it because of the slaveholders' Constitutional right to own slaves, and because, as he said, the new law "springs of necessity from the fact that the institution is among us."[21] To oppose the Fugitive Slave Law would be to oppose the Constitution, which unfortunately, yet explicitly, made provision for fugitives to be "delivered up."[22] In his Bloomington speech of September 12, 1854, he quipped, referring to the Fugitive Slave Law, "…if I were called upon by a Marshall, to assist in catching a fugitive, I should suggest to him that others could run a great deal faster than I could."[23]

Satan's success in contaminating the Constitution caused untold misery for the slaves in America and it opened the door for widespread

---

20. *Lincoln's Virtues,* William Lee Miller, p 235
21. Ibid. p 235
22. Ibid. p 239
23. Ibid. p 235

corruption and lawlessness. Looking at the Civil War in this light, it becomes clear that the Adversary's primary target was not slavery; he had always had success with slavery. It was not corruption and violence, he had perfected these depravities long before. It was not the ravages of war—war has been easy for him to provoke; he has caused and delighted in thousands of wars since the beginning. What he had in his sights was to collapse the Constitution. This remarkable and divine instrument formed a protective wall around the freedom of religious thought and expression that Satan for centuries had until now, successfully smothered. He was desperately determined to destroy the very United States Constitution that Abraham Lincoln and Joseph Smith were so determined to preserve.

7

Bondage

I N LATE 1862, Reverend Byron Sutherland and some friends called upon President Lincoln in the White House. Sutherland recalled that Lincoln "spoke for a half hour and poured forth a volume of the deepest Christian philosophy he ever heard."[1]

> The ways of God are mysterious and profound beyond all comprehension—"Who by searching can find Him out?" Now judging after the manner of men…if it had been left to us to determine it, we would have had no war. And, going further back to the occasion of it, we would have had no slavery. And, tracing it still further back, we would have had no evil.[2]

In the book of Moses chapter four we read of the origin of bondage, and that Satan is the author of it.

> 1 And I, the Lord God, spake unto Moses, saying: That Satan… came before me, saying—Behold, here am I, send me, I will be thy son, and I will redeem all mankind, that one soul

1. William J. Johnson, *Abraham Lincoln The Christian,* Mott Media, Milford Michigan, 1976, p 101
2. Ibid. p. 101

shall not be lost, and surely I will do it; wherefore give me thine honor.

2 But, behold, my Beloved Son, which was my Beloved and Chosen from the beginning, said unto me—Father, thy will be done, and the glory be thine forever.

3 Wherefore, because that Satan rebelled against me, and sought to **destroy the agency of man**...I caused that he should be cast down;

4 And he became Satan, yea, even the devil, the father of all lies, to deceive and to blind men, and to **lead them captive** at his will, even as many as would not hearken unto my voice.

Our Eternal Father's sublime gift in this mortal probation was freedom, agency to choose between the great opposites in all existence: good and evil. He would allow us to have an adversary to provide a sifting opposition, a second choice for us to prove through our actions, whom we would list to obey. By this only the Lord's elect would emerge from the mortal temptations as having chosen good above evil, of having repented of their erroneous choices and set their hearts on the redeeming power of Jesus Christ and his atonement for those sins.

Lucifer, the Son of the Morning, in his anger was cast down to earth and has led men and women to succumb to his temptations and into his captivity. To many of us the term "bondage" conveys the condition of slavery. But there are various forms of bondage. The bondage of sin or the "captivity of the devil" is the most eternally damaging because its victim is the soul; this impairment lives on into the eternities. In spite of the cruel and life-long suffering of the African slaves in America, in the end, many whose hearts remained pure, even in their horrible afflictions, will earn their exaltation. The bondage of the body through slavery could not captivate the soul of the pure in heart. Such was also the case of the ancient Israelites in their 400 years of slavery in Egypt.

In the Doctrine and Covenants section 101, verses 76 and 77, God reminds Joseph Smith a second time to,

> Continue to importune for redress, and redemption by the hands of those who are placed as rulers and in authority over you. According to the laws and constitution of the people, which I have suffered to be established and should be maintained for the rights and protection of all flesh, according to just and holy principles.

Sandwiched between this commandment and God's declaration that he had established the unspeakable gift of the Constitution that follows in verse 80, he gives this significant and elucidating statement. "It is not right that any man should be in bondage one to another."[3] Of all the conditions the Constitution would impact, freedom from bondage would be its primary purpose. To whom or what was He referring with this statement? Quite possibly it was concerning the four million slaves in America. Joseph Smith was deeply troubled over the slavery issue saying, "It makes my blood boil." But in searching scripture on this subject of bondage we can conclude that God may have been making reference to some of the other forms of captivity as well.

The Egyptians held the people of Israel captive for four centuries before being freed from their bondage by the hand of God through the great prophet Moses. Following the astounding success of the apostles in planting in the hearts of millions, Jesus Christ's holy name, the opposition of the father of lies was quick, violent and confining. The Roman

---

3. Doctrine and Covenants 101:79

Empire was baffled that their success in killing Jesus and his apostles did not stop the spread and strength of Christianity. Lehi and Nephi were privileged to see in their magnificent vision of the powers of good and evil in the advancing history of this world, "And after he [Jesus] was slain I saw the multitudes of the earth, that they were gathered together to fight against the apostles."[4]

It seemed to have been easy for Satan to instill in the hearts of Roman leaders the false notion that Christians were a threat to their empire and their own pagan religion. Through the Roman Empire, Lucifer waged war on believing Christians for the next three centuries. These faithful saints,[5] as Nephi identified them, lived under the bondage of oppression and religious persecution at the hand of their government, authored by Satan.

During this extended period of time, hostility toward these followers of Christ and his apostles fluctuated throughout the empire due to local events or individual officials' actions. Periods of peace were shattered by incidents like the great Rome fire of 64 A.D., which Emperor Nero blamed on the Christians. A belief in Jesus Christ was punishable by death to those who would not renounce their religion and then offer sacrifices to the emperor or Roman gods. The worship of Roman gods and goddesses was made a civic obligation and, at times, a law. With this Lucifer established a bondage of the heart and mind. This was much like King Nebuchadnezzar's religious restrictions of the captive prophet Daniel and the Jews in Babylon. Here again, Lucifer had at his disposal, a powerful government or kingdom to lead his fight to destroy the agency of the Israelites in their worship of Jehovah.

4. Book of Mormon, I Nephi 11:34
5. Book of Mormon, I Nephi 13:5

The year 313 A.D. brought an end to the 300 year Roman bondage for Christians, the enduring harvests of Christ and his holy apostles. Constantine I, who became the first Christian Emperor of Rome, collaborated with the Eastern Roman Emperor Licinius to ratify the Edict of Milan, which secured the first political tolerance for Christian worship throughout the Roman Empire, turning the government of Rome from persecutors to protectors of the faithful believers.

There is an important similarity between the Edict of Milan and the U.S. Constitution. They were both instruments of religious tolerance and freedom. These two great actions by governments brought great benefit to the Christian world. But in the case of the Constitution, Satan's success in infusing his two fatal flaws into it, also brought misery and violence. These contaminations nearly collapsed the Constitution, which was always Satan's intent. The Constitutional allowance of slavery with the three-fifths clause extended the cruelty of this bondage. The nation became so intensely divided over this issue that it turned a large portion of those blessed with the freedoms in the Constitution to take up arms against it. Satan's intent was to weaken and then discard the Constitution so he could resume his captivity of the soul by using churches or governments at his disposal to enforce his tyranny.

The president and Congress being constitutionally restricted from enforcing the Bill of Rights resulted in widespread civil and political corruption in America in just seven decades from the ratification of the Constitution. This not only climaxed in the Civil War, but it opened the door for Satan to establish yet another spiritual captivity—always his preferred form of bondage, this time in the United States. As both Abraham Lincoln and Joseph Smith observed and warned, the crippling of the Constitution, the rampant mob violence and the harsh disregard for the First Amendment right of free religious expression, could once again corrupt yet another government—this the American government. It could and likely would, under Satan's influence, become much like regimes of the European nations, the Roman Empire, King Nebuchadnezzar and other governments, restricting, instead of protecting religious freedom. With this Satan would once again have a compromised government in America to brandish his sword of tyranny, preventing the restored Church of Jesus Christ from flourishing. The stage was so very nearly set for Satan to extinguish the flickering flame of restoration—divine light and truth—in yet another dispensation.

The Edict of Milan was followed by the Nicene Creed where Constantine, seeking to establish unity in Christian doctrine, incorrectly defined the nature of the Godhead as being an equal divinity of the Holy Trinity. It would be taught that the Father and Son and the Holy Ghost were one and the same, without bodies, without parts, and without passions. Constantine had no living prophets on whom to rely for the unadulterated truths of the gospel of Jesus Christ. He was left with his scholars, some holy men and some not, to establish this definition, which was fundamentally wrong and diabolical in its origin.

With Constantine, Lucifer lost the Roman governmental influence but he gained a great conciliatory victory to his cause with the creed resulting from the Council of Nicaea. Through Constantine, he developed another ally in the emergence of a great and abominable church, which would indoctrinate this unusual fabrication within the minds of its parishioners. In creating a distortion of the true identity of the very Father and Redeemer and Comforter, Satan established a subtle impediment for the pure in heart that has endured since the dark ages.

For more than 1,700 years, this distortion of the true nature of the Godhead continues in its effect to mislead millions of Christian believers today. How it must please Lucifer that sincere seekers of their God and Creator are denied the pure knowledge of the true and divine nature of our Father, our Savior and the holy Comforter. Clarification of the true identity of the Godhead must wait until some 1,800 years after Christ's sojourn on earth, with the light of the Book of Mormon and modern day revelation through the prophet of the restoration. This grand truth was revealed on this continent, in this nation, which had as its governing beacon, an inspired Constitution designed to protect these truths from Satan's assaults.

> The Father has a body of flesh and bones as tangible as man's; the Son also; but the Holy Ghost has not a body of flesh and bones, but is a personage of Spirit. Were it not so, the Holy Ghost could not dwell in us.[6]

Satan hates this truth and the heavenly enlightening it brings, but in America, he was left with no established government or oppressive church dogma to fight against it.

The nature of God's identity was not the only doctrine that Lucifer was able to corrupt through those many years of his reign. In the centuries following Christ's earthly ministry, the writings of His life and

---

6. Doctrine and Covenants 130:22

teachings were compiled to become our Bible. Nephi was shown this book by the angel in his vison.

> And the angel said unto me, Knowest thou the meaning of the book? And I said unto him; I know not.

> And he said, The book that thou beholdest is a record of the Jews, which contains the covenants of the Lord...and it also containeth many of the prophesies of the holy prophets... they are of great worth unto the Gentiles. ...it contained the fullness of the gospel of the Lord, of whom the twelve apostles bear record.

> Wherefore, thou seest that after the book hath gone forth through the hands of the great and abominable church, that there are many plain and precious things taken away from the book, which is the book of the Lamb of God.[7]

Over the centuries this sacred work was copied, revised and translated hundreds of times and into various languages. We believe in the integrity of the written word by the holy prophets; we also believe that in the numerous translations and copies over the centuries, changes occurred to the original texts. Research of various Bible translations has confirmed that numerous passages are clearly mistranslated, and some of those changes were intentional. Dr. Bart D. Ehrman, writes an exhaustive treatment on these Biblical losses in his book, *The Orthodox Corruption of Scripture*. In it he describes in abundant detail, the numerous translation processes of the ancient biblical texts by scribes of the early Christians that spanned centuries. Ehrman declares, "My thesis can be stated simply: scribes occasionally altered the words of their

---

7. Book of Mormon, I Nephi 13:21-28

sacred texts to make them more patently orthodox and to prevent their misuse by Christians who espoused aberrant views."[8] He continues,

> The New Testament manuscripts were not produced impersonally by machines capable of flawless reproduction. They were copied by hand, by living, breathing human beings. Did the scribes' polemical contexts influence the way they transcribed their sacred Scripture? The burden of the present study is that they did, that theological disputes, specifically disputes over Christology, prompted Christian scribes to alter the words of Scripture in order to make them more serviceable for the polemic task. Scribes modified their manuscripts to make them more patently "orthodox" and less susceptible to "abuse" by the opponents of orthodoxy.[9]

Eusebius was the bishop of Caesarea, a contemporary with Constantine I and one of many who was distressed by the changes made in the sacred biblical texts of his day. He "accused the Roman adoptionists Theodotus, Asclepiades, and Hermophilus of tampering with the manuscripts of the New Testament in order to secure their own theology within them."[10] Over the centuries there were many like Eusabius who shared this concern. And there is ample evidence that there were others who were active in the modifications or corruptions of the original gospel texts as Dr. Ehrman described... Lucifer used these contaminated translations to cloud the plain truths of Christ's gospel, thus crafting a

---

8. Bart D. Ehrman, *The Orthodox Corruption of Scripture*, (New York, Oxford: Oxford University Press, 1993), p. xi.

9. Ibid., pp. 3-4.

10. Ibid., p. 47

spiritual bondage through confusion and engendering spiritual blindness among sincere European seekers of truth.

Nephi's marvelous vision of significant future events continued with the angel showing him a book, that was the Bible, "a record of the Jews, which contains the covenants of the Lord…and many prophecies…and they are of great worth unto the Gentiles."[11] His vision continues with a view of a great and abominable church that had, "taken away from the gospel of the Lamb, many parts which are plain and most precious; and also many covenants of the Lord are taken away."[12] Because of these omissions and variations with the written "gospel of the Lamb, an exceedingly great many do stumble, yea in so much that Satan hath great power over them."[13]

As much as Lincoln loved the Bible, as a young man he sometimes pointed out discrepancies found therein. This viewpoint incorrectly confirmed among many of his friends that he was in their minds, an infidel. But Lincoln's awareness of inconsistencies in the Bible, however, was in harmony with Latter-day Saint doctrine. The eighth Article of Faith states, "We believe the Bible to be the word of God as far as it is translated correctly; we also believe the Book of Mormon to be the word of God."[14]

Abraham Lincoln was one of those who stumbled with the Bible, but in a much different manner than did the Gentiles referenced in this scripture. Many sincere religions emerged from these European believers, such as Methodists, Presbyterians and Baptists, who brought their new found faith with them to America. Lincoln read the Bible with a

---

11. Book of Mormon, I Nephi 13:20-23
12. Book of Mormon, I Nephi 13:
13. Book of Mormon, I Nephi 13:29
14. Articles of Faith 1:8.

different set of eyes, and during his lifetime he declined many appeals
to join any of these sects. Lincoln had a remarkable and deep understanding of the Bible, he read it throughout his life, he attended church
meetings with his family, but never became a member of any.

This reluctance to join a church became a serious political liability;
many refusing to vote for him in his various campaigns for office because in their minds, Lincoln was an unbeliever, an infidel for refusing
membership in any one of the prominent Protestant religions of his day.
He could have averted a great deal of criticism and political angst by
simply choosing any of the various Protestant churches in his community. He was questioned often about his reticence to accept membership
in a church. Later in his life he wrote, "I planted myself upon the truth
and the truth only, so far as I knew it or could be brought to know it,
said Lincoln."[15] Referring to his reasons for not joining a church he said,

> Those days of trouble found me tossed amid a sea of ques-
> tionings. They piled big upon me… Through all I groped my
> way until I found a stronger and higher grasp of thought, one
> that reached beyond this life with a clearness and satisfaction
> I had never known before. The Scriptures unfolded before me
> with a deeper and more logical appeal, through these new ex-
> periences, than anything else I could find to turn to, or even
> before had found in them.[16]

---

15. Ibid., 9, p. 235.
16. William J. Wolf, *The Almost Chosen People*, Doubleday & Company, Inc., Garden City New,
York, 1959, p. 50-51

Is Lincoln describing here the experience of enlightenment through the Holy Ghost? He continues,

> I do not claim that all my doubts were removed then, or since that time have been swept away. They are not.

> Probably it is to be my lot to go on in a twilight, feeling and reasoning my way through life, as questioning, doubting Thomas did. But in my poor, maimed way, I bear with me as I go on a seeking spirit of desire for a faith that was with him of olden time, who, in his need, as I in mine, exclaimed, "Help thou my unbelief."[17]

Lincoln concluded, "I doubt the possibility, or propriety, of settling the religion of Jesus Christ in the models of man-made creeds and dogmas... I cannot without mental reservations assent to long and complicated creeds and catechisms."[18]

Henry C. Deming, member of Congress from Connecticut, in a memorial address given before his state's Legislature in June of 1865 (just days following Lincoln's assassination), shared this exchange when he had earlier asked Lincoln his reason for never joining any church:

> I have never united myself to any church, because I have found difficulty in giving my assent, without mental reservation, to the long, complicated statements of Christian doctrine which characterize their articles of belief and confessions of faith. When any church will inscribe over its altars, as its sole qualification for membership, the Savior's condensed statement of substance of both law and gospel, "Thou shalt love the Lord thy God with all thy heart, and with all thy soul, and with all

17. Ibid., p. 50-51
18. Ibid., p. 50-51

thy mind, and thy neighbor as thyself," that church will I join with all my heart and all my soul.[19]

Most of the prominent Protestant sects of today formulated their core beliefs and identities during an unprecedented period of Christian religious zeal in the late 1700s and early 1800s; the period known as the Second Great Awakening. Over time, some of these sects fragmented over doctrinal differences while others united. The Methodist, Baptist and Presbyterian religions originated in England during this period and rapidly spread across America, as did the American-born religions such as the Campbellites and Millerites, (later becoming the Seventh-Day Adventist Church), Assemblies of God, and Church of Christ, to name a few.

The Church of Jesus Christ of Latter-day Saints also emerged during this same era of religious revival but its followers alone encountered Satan's opposition and unrelenting persecution for their beliefs and practices. Virtually all of the emerging Protestant religions developed with general acceptance by the populace with little interference from secular authorities. This was not the case with the Mormons; they were met with intense persecution for their beliefs, much like the early religious reformers of Europe and much of this persecution from Protestant Christians.

Referring to his early days of attending these Protestant churches where he lived, Lincoln later wrote how, "The preacher bellowed and spat and whined, and cultivated an artificial 'holy tone' and denounced the Methodists and blasphemed the Presbyterians and painted a hell

---

19. William Barton, *The Soul of Lincoln* University of Illinois Press, Urbana and Chicago, 2005 pp. 244-245.

whose horror even in the backwoods was an atrocity."[20] Lincoln simply could not agree with their interpretations of the Bible; he seemed to see through the corruptions and omissions of the sacred text. For him as noted earlier, "The scriptures unfolded before me with a deeper and more logical appeal, than anything else I could find to turn to, or even before had found in them."[21]

Through Lincoln's personal records and of those who knew him, we learn that certain contemporary doctrines troubled him. He could find no peace in the doctrine regarding the endlessness of God's punishment that was propounded by nearly all of the Protestant and the Catholic churches—the belief that the benevolent Father would cause the punishments of His wayward children to go on forever. These tenets of eternal damnation and endless torment were pervasive in the "hellfire and damnation" sermons given throughout the country; most certainly heard by young Joseph Smith as well, in New York. On the doctrine of infinite punishment William Barton summarizes, "This dogma, the adult Lincoln denied upon two grounds: First, the justice and mercy of God; Second: the fact that according to the Biblical scheme of redemption, whatever right the human race had possessed to immortality and lost through sin, had been restored in Christ."[22]

---

20. William Barton, *The Soul of Lincoln* University of Illinois Press, Urbana and Chicago, 2005 p. 48.

21. William J. Wolf, *The Almost Chosen People,* Doubleday & Company, Inc., Garden City New, York, 1959, p. 50-51

22. William Barton, *The Soul of Lincoln* University of Illinois Press, Urbana and Chicago, 2005 p. 137.

On another occasion during a discussion on religion with some friends, Lincoln said,

> If justice requires that punishment be proportionate to the offense, then eternal damnation is intrinsically unjust and therefore unworthy of a just God. No finite offense (the only kind mortals are capable of committing) could fairly merit infinite punishment. But the Christian God is just, Lincoln continued, and the proof is in the 22nd verse of the 15th chapter of St. Paul's letter to the Corinthians: "For as in Adam all die, even so in Christ shall all be made alive."[23]

He went on to write his belief that "Christ's atoning death meant that punishment in the afterlife not only would fit the crime but also would be rehabilitative, designed to prepare the offender for eternal happiness."[24] His interpretation of this doctrine did not set well with the ministers or acquaintances of his day, serving as added evidence in their minds that he was an unqualified candidate for heaven. On this William J. Wolf commented, "This is hardly the statement of an 'infidel' position. It reveals rather a mind dissatisfied with the sectarian theology of his community probing deep into the Bible on his own. The unchanging affirmations for him in this process were man's need of salvation in terms of Adam's fall, God's loving purpose behind the infliction of punishment, and Christ's atoning work through His sacrificial death."[25] On this subject, Wolf concludes, "Lincoln's conviction that God would restore the whole of creation as the outcome of Christ's

---

23. Ibid., p. xxiv.

24. Ibid., p. xxiv..

25. William J. Wolf, *The Almost Chosen People*, Doubleday & Company, Inc., Garden City New, York, 1959, p. 47.

atonement would have been in itself a bar to membership in the Spring-field church he attended."[26]

Lincoln's solitary belief that all men could be saved, once just punishments for sins were exacted, was shared by Joseph Smith and his followers, and they too were derided for it. The third Article of Faith states: "We believe that through the atonement of Christ all mankind may be saved by obedience to the laws and ordinances of the Gospel."[27] As far as we know, Lincoln was unaware of this belief among the Mormons who had once lived in his state of Illinois before finding refuge in the Rocky Mountains. He was essentially alone on the Illinois western frontier with his personal view of a just God who would certainly bring judgment for unrepented sins, but also of a God who was filled with mercy and love for his children that would eventually allow for the blessed gift of eternal life, once the demands of justice and obedience had been fulfilled.

Latter-day Saints have always held to a similar belief as that embraced by Lincoln. Biblical references to eternal punishment is a reference of God's sovereign ownership in judging the world, not a measure of length of the course-corrective punishment. The Latter-day Saint belief that God has prepared three degrees or levels of glorious existence into which all of God's children will be assigned according to their levels of faithfulness, would likely have been of interest to Lincoln.

It was not Lincoln's nature to be critical of ideas or people but he did harbor other differences with the churches of his day, which he would only occasionally and guardedly express. His dissatisfaction with these religions was that they "neglected this fundamental love of God

---

26. Ibid., p. 104.
27. The Pearl of Great Price, articles of Faith #3

and of neighbor by too much introverted attention upon correctness in theological opinion."[28] He also "took a dim view of preachers who used the pulpit for politics" and said he preferred "those who preached the gospel."[29]

When Lincoln would express his doubts regarding certain Protestant beliefs, he would sometimes add, "but I have never denied the truth of the scriptures."[30] Lincoln's uncommon depth of Biblical knowledge and understanding led him to perceive and reject the "man-made abstracts" often present in the religious "frontier squabbles" of his day.[31] It can be inferred from these statements and many others throughout his life, that Lincoln's unwillingness to join any church was based on his unsuccessful search for a church that taught and practiced the pure doctrines and Heavenly truths as he perceived them in his lifelong reading of the Bible and through his humble prayers for guidance. "The Bible quite apart from the competing churches was his source of inspiration."[32]

Clarence E. Macartney wrote: "The ordinary daily speech of Lincoln was salted with timely and apt quotations from the Bible."[33] He cited President Lincoln's response to General George B. McClellan's complaints about the weather bogging down his army. Mr. Lincoln told his aide John Hay that the general "seemed to think, in defiance of Scripture, that heaven sent its rain only on the just, and not on the

28. William J. Wolf, *The Almost Chosen People,* Doubleday & Company, Inc., Garden City New, York, 1959, p. 92.

29. Ibid., p. 92.

30. Roy P. Basler, *Collected Works of Abraham Lincoln,* (New Brunswick, N.J.: Rutgers University Press, 1953), vol. I, p. 256

31. Ibid., 5, p. 75.

32. Ibid., 5, p. 42.

33. Clarence Edward Macartney, *Lincoln and the Bible,* p. 84. (See William E. Barton, *The Soul of Abraham Lincoln),* pp. 93-94.

unjust."[34] Also during the presidential campaign, Mr. Lincoln had a long conversation with State Superintendent of Instruction Newton Bateman. Bateman wrote that in October 1860, Mr. Lincoln "repeated many passages of the Bible, in a very reverent & devout way, & seemed especially impressed with the solemn grandeur of portions of revelation describing the wrath of Almighty God."[35] On another occasion Lincoln told a friend,

> I decided a long time ago that it was less difficult to believe that the Bible was what it claimed to be than to disbelieve it. It is a good book for us to obey – it contains the Ten Commandments, the Golden Rule, and many other rules which ought to be followed. No man was ever the worse for living according to the directions of the Bible.[36]

Lincoln's long-time friend, Joshua F. Speed recalled a visit to President Lincoln at the Soldiers' Home in Washington:

> As I entered the room, near night, he was sitting near a window intently reading his Bible. Approaching him I said: 'I am glad to see you so profitably engaged.' 'Yes,' said he, 'I am profitably engaged.' 'Well,' said I, 'if you have recovered from your skepticism, I am sorry to say that I have not.' Looking me earnestly in the face and placing his hand on my shoulder, he said: 'You are wrong, Speed. Take all of this book upon

---

34. Allen C. Guelzo, *"Holland's Informants: The Construction of Josiah Holland's 'Life of Abraham Lincoln,'" Journal of the Abraham Lincoln Association, (Letter from Newton Bateman to Josiah G. Holland, June 19, 1865),* Winter 2002, p. 28.

35. Clarence Edward Macartney, *Lincoln and the Bible*, p. 74-75.

36. Ibid., 5, p. 136.

reason that you can and the balance on faith, and you will live and die a happier and better man.'[37]

To a group of free Blacks who had just presented him with a beautifully bound Bible, Lincoln said:

In regard to this Great book, I have but to say, it is the best gift God has given to man. All the good the Savior gave to the world was communicated through this book. But for it we could not know right from wrong. All things most desirable for man's welfare, here and hereafter, are to be found portrayed in it.[38]

As President, Lincoln would refer to God in his speeches, his conversations and his writing more than any other President before or after him. He was the first and only American president to publicly call for the intervention of the Holy Spirit. On July 15, 1863, in the midst of the Civil War, Lincoln wrote in an official proclamation to the American people,

I invite the people of the United States to invoke the influence of the Holy Spirit ... to guide the counsels of the government with wisdom adequate to so great a national emergency, and to visit with tender care and consolation throughout the length and breadth of our land all those who, through the vicissitudes of marches, voyages, battles, and sieges, have been brought to suffer in mind, body or estate.[39]

37. Wayne Temple, *From Skeptic to Prophet,*

38. Roy P. Basler, Editor, *Collected Works of Abraham Lincoln (Statement by S. W. Chase to President Lincoln, Washington Chronicle),* September 8, 1864, Volume VII, pp. 543.

39. Abraham Lincoln, Speech on July 15, 1863 see Walking with Lincoln... by Thomas Freiling

Lincoln seemed to always be reaching for and operating from, a higher spiritual plane than those around him. In one of his debates with Stephen A. Douglas over slavery in America he said, responding to an accusation made by Douglas,

> My friend has said to me that I am a poor hand to quote Scripture. I will try it again, however. It is said in one of the admonitions of the Lord, 'As your Father in Heaven is perfect, be ye also perfect.' The Saviour, I suppose, did not expect that any human creature could be perfect as the Father in Heaven; but He said, 'As your Father in Heaven is perfect, be ye also perfect.' He set up that standard, and he [Jesus] who did most toward reaching that standard, attained the highest degree of moral perfection. So I say in relation to the principle that all men are created equal, let it be as nearly reached as we can.[40]

Vision of Captivity

Nephi's prophetic vision of the Promised Land includes ten references to the captivity of the Gentiles in Europe, where Satan had significant success in destroying the agency of truth seeking Gentiles throughout Europe. He saw Jehovah's great process of enlightenment brought on with the translation of the Bible and the mass production of the

40. Ibid., 5, p. 98.

same. He also saw Satan's disturbing attacks upon those saints where he brought "them down into captivity."[41] Nephi records,

> I saw among the nations of the Gentiles the formation of a great church.
>
> And the angel said unto me: Behold the formation of a church which is most abominable above all other churches, which slayeth the saints of God, yea, and tortureth them and bindeth them down, and yoketh them with a yoke of iron, and bringeth them down into captivity.
>
> And it came to pass that I beheld this great and abominable church; and I saw the devil that he was the founder of it.[42]

In their vision of the dramatic future events leading to Christ's return in glory, Lehi and Nephi were shone Satan's horrific bondage and oppression unjustly imposed upon the Lord's European Gentiles during the dark ages. It is important to recognize that there were saints among these Gentiles, as Nephi identified them in verse five. Much of this persecution and tyranny came through the Inquisition, an ecclesiastical court and process of the Roman Catholic Church in which they slayed, tortured, bound, yoked and brought the saints of God into captivity. It was established to identify and punish heretics. In the case of the Inquisition, a heretic was defined as any person having a belief, practice or conversation that was outside of the Catholic Church dogmas. This of course included believers in heavenly truth, in other words, the saints. Satan's target with the Inquisition was primarily those individuals who were sincere seekers of the eternal truths that were coming to light

41. Book of Mormon, I Nephi 13:5
42. .[40] Book of Mormon, I Nephi 13: 4-6

through the translations of the Bible into European languages. Estimates of number of innocent people who were tortured and murdered, and their belongings confiscated by the church during these harrowing years of the Inquisition range from 600,000 to a million.[43]

The Inquisition or inquiry wielded immense and brutal power throughout the medieval times. Its function was to repress all heretics of their rights and then to confiscate the estate and assets of those convicted. These possessions would then be added to the Catholic treasury. Nephi's vision confirms,

> I beheld this great and abominable church; and I saw that the devil was the founder of it. And I also saw gold, and silver, and silks, and scarlets, and fine-twined linen, and all manner of precious clothing; and I saw many harlots. [These things] are the desires of the great and abominable church. And for the praise of the world do they *destroy the saints of God,* and *bring them down into captivity*[44] (emphasis added).

Lucifer Rages

For nearly six centuries potential heretics were sought out and destroyed for thoughts or speech in opposition to the dominant religion, a system that became the legal framework throughout much of Europe, orchestrating the most abominable religious order in the history of mankind. Pope Innocent III declared that, "Anyone who attempts to

43. The Horrors of the Church and its Holy Inquisition, http://www.bibliotecapleyades.net/vatican/esp_vatican29.htm#The%20Church
44. Book of Mormon, I Nephi 13: 6-9

construe a personal view of God which conflicts with Church dogma must be burned without pity."[45]

In 1252, Pope Innocent IV officially authorized the creation of the horrific Inquisition torture chambers. His edict also included a new perpetual sentence of imprisonment or death at the stake. It made acquittal of anyone merely accused, virtually impossible to be obtained. Thus, with a license granted by the pope himself, Inquisitors were free to explore the depths of horror and cruelty. Dressed as black-robed fiends with black cowls over their heads, the Inquisitors' torture could extract confessions from just about anyone, including children. Many innocent Gentile "saints" were thus tortured and murdered. The Inquisition invented every conceivable device to inflict pain by slowly dismembering and dislocating the body.

Prominent inquisitors included Peter of Verona, Italy, Robert le Bougre in northeastern France and Bernardus Guidonis in Toulouse. Guidonis was renowned for his ruthlessness, condemning roughly 900 heretics, some of whom were saints, sincere believers in Jesus Christ, as Nephi was shown. Not only was a victim's property confiscated, but his heirs were subjected to still further penalties. In the north of France, Robert le Bougre, spent six years going through the areas of Nivernais, Burgundy, Flanders and Champagne, burning at the stake in each place, unfortunate victims condemned with unjust trials.

The Spanish Inquisition terrorized virtually everyone in that country for some 350 years. It was established in 1478 with the papal approval of Pope Sixtus IV, just 14 years prior to Christopher Columbus' ocean voyage to the Americas. Many Jews had taken residence in Spain

---

45. The Horrors of the Church and its Holy Inquisition, http://www.bibliotecapleyades.net/vatican/esp_vatican29.htm#The%20Church

prompting the Inquisitors to expand their inquiries, intent upon discovering Muslims and Jews performing their religious expressions and traditions in secret, torturing and murdering them for their faith.

Over these centuries of tyranny, this church-sponsored torture, robbery and murder were so vast that it actually diminished the population of Spain, depleting its resources and political strength. This diabolical bondage and oppression in Spain was considered the most deadly and notorious of all Inquisitions. It received praise from the Catholic hierarchy for its highly organized and efficient operations of torturing and slaying innocent people.

The first two Inquisitors in the districts of Seville were appointed in 1480 by cash-strapped King Ferdinand and Queen Isabella. Their royal charge was to round up the wealthiest heretics in Seville. Once confessions were extracted through their torture, the property of the accused was expropriated and divided between the Spanish throne and the church. King Ferdinand and Queen Isabella conspired with the church to directly pay the expenses of the inquisitors, and then receive the net income from the stolen estates and assets of the accused.

Tomas Torquemada was appointed Inquisitor General for all of Spain. His duty was to expand the inquisition process to the populations in Castille and Aragon. He boasted that his work of torture, theft and murder for the heretics was the only way to achieve political and religious unity in Spain. Those refusing to accept Catholicism were convicted and then paraded in processions to public squares where they were burnt alive at the stake in front of large crowds who were ordered to watch the brutality. This Catholic ceremony in Spain was paradoxically known as the auto de fe, or act of faith.

The Roman Inquisition, which emanated from Italy, sowed its terror from 1542-1700. In the early 1500s the Catholic Church had assumed a defensive reaction against the growing Reformation, the movement spawned by Martin Luther in 1517 that gave birth to Protestantism. His Ninety-Five Theses enumerated the crimes and false dogmas of the Catholic Church. But the real impact of his protestations came by way of the newly invented printing press. He blanketed Europe with tens of thousands of printed pamphlets containing his protests. This Reformation movement was so strong that a vast number of Gentiles in Europe embraced it; but they had to do it secretly to escape the treacherous measures of the Inquisition. In 1542, Pope Paul III established the Holy Office as the final court of appeal in trials of heresy to combat the dramatic impact of Martin Luther's revolt.

The church also identified books and pamphlets that were forbidden to read, including those of Luther and the Bible. The Roman Catholic Church managed to influence governments to censor these writings, especially religious tracts of the Reformation. These Gentiles were drawn by the light of God's opening process of restoration, but lived in unending fear of surprise home-invasions by officers of the Inquisition who would ransack the home looking for any publication or other piece of evidence that might be construed to be heretical. Every book encountered was minutely scrutinized with the express object of finding any word, phrase or passage that might be interpreted as contrary to the creeds or interests of the dominant church. If judged to be heretical, the owner, or his or her family would become subject to the questioning, harassment, beating, torture and murder by these servants of Satan.

These horrors were described by Nephi to be the captivity of the devil. Nearly everyone lived in constant dread of being accused by a disgruntled neighbor or an offended churchman because once accused, few, even if innocent, escaped the torture and murder of the great and abominable church's Inquisition. This bondage of the European Gentiles was different from the bondage of the American slaves, but also traumatizing. The longings of their hearts for the liberating points of heavenly light were simply not permitted to gain full expression. This was the captivity that Nephi saw and recorded in his vision.

When God's appointed time arrived, he provided for a large scale and dramatic escape for these European Gentile saints out of this tyranny, "the captivity of the devil."[46] This escape would release them from the grip of Satan's church used for centuries to blind, bind, yoke, torture and slay the Gentile saints for their desires to look for and find their true God. Their flight to freedom would eventually entail a literal removal to a land far distant from Europe—the promised land of the people of Lehi on the American continent. The Holy Spirit would inspire them, like Lehi, to cross the great Atlantic Ocean. Nephi beheld that in this land God would perform a "great and marvelous work."[47] In his record he continues: "And it came to pass that I beheld the Spirit of God, that it wrought upon other Gentiles; and they went forth out of captivity, upon the many waters"[48]

God revealed to Nephi that he would open the way for the Gentiles to escape from centuries of Satan's captivity by inspiring a man to do what no Gentile thought could be done:

> I looked and beheld a man among the Gentiles, who was sep-
> arated from the seed of my brethren by the many waters; and

---

46. Book of Mormon I Nephi 14: 7
47. Book of Mormon I Nephi 14: 7
48. Book of Mormon, I Nephi 13:13

I beheld the Spirit of God, that it came down and wrought upon the man; and he went forth upon the many waters, even unto the seed of my brethren, who were in the promised land.[49]

Modern day prophets have confirmed that this man among the Gentiles whom Nephi saw in vision was Christopher Columbus. Brigham Young declared:

The Almighty…moved upon Columbus to launch forth upon the trackless deep to discover the American Continent; he moved upon the signers of the Declaration of Independence; and he moved upon Washington to fight and conquer, in the same way as he moved upon ancient and modern Prophets, each being inspired to accomplish the particular work he was called to perform in the times, seasons, and dispensations of the Almighty.[50]

Americans in this country have revered Columbus for his so-called discovery of America. While it was a discovery for the European and Eastern world, it was a land well known to the Creator and its millions of inhabitants who were of the house of Israel through Lehi and Sariah. What God revealed to Columbus and the Gentile world was a land of promise, a land that had been held in reserve for many great and marvelous works of God to be performed by his prophets and Gentile saints.

Only a few of the teachings of Christ in the Americas had survived the centuries among the Lamanites. Columbus' ocean voyage to the Americas in 1492 and the millions of Europeans who would follow

---

49. Book of Mormon, I Nephi 13:12

50. Reported by G. D. Watt, *Journal of Discourses,* Liverpool, England, Published by S.D. &S. W. Franklin, 1851, Vol. 7, p. 13

him, clearly played a role in this phenomenon of religious fervor and freedom of thought that would eventually cover the globe. It is a marvel that the testimonies of the Holy Apostles and the emergence of the Holy Bible would establish such a lasting faith on the name of Jesus Christ that endured the horrors of the Dark Ages throughout the Old World. The memory of their spiritual captivity in Europe drove the new residents of the North American Colonies to establish and fiercely defend their liberated state of freedom of worship by placing few restrictions on how their citizens could worship God. In America, one could freely choose which set of religious tenets he or she would follow.

It is interesting that Christopher Columbus was driven to his courageous voyage by what he felt to be a higher purpose. He said of his voyage in 1492 to his son, "God gave me the faith, and afterwards the courage so that I was quite willing to undertake the journey."[51] And in his will he wrote: "In the name of the most holy trinity, who inspired me with the idea and afterwards made it perfectly clear to me that I could navigate and go to the Indies from Spain, by traversing the ocean westward."[52]

There is a noteworthy parallel between Abraham Lincoln and Christopher Columbus. Both harbored strong inner premonitions that they were placed on this earth with a high and sacred work to perform. The fact that Lincoln believed that he was also raised up by God, as were the framers of our Constitution, is supported by frequent statements of

51. "*The Great Prologue,*" Mark E. Petersen, Brigham Young University, 29 September 1974, speeches.byu.edu/?act=viewitem&id=1024.

52. Jacob Wassermann, *Columbus, Don Quixote of the Seas,* (Little, Brown, and Company, 1930, Trans., Eric Sutton) pp. 46, 61. Christopher Columbus' Last Will and Testament

his own and of those who knew him. Columbus' road to fulfillment of prophecy seemed also to be under holy and heavenly direction. He said,

> At a very early age I began to navigate upon the seas, which I have continued to this day. . . . Such has been my interest for more than forty years. . . . I prayed to the most merciful Lord concerning my desire, and he gave me the spirit and the intelligence for it.[53]

On another occasion he wrote to Amerigo Vespucci that,

> I feel persuaded by many and wonderful manifestations of Divine Providence in my special favour, that I am the chosen instrument of God in bringing to pass a great event—no less than the conversion of millions who are now existing in the darkness of Paganism.[54]

Dr. Arnold K. Garr in his book *Christopher Columbus: a Latter-day Saint Perspective* shares an interesting insight about this man.

> Christopher's son, Ferdinand, believed that God directed the choice of his father's names. For example, the name Christopher means Christ-bearer. The Columbus surname was common in Southern Europe, and means "dove." Ferdinand also believed that this name was providential because his father, "carried the grace of the Holy Ghost to that New World . . . showing those people . . . God's beloved son, as the Holy Ghost did in the figure of the dove when St. John baptized Christ (Ferdinand 4).

---

53. Dr. Arnold K. Garr, *Christopher Columbus: A Latter-day Saint Perspective,* Deseret Book, Salt Lake City, Utah, 1992, p. 17
54. Ibid., p. 41

The religious symbolism of his name does seem significant, considering the Admiral's professed faith and the inspiration to which he attributed his great success.

Perhaps the most intriguing aspect of Columbus' name, however, is the way in which he signed it after he returned home from his first voyage to the New World. Although there were several variations, the most common rendering was as follows:

.S.

.S.A.S.

X M Y

Xpo FERENS

The most complete explanation of this curious cryptic autograph by Columbus himself is, at best, vague. In his will, he simply instructed his heirs on the mechanics, spacing, and punctuation of the signature. Though he left no clues as to its meaning, he directed them to use the cryptic signature, thereafter, as their own (Thacher 3:455; this volume has 371 pages on Columbus' handwriting). Scholars generally agree that the signature denotes some kind of tribute to Christianity. On the bottom line, Xpo is Greek for "Christ," and FERENS is Latin meaning "bearer." Many interpretations suggest that the X M Y, one line above, stand for "O Christ, Mary, Joseph!" The top four letters of the pyramid may stand for either, "Save me" or, "I am the servant of the Most High Saviour." According to Thacher (3:456-57), the complete message might well be:

I am the servant of the Most High Saviour

O Christ, Mary, Joseph!

Christ-bearer[55]

55. Dr. Arnold K. Garr, *Christopher Columbus: A Latter-day Saint Perspective,* Deseret Book, Salt Lake City, Utah, 1992, pp 19-20

By opening the seaways to the American Continents, Christopher Columbus, the Christ Bearer truly did open an entire Continent to a knowledge and belief of Jesus Christ. And ironically it was the Catholic Church that was zealous to teach their version of Christianity to the native peoples of the newly discovered West Indies. Many Spanish Catholic priests crossed the sea to establish missions and build their Cathedrals. By means of the Spanish Inquisition, many natives of Central and South America were effectively compelled to embrace the dogmas of the Catholic Church.

Bartolome de las Casas a 16th century Spanish historian chronicled the atrocities committed in the name of the Church.[56] By the time of the restoration of the gospel, the vast majority of inhabitants of the new Spanish empire had accepted (first by force and then tradition) Christianity and the name of Jesus Christ. This rather strained foundation of faith in Christ nonetheless prepared millions to embrace the fullness of the Savior's revealed truths revealed through the Prophet Joseph Smith in the New World in modern times.

De Las Casas also chronicled the Admiral's fervent desire to carry the message of Christ to the world:

> He was extraordinarily zealous for the divine service; he desired and was eager for the conversion of these people [the native Indians], and that in every region the faith of Jesus Christ be planted and enhanced . . . ever holding great confidence in divine providence.[57] (Morison 1:63-64).

56. http://origins.osu.edu/milestones/july-2015-bartolom-de-las-casas-and-500-years-racial-injustice
57. Dr. Arnold K. Garr, *Christopher Columbus: A Latter-day Saint Perspective,* Deseret Book, Salt Lake City, Utah, 1992, p 24

Las Casas also claimed that,

> Columbus was the most outstanding sailor in the world, versed like no other in the art of navigation, for which divine Providence chose him to accomplish the most outstanding feat ever to be accomplished in the world until now.[58] (Las Casas 17)

In these later years, however, the revered name of Columbus has declined in its level of respect as modern Americans malign him for having brought disease, death and destruction with his discovery. The angel makes reference to this to Nephi in the verse preceding Nephi's view of a man crossing the ocean to the Promised Land. And it came to pass that the angel said to me: Behold the wrath of God is upon the seed of thy brethren.[59]

This is followed in verse 14 with,

> And it came to pass that I beheld many multitudes of the Gentiles upon the land of promise; and I beheld the wrath of God, that it was upon the seed of thy brethren; and they were scattered before the Gentiles and were smitten. [60]

In North America—which the scriptures reveal to be the original Land of Promise, beginning with the Garden of Eden, the Ancient-of-Days, the City of Enoch and future location of the City of Zion—the works of God would move forward in an unprecedented degree. Judgments upon the Lamanites were in full swing as those native tribes were driven and scattered from their homelands in the eastern United

---

58. Dr. Arnold K. Garr, *Christopher Columbus: A Latter-day Saint Perspective,* Deseret Book, Salt Lake City, Utah, 1992, p 34
59. Book of Mormon, I Nephi 13:11
60. Book of Mormon, I Nephi 13:14

States. They retreated before the European settlers who were coming out of "captivity" in great numbers from their Gentile nations, just as Nephi had foreseen. These immigrants were seen by Nephi to be Israelites, unaware of their own identity mostly through the lineage of Joseph by Ephraim.[61] These Gentile saints carried with them a book (the Bible) which, unlike their gold-seeking Gentile cousins to the south, these "Gentiles" were seeking a place to worship and freely practice their Bible-based religion according to the dictates of their own conscience. The hearts of so many men and women thus inspired by the light of the newly translated and mass-produced Bible could finally begin to enjoy the free exercise thereof.

This incoming wave of Christian pilgrims became fertile ground for fulfillment of perhaps the most important aspect of Nephi's vision. The formation of a new, independent and powerful nation eventually to be governed by a most unique Constitution, one that was inspired by the Almighty God. Not only would this Constitution champion religious freedoms, it would also be surrounded and protected by a nation so powerful that the only forces that could threaten these freedoms would be those residing within its own borders. This would be a nation with a government the world had never known. Lucifer's forces of darkness that had ruled the Dark Ages, met obstacles that he had not as yet seen with this remarkable Promised Land.

On the Colonies' fight for independence, the Book of Mormon prophet Nephi described what he saw,

> And it came to pass that I Nephi, beheld that the Gentiles
> who had gone forth out of captivity did humble themselves
> before the Lord; and the power of the Lord was with them.

61. 2 Nephi 3

And I beheld that their mother Gentiles were gathered together upon the waters, and upon the land also, to battle against them. And I beheld…that the wrath of God was upon all those that were gathered together against them to battle… and the Gentiles that had gone out of captivity were delivered by the power of God out of the hands of all other nations."[62]

Our founding fathers and Revolutionary patriots would win their freedom from England and would establish this government whose extraordinary liberties would insulate the right to worship and foster the development of the resulting Protestant churches so prominent in America today. The religious freedoms in 19th Century America would provide a safe haven for all of these newly established religious groups, all, that is except for the Latter-day Saints. The Mormons were met with instant opposition as Satan raged in the hearts of many Protestant Gentiles who unleashed their persecutions upon the Saints of these latter days, just as he had done in all other dispensations.

62. Book of Mormon, I Nephi 13:16-19

8

Joseph Smith for President!

B y 1843, Joseph Smith had been the Prophet of the Restoration for 23 years, beginning on that glorious spring day in 1820 when he had an experience, even unique to most of the mortal prophets in our history. God the Father and His Son Jesus Christ chose to appear before the young 14 year-old boy and initiate the glorious restoration of all things as promised through prophets who had gone before. Few prophets of God have experienced as many manifestations of ministering angels as did Joseph Smith. He received counsel through multiple visits from the great prophet Moroni, a visit and ordination from John the Baptist, an appearance and ordination from the noble Apostles Peter, James and John. In 1836 he along with Oliver Cowdery, saw the Divine Redeemer again in the holy Temple at Kirkland, Ohio. This glorious manifestation was followed by the appearance of Moses, Elias and Elijah.

He heard the voice of the Lord in the wilderness of Fayette, New York, and the voice of Michael on the banks of the Susquehanna River.[1] "And again, the voice of God in the chamber of old Father Whitmer... and the voice of Michael, the archangel; the voice of Gabriel, and of

---

1. Doctrine and Covenants 128: 20

Raphael, and of divers angels from Michael, or Adam down to the present time, all declaring their dispensations, their rights, their keys, their honors, their majesty and glory, and the power of the priesthood."[2]

By 1843, Joseph Smith had accomplished the unthinkable. Nauvoo, with its dramatically beautiful Temple abuilding and its 20,000 followers was the subject of dozens of newspaper articles across the country. So remarkable had been the resilience of the beleaguered Mormons that Nauvoo, the largest city in Illinois, had become a destination point for hundreds of curious travelers, ministers and politicians from around the country, determined to see the phenomenon of the Mormons for themselves. Joseph and Emma seemed always to have visitors to entertain and board in their home. God gave him the power to translate the Book of Mormon; he had received more than 100 revelations from the Lord, which he compiled in the Book of Revelations now named the Doctrine and Covenants.

Missionaries were covering the continent and Europe, bringing in thousands of new converts each year. And the fullness of the gospel, with the holy priesthood, doctrines and ordinances, which Satan had removed from the earth during the captivity of his Dark Ages reign, had all been restored. The eternal light of heaven, that pearl of great price, was emerging under the protective, yet precarious and broken umbrella of Constitutional civil and religious freedoms. Looking back, it becomes clear that Joseph Smith was very near to completing all that the Great God in Heaven had ordained him to do.

During this last full year of his life, he and the Saints rejoiced in the newly revealed doctrine of baptisms for the dead and the marvelous principle that vicarious Temple ordinances of eternal salvation could be

---

2. Doctrine and Covenants 128: 20, 21

extended to all who had gone before. The elation of the Nauvoo saints could not be contained over this new revelation that now, many of their loved ones, to whom they had bidden farewell so they could gather in the American west, could be blessed by them with the ordinances of salvation. In these joyous yet still perilous days, the spirit of Elijah had rested upon them, and the hearts of the children turned with inexpressible joy to their beloved fathers. Day after day the Saints would gather at the banks of the Mississippi River to be baptized for loved ones past.

Politics

Remarkably, in Joseph's final year, his focus turned to the government of the United States, and this objective would be his final priority until his enemies would succeed in gaining his earthly demise. Joseph Smith is not often thought of as a political figure in light of the magnitude of his role in the great and marvelous work of the restoration. But a closer analysis will show that in the twilight of his earthly ministry, he was very involved with a number of high level officers of the government, and his objective was of the highest importance—to fix the broken and weakened Constitution. This he did with a determination to influence the just and righteous implementation of the unspeakable heavenly gift of Constitutional law for his saints and for all Americans.

On April 11, 1844 the minutes of the Council of Fifty record Joseph's numerous statements on the topic of religious freedom. In it he asked that the minutes include the fact that at least three members of the council were men of other faiths or no professed religious affiliation at all. He wanted it clearly noted the Council of Fifty was one where "men are not consulted as to their religious opinions or notions... and we act upon the broad and liberal principle that all men have equal rights and ought to be respected. God cannot save or damn a man only on the principle that every man acts, chooses and worships for himself; hence the importance of thrusting from us every spirit of bigotry and intolerance towards a man's religious sentiments, that spirit which has drenched the earth with blood."[3]

Joseph was determined to teach and demonstrate that the very people whose civil and religious rights had been violently denied multiple times, would not be guilty of denying it to others. John Finch, an Owenite socialist, visited Nauvoo in September 1843 and commented on the religious tolerance he experienced in Nauvoo. He said that Joseph Smith was "liberal and charitable, in speaking of other sects, said he considered that the great principle of Christianity was love and affirmed that there was more of that love-spirit among his followers than is to be found in any other sect."[4] Joseph invited Mr. Finch to remain in Nauvoo for some days and to address his followers.

As noted earlier he had written to President Andrew Jackson in 1833 after receiving no lawful support from Governor Daniel Dunklin of Missouri in consequence of the violent removal of the Saints from Jackson County. In 1838, he appealed to Missouri Governor Lilburn W. Boggs after his extermination order resulted in the expulsion of thousands of saints from their homes in Far West, again to no avail. He personally met twice with President Martin Van Buren in the White House, once in November 1839 and again in February 1840. While in Washington, he met with the powerful proslavery champion and former U. S. Vice President, Senator John C. Calhoun from South Carolina, who later

---

3. *Twenty-Sixteen,* Publications from The Church Historian's Press, 2016 Salt Lake City, Utah, p. 57

4. *Twenty-Sixteen,* Publications from The Church Historian's Press, 2016 Salt Lake City, Utah, p. 58

became one of those curious travelers to Nauvoo from the east. Joseph also met often with John Todd Stuart, Illinois Congressman and former law partner with Abraham Lincoln, along with others of the Illinois delegation in Washington. From these men from Illinois, he received kind and sincere, albeit unproductive assistance with his personal appeals for justice for the crimes committed against the Saints in Missouri.

The timing for this journey to Washington to comply with God's command to appeal for "redress and redemption,"[5] could not have been more difficult. In April of that year he was freed from the cold and bitter confinement at Liberty jail. In May he completed his purchase transactions with Isaac Galland for the township of Commerce. That done, the Saints, with gratitude for the unprecedented kindness of the Quincy, Illinois citizens for sheltering and feeding them through the harsh winter months, moved to their new settlement that Joseph would name the City Beautiful, or Nauvoo.

The summer months were a flurry of projects under the young Prophet's guiding hand: the draining of the swampland around Commerce, laying out the town, planning for the new Temple, building hundreds of shelters, planting acres of crops, heeding unending requests for him to speak at a seemingly endless number of funerals for those faithful saints who succumbed to the malaria outbreak from the swamp project, and receiving a constant stream of additional faithful, yet also homeless converts from the east who had heeded the call from the Lord to "flee to the west."[6] In early October 1839, Joseph walked away from this dizzying flurry of activity to embark on a journey to Washington DC, the same month that nine of the Apostles began their journey

5. Doctrine and Covenants 101:76

6. Doctrine and Covenants 42:64

to England to preach the gospel message there. These Apostles, much like the Twelve Apostles of the Lamb, would have remarkable success in introducing the fullness of the gospel to thousands of truth seeking Gentiles in Europe, releasing them from Satan's captivity of spiritual blindness and deception. Most of these faithful Gentile converts would feel that same prompting of the Holy Spirit that had inspired their European ancestors in the centuries before to cross the great Atlantic to the promise of religious freedom in America.

Joseph must have felt assurance from the Lord that the Saints were in His hands and that he and his Apostles could continue their separate, yet vital missions. The fact that he would leave his family and thousands of virtually homeless Church members as they were just establishing their new lives in Nauvoo demonstrated the degree of importance he placed on correcting the growing misperception that the bleeding Constitution was unable to remedy. He had been commanded by God six years earlier in 1833 to importune for justice at the feet of judges, governors and presidents; he clearly continued to take that, as well as all commandments from the Lord, very seriously.

In these Nauvoo years he was also engaged with state and local authorities in the government. With the help of Robert B. Thompson and John C. Bennett, Joseph drafted the Nauvoo Charter and commissioned Bennett to present their proposed Charter before the Illinois Legislature in October of 1840. Young Assemblyman Abraham Lincoln and the vast majority of the Illinois Legislature gave resounding approval for the Charter. They, as were most of the rest of the country, appalled by the atrocities of the Missourians. In 1841, Joseph called upon Illinois Governor Thomas Carlin at his home in Quincy. In January 1843, he was invited to a cordial lunch with Governor Thomas Ford and Judge

Nathaniel Pope while in Springfield, Illinois. He became a close friend to Senator and future presidential candidate Stephen A. Douglas. He and Emma hosted Judge Douglas in their home at least twice. Douglas literally saved Joseph's life with his impartial and strong defense of justice in 1841 by calming a violent mob bent on his death.

The 1844 Presidential Election

The Mormons faced a growing problem in 1843. It was an election year and this meant sure criticism for the Saints. Their sheer numbers in Illinois brought them immense political power at the ballot boxes. Most of the candidates they voted for won their elections. The Illinois Mormons did not generally adhere to either the Whig or the Democratic Parties but often voted for men from both parties. Whomever could get the Mormon support in Illinois was seen as sure to win; this infuriated supporters of opposition candidates. In an 1842 editorial, Apostle John Taylor, the editor of Nauvoo's *Times and Seasons* and future president of the Church described their dilemma.

> There were always two parties, the Whigs and Democrats, and we could not vote for one without offending the other; and it not unfrequently [sic] happened that candidates for office would place the issue of their election upon opposition to the Mormons, in order to gain political influence from the religious prejudice, in which case the Mormons were compelled, in self-defense, to vote against them, which resulted almost invariably against our opponents. This made them angry... yet they raged on account of their discomfiture, and sought to wreak their fury on the Mormons.[7]

7. B.H. Roberts, *The Rise and Fall of Nauvoo* (Provo, UT: Republished by Maasai, Inc., 2001), p. 416.

Joseph Smith addressed the citizens of Nauvoo regarding this growing political quandary following the Illinois gubernatorial election. This message gained coverage in a number of newspapers throughout Illinois. The candidates for governor were Joseph Duncan and Thomas Ford.

> With regard to elections, some say all Latter-day Saints vote together and vote as I say. But I never tell any man how to vote, or who to vote for. But I will show how we have been situated by bringing comparison. Should there be a Methodist society here and two candidates running for office, one says, 'If you will vote for me and put me in [as] Governor I will exterminate the Methodists, take away their charters, etc.' The other candidate says 'If I am Governor, I will give all equal privilege.' Which would the Methodists vote for? Of course they would vote en masse for the candidates that would give them their rights. Thus it has been with us. Joseph Duncan said, if the people would elect him, he would exterminate the Mormons and take away their charters. As to Mr. Ford he made no such threats, but manifested a spirit in his speeches to give every man his rights; thence the Church universally voted for Mr. Ford, and he was elected governor.[8]

This message was given to once again describe the ongoing political quandary that the Mormon citizens faced. But Joseph also expressed his overriding concern that the Constitutional rights of the Mormons as American citizens had been severely abused and, at this time in Illinois, continued to be threatened.

It was under this cloud of confusion that the Mormons faced the presidential election of 1844. As noted earlier, Joseph Smith wrote to

8. Millennial Star, (Liverpool: Asa Calkin, 1859), vol. XXL, p. 668.

the five leading candidates for president. The glaring fact that this government under the Lord's sacred Constitution would allow such blatant crimes against a religion, bode poorly for the future of the Saints and all Americans. Joseph seemed very preoccupied by this fact. He, better than anyone else could see that Lucifer had a firm grip in his war against the "agency of man," and was wreaking his havoc by blinding the eyes and minds of Americans; leading them "captive at his will, even as many as would not hearken unto [God's] voice."[9]

Joseph's letters to these candidates for president asked one question, what would they do if elected, to bring justice to the Mormons for the crimes committed against them by the state of Missouri in 1833 and 1838? These letters were written on November 4, 1843; five years had passed since the second violent expulsion, theft and murder in Far West. Only John C. Calhoun and Henry Clay responded. Martin Van Buren who was running for a second term and the other lesser candidates gave no response to the prophet. This passage of time took much of the pressure to respond off the presidential candidates. Joseph Smith, the Mormon Prophet was the only American pressing this issue. It was a much forgotten issue by most Americans, but God had commanded that these cries for redemption should be made. And Joseph diligently and heroically complied because he knew that great peril was in the path of America if these two fatal Constitutional flaws—the three-fifths clause allowing for slavery and the optional compliance clause—be not corrected.

It is remarkable that for some fifty years this Constitution, even though highly regarded and revered by Americans, was allowed to continue in its weakened condition, with no real effort to correct it. Since

9. Pearl of Great Price, Book of Moses 4:3,4

no one felt inclined to fix the problem, Joseph Smith, the Prophet of the Restoration, seemed determined to do it himself. There was likely another reason why he pressed so hard to have these flaws addressed. He had a clear view of the even more intense persecutions for the Saints that were smoldering in Illinois.

It was one year earlier, in the month of August 1842 that Joseph Smith made a disquieting prophecy of their approaching expulsion from Illinois, declaring to a group of his followers:

> That the Saints would continue to suffer much affliction and would be driven to the Rocky Mountains, many would apostatize, others would be put to death by our persecutors or lose their lives in consequence of exposure or disease, and some of you will live to go and assist in making settlements and build cities and see the Saints become a mighty people in the midst of the Rocky Mountains.[10]

This prophecy was disconcerting to his followers with its predictions of yet another expulsion and death by persecutors and exposure. They had been yearning, working and praying for a successful and peaceful settlement in Nauvoo, and for an end to their persecutions. But their Prophet informed them that not only would persecutions mount once again, but; they would be driven to an ominous and unknown place—the Rocky Mountains. And as if this troubling prophecy was not enough, Joseph punctuated this ominous message a month later by saying,

> My bosom swells, with unutterable anguish when I contemplate the scenes of horror that we have pass'd through in the State of Missouri and then look, and behold, and see

---

10. B.H. Roberts, *History of the Church*, (Salt Lake City, UT: Deseret Book, 1949), vol. 5, p.85.

the storm, and cloud, gathering ten times blacker—ready to burst upon this innocent people. Shall we bow down as slaves? The [Nauvoo] Legion would willingly die in the defence [sic] of their rights; but what would that accomplish? I have kept down their indignation, and kept a quiet submission on all hands, and am determined to do so at all hazards. Our enemies shall not have it to say, that we rebel against government, or commit treason; however much they may lift their hands in oppression, and tyranny.[11]

Rebukes

Once again Joseph Smith was speaking about the Constitutional rights that were denied the Latter-day Saints and Lucifer's continued and relentless pursuit of the captivity of the Saints.

It is noteworthy to see in Joseph's rebuttal to Calhoun and Clay the deep intensity of Joseph's demand that justice be served to the victimized Latter-day Saints. John C. Calhoun was cordial in his response but offered no assistance, citing the same reason as he had expressed to Joseph in person while he was in Washington DC four years earlier. Calhoun read in the Constitution, and correctly so, that the Federal government may not be permitted to intervene in state matters unless requested by that state governor. Clay responded that if elected it would be with promises to no one prior to his taking office. Joseph lashed back at both of them.

Again those two original flaws infused into the Constitution gave these politicians an easy out and gave the Adversary access to yet an-

11. Richard Lyman Bushman, *Joseph Smith: Rough Stone Rolling*, (New York: Alfred A. Knopf, 2005), pp. 475-476.

other government to wield the club of oppression against the Saints of God. To be sure, he had no tyrant or despot through whom he could again bring directly by a government, more violence to the Saints as he had with the Roman Empire and the Roman Catholic Church. But in these two defects he did have soft Constitutional provisions giving the weak of heart a comfortable way of evading the unpopular *"Mormon Problem."* In the public eye, it was a matter that was easily put aside and none of these presidential candidates felt the responsibility to defend the Saints for the crimes Missouri committed five years earlier.

Joseph responded to Calhoun's dodge with a righteous indignation.

> ...you say that 'according to your view, the federal govern-
> ment is one of limited and specific powers', and has no ju-
> risdiction in the case of the Mormons. So then a State can at
> any time expel a portion of her citizens with impunity, and,
> in the language of Mr. Martin Van Buren,...though the cause
> is ever so just, Government can do nothing for them, because
> it has no power.

> Go on, then, Missouri, after another set of inhabitants (as
> the Latter-day Saints did) have entered some two or three
> hundred thousand dollars' worth of land; and make exten-
> sive improvements thereon. Go on, then, I say; banish the
> occupants or owners, or kill them, as the mobbers did many
> of the Latter-day Saints, and take their land and property as
> spoil; and let the legislature, as in the case of the Mormons,
> appropriate a couple of hundred thousand dollars to pay the
> mob for doing that job...[12]

12. Joseph Smith, *The Prophet Joseph Smith's Views on the Powers and Government of the United States*, Jos. Hyrum Parry & Co., Salt Lake City, 1886, p 28, 29

He continued his denunciation against these obvious misinterpretations of the law:

> ...and when you have learned that fifteen thousand innocent citizens, after having purchased their lands of the United States and paid for them, were expelled from a "sovereign State" by order of the governor, at the point of the bayonet, their arms taken from them by the same authority, and their right of migration into the said State denied, under pain of imprisonment, whipping, robbing, mobbing, and even death, and no justice or recompense allowed; and, from the legislature with the governor at the head, down to the justice of the peace, with a bottle of whiskey in one hand and a bowie-knife in the other, hear them all declare that there is no justice for a Mormon in that State; and judge ye a righteous judgment, and tell me when the virtues of the States was stolen, where the honor of the General government lies hid...
>
> If the General government has no power to reinstate expelled citizens to their rights, there is a monstrous hypocrite fed and fostered from the hard earnings of the people![13]
>
> While I have power of body and mind...I or my posterity will plead the cause of injured innocence, until Missouri makes atonement for her sins..."[14]

13. Joseph Smith, *The Prophet Joseph Smith's Views on the Powers and Government of the United States*, Jos. Hyrum Parry & Co., Salt Lake City, 1886, p 29, 30
14. Ibid., p 31

Joseph concluded his rejection of Calhoun's recalcitrance with,

> And let me say that all men who say that Congress has no power to restore and defend the rights of her citizens have not the love of the truth abiding in them. Congress has power to protect the nation against foreign invasion and internal broil; and whenever that body passes an act to maintain right with any power, or to restore right to any portion of citizens, it is the SUPREME LAW OF THE LAND; and should any state refuse submission, that state is guilty of insurrection or rebellion, and the President has as much power to repel it as Washington had to march against the 'whiskey boys' at Pittsburg,' or General Jackson had to send an armed force to suppress the rebellion of South Carolina.[15]

Joseph would sum up his hot anger against this Constitutional flaw when he condemned in no-uncertain-terms the doctrine of states' rights:

> The States' rights doctrine are what feed mobs. They are a dead carcass, a stink and they shall ascend up as a stink offering in the nose of the Almighty.[16]

Joseph's response to Henry Clay did not come until May 13, 1844, some five months after Clay's letter to him and just six weeks before his martyrdom. Joseph was waiting for some declaration of Clay's campaign position regarding the various issues facing the American public, but no such clarification came. Like Calhoun, Joseph excoriated Clay for his passivity to the great injustice against the Mormons in Missouri during

15. Joseph Smith, *The Prophet Joseph Smith's Views on the Powers and Government of the United States*, Jos. Hyrum Parry & Co., Salt Lake City, 1886, p 33
16. Bushman, *Rough Stone Rolling*, 514.

this, his election campaign, and for his inaction four years earlier when Clay served in Congress and Joseph personally sought his assistance.

O frail man, what have you done that will exalt you? When fifteen thousand free citizens were exiled from their own homes, lands and property, in the wonderful patriotic state of Missouri, and you then upon your oath and honor occupying the exalted station of a Senator of Congress from the noble-hearted State of Kentucky, why did you not show the world your loyalty to law and order, by using all honorable means to restore the innocent to their rights and property?[17]

And when fifteen thousand free citizens of the high blooded republic of North America are robbed and driven from one State to another without redress or redemption, it is time for a candidate to the presidency to pledge himself to execute judgment and justice in righteousness, law or no law.[18]

But during ten years, while the Latter-day Saints have bled, been robbed, driven from their own lands, paid oceans of money into the treasury to pay your renowned self and others for legislating and dealing out equal rights and privileges to those in common with all other religious communities, they have waited and expected in vain![19]

17. Joseph Smith, *The Prophet Joseph Smith's Views on the Powers and Government of the United States*, Jos. Hyrum Parry & Co., Salt Lake City, 1886, p 37, 38

18. Joseph Smith, *The Prophet Joseph Smith's Views on the Powers and Government of the United States*, Jos. Hyrum Parry & Co., Salt Lake City, 1886, p 44

19. Ibid., p 45

Resolution

What was driving Joseph Smith to press with such zeal and determination for justice for the Latter-day Saints? What was he thinking to gain after ten years of complacency in the face of the grossest crimes committed in America, second only to slavery. First and foremost, Joseph had been commanded by Jehovah to do so, and it is significant to note that even after so much time elapsed, the Prophet of the Restoration still felt compelled to continue in obedience to this commandment of God.

A second reason was that with this lapse of time in which the United States government, guided by the Declaration of Independence and the sacred Constitution, was itself now guilty of yet another transgression through its inaction. This dereliction of duty was worthy of the "wrath, indignation and chastening hand of an Almighty God."[20] These unwise stewards, Jackson, Boggs, Clay, Calhoun, Van Buren and others had committed a crime against God and his chosen people, for failing to righteously apply the civil and religious rights to the offended Latter-day Saints. Now this nation was ripe for the judgments of God in the form of the horrendous Civil War. Joseph, the prophet would not let them forget these crimes; it was the role of a prophet to warn of God's impending judgments.

Upon ascertaining that none of the presidential candidates would step forward in defense of the beleaguered Mormons, Joseph's incomparable mind began contemplating other avenues. Meetings were held in Nauvoo to find amelioration for the local political turmoil that was again brewing against them for the 1844 election. Much of their delib-

---

20. Doctrine and Covenants 87:6

erating centered on finding ways to avoid the certain blame that would stem from the defeated political party in Illinois.

The more they discussed the matter the more they warmed to the most dramatic of their options: They would nominate Joseph Smith as a candidate for the President of the United States. By doing so the Mormons and the rest of the country would have a candidate, who was neither Whig nor Democrat as a choice. And importantly, it gave the Mormons a candidate for whom they could vote and not be blamed for the defeat of the losing candidates. To this solution, Joseph agreed, then Willard Richards stood and introduced a motion that they nominate Joseph Smith as a candidate for President of the United States. The motion was resoundingly seconded. The announcement of his candidacy shocked the citizens of Illinois. To the dismay of many, the first native son in their state history to run for president would be the controversial Joseph Smith.

But there were other more compelling reasons in Joseph's decision to run for President of the United States. He had known since 1832 that a great war between the Northern and Southern States caused by the rebellion of South Carolina was on the horizon through a revelation from God.[21] By 1844 the signs were trending toward this mighty collision. Joseph knew that it pained the heart of God that such judgments lay in wait for the people. He also knew that a strong course correction by this people and the government had the distinct possibility of averting the great Civil War altogether. We were told plainly in 1833 through revela-

21. Doctrine and Covenants section 87

tion instructing Joseph to importune for redress and redemption for the crimes committed against the Saints in Missouri. He said,

> And if the president heed them not, then will the Lord arise and come forth from his hiding place, and in his fury vex the nation.
>
> Pray ye therefore, that their ears may be opened unto your cries, that I may be merciful unto them, that these things may not come upon them.[22]

How could Joseph Smith have turned the course of history and prevented the Civil War? He explained it clearly in a twelve-page pamphlet that informed the leaders and citizens of the United States just how he would save the nation if elected President.

Joseph Smith for President

The announcement of Joseph Smith's candidacy infuriated his enemies in Illinois and Missouri but remarkably it is noted that across the country, his candidacy was warmly received in many places. He had as much name recognition throughout the country as did the other candidates. Even though it was believed from the beginning by those who nominated him that the probability of his success in the election was somewhat remote, his supporters developed an extensive national campaign strategy across the country for his election. Springfield's newspapers like the Democratic *Illinois Register* carried the announcement, which Lincoln was very likely to have read:

22. Doctrine and Covenants section 101: 89-92

Illinois Register.

Vol. V.   Springfield, Friday, February 16, 1844.   No. 29.

PRESIDENTIAL.

The Nauvoo Neighbor of the 7th inst. contains the following paragraph:

"Who shall be our next President? Do you want to know? We will let it out soon. We have our eye upon the man and when the proper time comes we will publish it from "Dan to Beersheba," and then as American citizens, we will go to it with a rush."

The Neighbor has since announced Jos. Smith, the Mormon Prophet, as its candidate.

Days later this same Springfield *Illinois Register* reported the following:

It appears by the Nauvoo papers that the Mormon Prophet is actually a candidate for the Presidency. He has sent us his pamphlet, containing extracts of his principles... On these points he is much more explicit than Mr. Clay... General Smith...comes right out in favor of a bank and a tariff, taking the true Whig ground, and ought to be regarded as the real Whig candidate for President, until Mr. Clay can so far recover from his shuffling and dodging as to declare his sentiments like a man.[23]

In the pamphlet, Joseph acknowledged the presidents who had gone before, noting their accomplishments. "One of the most noble fathers of our freedom and country's glory"[24] was George Washington. Then

23. George Q. Cannon, *Life of Joseph Smith the Prophet,* (Salt Lake City, Utah: Deseret Book Company, 1972), p. 550.

24. Joseph Smith, *The Prophet Joseph Smith's Views on the Powers and Government of the United States,* Jos. Hyrum Parry & Co., Salt Lake City, 1886, p 4

he honors John Adams, Thomas Jefferson and James Madison, all of whom labored, "to avoid the slightest interference with the rights of conscience or the function of religion."[25] He commended John Quincy Adam's leadership and praised Andrew Jackson for "paying off the national debt."[26]

His praise ended when he came to the administration of Martin Van Buren saying that at the nation's 60th year, "our blooming Republic began to decline under the withering touch of Martin Van Buren! Disappointed ambition, thirst for power, pride, corruption…priestcraft, and spiritual wickedness in *high places* struck hands and reveled in midnight splendor."[27]

At the age of 69, General William Henry Harrison became the ninth U.S. president, succeeding Van Buren in 1841, but he died in office just 31 days after his inauguration. Like Lincoln, Joseph Smith had high hopes in Harrison. In Joseph's pamphlet he referred to Harrison's inaugural address saying, "while descanting upon the merits of the constitution and its framers," Harrison described features of this nation that were out of harmony with a Republic. "Predictions were made that, at no very remote period, the Government would terminate in virtual monarchy."[28] Joseph agreed with President Harrison's assessment of this faltering Republic, and their views were consistent with Abraham Lincoln's warnings that a lawless nation, divided against itself had little hope for survival.

---

25. Joseph Smith, *The Prophet Joseph Smith's Views on the Powers and Government of the United States*, Jos. Hyrum Parry & Co., Salt Lake City, 1886, p 10

26. Ibid., p 13

27. Ibid., p 13

28. Ibid., p 13

With this summary of the nation's progress and decline Joseph Smith declared his intent to run for President of the United States. "I have heretofore given my determination to arrest the progress of that tendency...and restore the Government to its pristine health and vigor."[29] "No honest man can doubt for a moment but that the glory of American liberty is on the wane, and that calamity and confusion will sooner or later destroy the peace of the people."[30] "Now, Oh People! People! Turn to the Lord and live, and reform this nation."[31]

Other prophets of God had served as the political leader of the people. Enoch's prophetic leadership transformed the city of Enoch into Zion, a land of the pure in heart; his entire city was so pure and righteous that God took it up unto himself. Moses, the Prince of Egypt was the instrument through whom God freed his people Israel from the Pharaoh Ramses. Kings Benjamin and Mosiah also governed their people with an eye single to God's glory. Joseph Smith was the first among the Prophets of God to be His spokesman in a Republic, in the land of promise, which had received the Constitution from God Himself, to be its ruling guide. If he were to be President of this nation, it would be by the vote of the people.

This begs the question, what was to be gained by Joseph Smith's run for president? The answer: much. Had Joseph Smith been elected, Americans would have learned that they had elected the very man who received the revelation from heaven that God was the grantor of the U. S. Constitution. It was to this man, Joseph Smith that God revealed that He had inspired certain wise men whom He raised up for the purpose

---

29. Ibid., p 13

30. Joseph Smith, *The Prophet Joseph Smith's Views on the Powers and Government of the United States*, Jos. Hyrum Parry & Co., Salt Lake City, 1886, p 15

31. Ibid., p 16

of crafting the Constitution.[32] This Constitution was a gift to the world that the adversary had infiltrated with two very destructive contaminations; their damage had been enormous. The three-fifths clause sent the nation tumbling into civil war over slavery and the optional compliance clause brought the "wrath and indignation and chastening hand"[33] from the Great God in heaven.

The Constitution had to be repaired and no government official had stepped forward to fix it. But the Prophet of the Restoration did; he knew that it had to be repaired and his plan was plausible. If elected, Joseph Smith would have become the first American President with the pledge to end more than two centuries of slavery in America; he outlined his plan in his pamphlet. Through Joseph, the demise of slavery would have been sealed with the removal of three-fifths clause from the sacred Constitution. This would have been followed by the ratification of a new Amendment to the Constitution ending slavery forever in this land. A peaceful closure of slavery through his proposed compensated emancipation would have negated the entire cause of the Civil War! It appears that God, through his Prophet was offering America one final opportunity to steer the nation off this course toward disaster.

This Prophet for a President would also have repaired the second Constitutional flaw by giving the Federal government the power to enforce the protection of all citizens being persecuted by rogue state leaders. In order to accomplish this Joseph would have collaborated with Congress to remove or rewrite Article IV, Section 4 of the Constitution, which was placed there by the small number of errant framers of the original Constitution, who were unwilling to bind the states to full

---

32. Doctrine and Covenants 101:80

33. Doctrine and Covenants 78:6

compliance to the Constitution. It was this article that allowed Missouri and Illinois to commit their crimes against the Mormons with no interference from the federal government.

Joseph's plan would have ensured that all states would act as one in defense of all people and in compliance with the Constitution. This was the very intent of the "wise men whom God raised up" in that Constitutional Convention. No more could a state like Missouri and Illinois allow its citizens to be singled out, driven and persecuted because the federal government would be empowered and obligated to intervene for the wellbeing of the people.

How serious was Joseph Smith in his bid for the Presidency? The following facts will indicate that he ran for President with the intent to win the election.

A Remarkable Campaign

On February 7, 1844, Joseph laid out his political platform as a candidate for President of the United States when he completed and signed the twelve-page pamphlet entitled, *General Smith's VIEWS on the Powers and Policy of the Government of the United States.*

On February 24, 1,500 copies of the pamphlet were in hand. On February 27, *General Smith's Views* was sent to the President of the United States, John Tyler. On that date, his *View's* pamphlet was also sent to the Vice President, all members of the Cabinet, all members of Congress and all members of the Supreme Court. It was sent to postmasters and to nearly every newspaper in the country. At least 45 of these newspapers in twenty-two of the twenty-six states published articles on Joseph Smith's candidacy for President. On March 11th the Council of Fifty was organized in Nauvoo; much of their function was to aid in the campaign of Joseph Smith. In General Conference on April 9th a call for volunteer electioneering missionaries was issued; 244 stepped forward. On April 15th, members of the Quorum of the Twelve Apostles appointed 337 volunteer electioneer missionaries to travel to every state in the Union and to the Wisconsin Territory. Nine of the Quorum of the Twelve traveled east to direct the campaign effort, leaving Willard Richards, John Taylor and William Smith back in Illinois to support the Prophet there.[34] These volunteers would hold conferences with the member branches still functioning in the eastern states, with a campaign meeting for Joseph Smith in the following days.

Here are segments of his political agenda, addressed to the American people in his *Views* pamphlet.

> I feel a double anxiety for the happiness of all men, both in time and in eternity."[35] "My cogitations, like Daniel's have for a long time troubled me..." "...the Declaration of Independence, 'holds these truths to be self-evident, that all men are created equal: that they are endowed by their creator with certain unalienable rights; that among these are life, liberty, and the pursuit of happiness;' but at the same time some two or three millions of people are held as slaves for life, because the spirit in them is covered with a darker skin than ours..."[36]

34. Arnold K. Garr, *Setting the Record Straight, Joseph Smith: Presidential Candidate*, Millennial Press, Inc., Orem, Utah, 2007, pp. 2-3

35. Joseph Smith, *The Prophet Joseph Smith's Views on the Powers and Government of the United States*, Jos. Hyrum Parry & Co., Salt Lake City, 1886, p 3

36. Ibid., p 3

Joseph then elaborates on this hypocrisy in the government.

When in the Constitution it says, 'We the people of the United States, in order to form a more perfect union, establish justice, ensure domestic tranquility, provide for the common defence, promote the general welfare, and secure the blessings of liberty to ourselves and our posterity, do ordain and establish this Constitution for the United States of America', meant just what it said without reference to color or condition, ad infinitum."[37]

Joseph Smith now turns to his solutions for repairing the first flaw in the Constitution with a clear and straightforward proposal to end slavery.

Petition, ye goodly inhabitants of the slave States, your legislators to abolish slavery by the year 1850. Pray Congress to pay every man a reasonable price for his slaves out of the surplus revenue arising from the sale of public lands...hire the black man to labor like other human beings.[38]

Joseph then addressed the second flaw in the Constitution:

Give the President full power to send an army to suppress mobs, and impugn that relic of folly which makes it necessary for the Governor of a State to make the demand of the President for troops, in case of invasion or rebellion.[39]

---

37. Ibid., p 4

38. Joseph Smith, *The Prophet Joseph Smith's Views on the Powers and Government of the United States*, Jos. Hyrum Parry & Co., Salt Lake City, 1886, p 17

39. Ibid., p 19

Then Joseph Smith spoke to Americans as their Prophet, an office that he already held, not by the voice of the people, but by the voice of God and by the order of heaven.

> Make HONOR the standard with all men. Be sure that good is rendered for evil in all cases, and the whole nation, like a kingdom of kings and priests, will rise up in righteousness, and be respected as wise and worthy on earth, and as just and holy for heaven, by Jehovah, the author of perfection.[40]

He continues, outlining his course of action as the leader of the nation:

> In the United States the people are the sovereign that should rule, the only power that should be obeyed..." Wherefore, were I President of the United States, by the voice of a virtuous people, I would honor the old paths of the venerated fathers of freedom; I would walk in the tracks of the illustrious patriots who carried the ark of the Government upon their shoulders with an eye single to the glory of the people; and when the people petitioned to abolish slavery in the Slave states, I would use all honorable means to have their prayers granted, and give liberty to the captive by paying the southern gentlemen a reasonable equivalent for his property, that the whole nation might be free indeed![41]

> And God, who once cleansed the violence of the earth with a flood, whose son laid down His life for the salvation of all His father gave Him will come and purify the world again with

40. Ibid., p 17

41. Joseph Smith, *The Prophet Joseph Smith's Views on the Powers and Government of the United States*, Jos. Hyrum Parry & Co., Salt Lake City, 1886, p 22

fire in the last days, should be supplicated by me for the good of the people.[42]

To his beloved followers in Nauvoo he explained his decision to run for president on this wise,

> I would not have suffered my name to have been used by my friends on anywise as President of the United States, or candidate for that office, if I and my friends could have had the privilege of enjoying our religious and civil rights as American citizens, even those rights which the Constitution guarantees unto all of her citizens alike. But this as a people we have been denied from the beginning. Persecution has rolled upon our heads from time to time, from portions of the United States, like peals of thunder, because of our religion; and no portion of this government as yet has stepped forward for our relief. And in view of these things, I feel it to be my right and privilege to obtain what influence and power I can, lawfully, in the United States, for the protection of injured innocence.[43]

It is submitted here that Joseph Smith's chances to win the election were not as remote as might be thought. No other candidate for that election had an army of 300+ full-time campaigners methodically operating in every state. No candidate had Apostles of the Lord directing the campaign. These electioneering missionaries often reported that the response by the citizens who attended their rallies and heard Joseph's platform, were often favorable and many left the meetings with the intent to vote for the Mormon Prophet.

---

42. Ibid., p 23

43. Joseph Smith, *History of the Church*, Bookcraft, Salt Lake City, vol. 6 p. 210-211

The electioneering missionaries began their campaigns in April and they would have remained in their endeavor for an additional seven months until the general election would take place in November of 1844. And it is certainly plausible, given the remarkable resilience and dedication of the Latter-day Saints, that the number of electioneering missionaries could have doubled or tripled during that time.

Had Joseph Smith been President, two and a half centuries of slavery could have been peacefully abolished at his hand. The U. S. Constitution could have been repaired under his leadership, restored to its intended and inspired perfection. He would have cleansed it from the adversary's contaminations, which Satan managed to infuse into the sacred document. It is noteworthy that these important corrections to the Constitution would have been accomplished by the Prophet of God, the personal and only witness of Constitution's Divinity through a revelation—if only the people of America would have allowed him to do it. They would not.

This unprecedented political effort ended abruptly in June, when Joseph Smith, Prophet of God and candidate for President of the United States was assassinated on June 27, 1844. The nine members of the Quorum of the Twelve Apostles and 337 electioneer missionaries would continue their campaigns for several days after until the tragic news could reach them. He was murdered just five months into his campaign, the first American candidate to be assassinated in pursuit of the Presidency. Joseph Smith was also the first presidential candidate to run for the office with a clear and lucid purpose for repairing the two greatest challenges of civil and religious freedom in America. Disastrously, Lucifer succeeded again in killing another Prophet of God and States would continue to abuse slaves and religious groups with impunity and the federal government would remain unaccountable to end the atrocities. The gates of hell had opened even wider upon this Promised Land, and the captivity of Satan would continue in its insidious advance.

9

O the Cunning Plan
of the Evil One

JUST TWO YEARS after Joseph Smith's martyrdom some 20,000 Latter-day Saints were, at the threat of death, forcefully driven from Illinois, again by rogue lawless mobs. The Mormons were evicted from their own homes, farms, businesses, and their magnificent Temple because of the hatred of their neighbors for their religion. In 1846, Governor Thomas Ford, passively observed these crimes, just as he did the killing of Joseph Smith and his brother Hyrum two years earlier. He and the state of Illinois convicted no one for the Smiths' murder or for the dreadful crimes of violence, robbery and mayhem against 20,000 of his innocent citizens. And again, Lucifer's contamination of the Constitution had its continued effect as President James K. Polk and the federal government laid back, offering no help in prosecuting the guilty or restoring the oppressed Mormon citizens to their Constitutional civil and religious rights in Illinois.

Many Latter-day Saints would succumb to the harsh elements due to their hasty winter escape from the Illinois mobs. Ill prepared for the forced arduous trek across the American plains, thousands of graves of these oppressed men, women and children were tearfully dug at their makeshift Winter Quarters in Nebraska, along the North Platte River, along the Sweetwater River and along the Rocky Mountain trail to the Great Salt Lake Valley. Three U. S. Presidents, Andrew Jackson, Martin Van Buren, and now James K. Polk, elected and sworn defenders of the peoples' freedom under the Constitution proved themselves, in the eyes of God, to be "unjust stewards"[1] of the Mormon citizens' rights of civil and religious freedom. In this case, Lucifer did not need despots or tyrannical presidents of the United States; he just needed complacent ones to aid and abet his perversions to the Constitution.

Article IV Section 4

With his Constitutional corruptions, he was able to establish his bondage of the American Saints of God, similar to the captivity of the early Disciples of Christ and his Apostles, and the European Gentiles. This time the adversary raged in the hearts of localized lawless mobs, while judges and governors and presidents passively looked on. These presidents hid behind the unfortunate Article IV, Section 4 of the U. S. Constitution, which placed in question a president's responsibility to intervene in crimes against their own citizens until the governor requested federal government protection. It is likely that the three rogue Constitutional delegates who forced the compromise in this Article of the Constitution did not anticipate such ill-fated consequences for their short-sightedness, but it is certain that Lucifer did. His deceit and cunning are evident here; just as he corrupted the Bible, he was able to corrupt the sacred Constitution. His aim has always been since the beginning, to collapse and ruin our Father's gift of agency with the darkness of spiritual captivity.

---

1. Doctrine and Covenants 101: 89, 90

Article IV Section 4 of the original Constitution read:

> The United States shall guarantee to every State in this Union a Republican Form of Government, and shall protect each of them against Invasion; and on Application of the Legislature, or of the Executive (when the Legislature cannot be convened) against domestic Violence.

No governor or legislative appeals were made, and none of these presidents, state legislatures, governors or judges had the inclination to pursue justice for the oppressed Latter-day Saints.

Over a thirteen-year period, these crimes against the same group of sincere worshipers of the Great God in Heaven occurred not just once but in three appalling and illegal removals of tens of thousands of citizens from their lawfully purchased and rightfully owned homes and properties. Given the freedoms we so glibly take for granted in America today, the fact that these atrocities were committed against an innocent minority and not redressed, is galling; that they were repeated two more times is beyond comprehension! As promised by the voice of the Almighty God himself,

> if the judges, governors and presidents, heed them not, then will the Lord arise and come forth out of his hiding place, and in his fury vex the nation; and in his hot displeasure and in his fierce anger, in his time will cut off those wicked, unfaithful

and unjust stewards, and appoint them their portion among hypocrites and unbelievers.

What I have said unto you must be, that all men may be left without excuse. That wise men and rulers may hear and know that which they have never considered.

That I may proceed to bring to pass my act, my strange act, and perform my work, my strange work, that men may discern between the righteous and the wicked, saith your God.[2]

Black Laws

From the early colonial period, various colonies and states had passed laws that applied only to Blacks. Some of these Black laws, as they were called, applied to free Blacks and other laws applied to slaves. Almost all Black laws were openly discriminatory, intended to restrict and control the Blacks living in America. With the three-fifths clause in the Constitution acknowledging the legitimacy of slavery, even those whites who saw the injustice of these laws remained virtually powerless to oppose them. How these injustices could be perpetrated in light of the Declaration of Independence and the Constitution is a travesty of the worst kind.

In the remarkable process of successes that contributed to this nation's establishment and survival, slavery remained an insidious threat to these freedoms and government. The inalienable rights and dignity of millions of African men, women and children were trampled because of the color of their skin. There developed a web of deceit fueled by unparalleled wealth on the part of the slave owners and pro-slavery pol-

---

2. Doctrine and Covenants 101:89-95

iticians. This wealth would move men and women to accept and then embrace, every conceivable measure, including the creation of laws and judicial rulings, to protect the abominable practice of enslavement for the purpose of protecting their river of free-flowing revenue.

"If Slavery Is Not Wrong, Nothing Is Wrong" Abraham Lincoln

The three defiant Constitutional Convention delegates from South Carolina who forced the slavery compromise not only threatened to leave the convention, knowing that their exit would completely derail the Constitution building and ratifying process, but insisted that the three-fifths clause be added, thus defiling the sacred document. They held the Constitution hostage so that they could preserve slavery in all its many manifestations, leaving the inspired men raised up by God himself, no choice but to surrender to their demands. The damage done by these slave owning delegates brought incalculable suffering and anguish to millions of slaves and their posterity over the next 75 years. During this same period they also brought damnation to themselves and hundreds of thousands of white slave-owning families, men and women, who embraced the Constitutional right to brutally abuse the unfortunate slaves in their bondage.

The life experiences of Frederick Douglass speak for millions of other slaves like him. One of the few slaves to learn to read and write, he escaped and became a powerful voice against the horrors of servitude and for emancipation of all slaves in America. He was a strong critic of President Lincoln for not acting sooner on freeing the slaves. But when Lincoln invited him to the White House to hear Douglass' advice for him (the first time in history that a Black man had been consulted by a

President) Douglass became a sincere admirer of this modern-day Moses who freed the American slaves. Douglass was born a slave but was separated from his mother at about the age of one year. It was a common practice for slave owners to sell the mother of an infant to another plantation, and then give the baby to an older slave woman to raise. Family ties were a hindrance to slave owner's control so the breaking up of families through slave sales and auctions was common practice.

As a child Douglass was horrified at the cruel reality of the slave masters.

> I have often been awakened at the dawn of day by the most heart-rendering shrieks of an own aunt of mine, whom he used to tie up to a joist, and whip upon her naked back till she was literally covered with blood. No words, no tears, no prayers, from his gory victim, seemed to move his iron heart from its bloody purpose. The louder she screamed, the harder he whipped; and where the blood ran the fastest, there he whipped longest.[3]

Douglass described Mr. Gore, a particularly cruel owner as one who could,

> torture the slightest look, word, or gesture, on the part of the slave, into impudence, and would treat it accordingly. There must be no answering back to him; no explanation was allowed a slave, showing himself to have been wrongfully accused. Mr. Gore acted fully upon the maxim laid down by slaveholders— 'It is better that a dozen slaves suffer under the lash, than that the overseer should be convicted, in the

---

3. Frederick Douglas, *Narrative of the Life of Frederick Douglass, An American Slave,* Bedford Books of St. Martin's Press, Boston, New York, 1993, p 40, 42

presence of the slaves, of having been at fault.' No matter how innocent a slave might be—it availed him nothing, when accused by Mr. Gore of any misdemeanor. To be accused was to be convicted, and to be convicted was to be punished; the one always follows the other with immutable certainty.

The feelings of racial superiority of the white or Aryan race were deeply instilled in the minds of Europeans generations before they crossed the Atlantic to America.[4] There was hardly a dissenting voice in the frequent passage of these Black laws. Of course, the Blacks were deeply opposed, but these laws forbade them from voting or participating in any governing effort. The Black laws were more prevalent in the South and were openly intended to manage and maintain their masters' cruel dominance. Restrictions prohibited them from voting, bearing arms, gathering in groups for worship, learning to read and write, exercising free speech, and testifying against white people in court, no matter the crime.

In the years following the Civil War, white-dominated southern legislatures passed Black Codes modeled after the earlier Black laws. Their purpose was to control the movement and labor of the now freed Blacks, as slavery had given way to a free labor system. Although freedmen had been emancipated, their lives remained greatly restricted by these laws. Over the period of 1687-1865, the state of Virginia alone enacted more than 130 slave statutes.[5]

Many descendants of the once oppressed Gentiles of Europe, who escaped religious tyranny by coming to America under the guidance

---

4. James Bradley, *The Imperial Cruise,* Back Bay Books/ Little, Brown and Company, New York, 2009, pp. 22-33

5. https://en.wikipedia.org/wiki/Black_Codes_(United_States)

of the Holy Spirit had themselves become the oppressors of civil and religious freedom of Blacks and Latter-day Saints. And this, in a nation that had received the Heavenly gift of the Declaration of Independence, establishing that God created all men, and that all men are equal in importance to Him. God also gave them the U. S. Constitution, whose Bill of Rights lists the freedom of religious expression as first and foremost of the inalienable rights to be upheld.

Ever so carefully, Satan employed his weapons of slavery and religious intolerance to blind the minds and harden the hearts of the now freed Gentiles of America. Many Americans came to believe that God approved of enslaving Blacks and of persecuting Mormons. Many Gentile Americans had become unwitting servants of Satan, blinded in their willingness to bring upon other minorities the very oppressions their ancestors had suffered in Europe under the domination of the Inquisition.

> …there are many plain and precious things taken away from the book, which is the book of the Lamb of God. And after it goeth forth unto all nations of the Gentiles, yea, even across the many waters…thou seest…an exceeding great many do stumble, inasmuch that Satan hath great power over them.[6]

With the corrupted Bible and Lucifer's relentless distortions of truth, many white Americans were themselves brought into Satan's captivity. Satan's bondage had been established yet again, this time in the Promised Land. The great deceiver was at the doorstep of dividing this nation with a war over the cruelty of slavery, and this division would serve to weaken the U. S. Constitution—the great obstacle to global captivity in this last dispensation.

6. 1 Nephi 13: 28,29

O THE CUNNING PLAN OF THE EVIL ONE

In the years preceding the war, most free-worshipping Protestants approved of, or were indifferent to slavery and they had little or no concern with the religious persecution of the Mormons. After whipping, selling and raping his slaves, many an overseer would then piously attend their Sunday worship services. All the while these Christians were being pacified, first by pro-slavery activists and later by ministers at pulpits across America, who preached tacit approval of the brutal enslavement of the Blacks and of the assaults on the Latter-day Saints at the hands of his servants of darkness.

> O that cunning plan of the evil one! O the vainness, and frailties, and the foolishness of men! When they are learned they think they are wise, and they hearken not unto the counsel of God, for they set it aside, supposing they know of themselves, wherefore their wisdom is foolishness and it profiteth them not. And they shall perish.[7]

All of this racial and religious prejudice, much like the lie utilized by the great and abominable church in Europe resulted in Americans offering no more than a shrug at the oppression of the much maligned religious group called Mormons. In the minds of most Christian Americans, the Mormons were receiving what they deserved with their talk of prophets and apostles, of miracles and spiritual gifts and of new scrip-

---

7. Book of Mormon, II Nephi 9:28

tures, and of course, polygamy, as Satan's rage infiltrated the hearts of the most blessed people on the earth:

> For behold, at that day shall he rage in the hearts of the children of men, and stir them up to anger against that which is good.
>
> And others he will pacify, and lull them away into carnal security, that they will say: All is well in Zion, yea Zion prospereth, all is well—and thus the devil cheateth their souls, and leadeth them away carefully down to hell.[8]

Lucifer most certainly perceived that if this American Constitution were to be allowed to reach its full and divine potential, other nations would see its remarkable value for themselves. The people in those countries would rise up as did the Americans in their desire to have the same liberties for themselves as the Americans had been granted. He knew that the Divine nature in all of God's children throughout the world would long for the pure and holy principles of civil and religious liberty for their own lands.

In all of history, the great adversary had never had to contend with such a formidable obstruction to his work of bondage and oppression like the U.S. Constitution. For his work to go forth, that barrier had to be taken down. If not, the protected liberties of civil and religious freedom would have to be contended with not only in America but in the vast majority of the nations of his world. These Constitutions would all have the power to remove the repression against religious expression from the hands of tyrants. No majority of people have ever been in fa-

---

8. II Nephi 28: 20,21

vor of tyrants as their rulers, who for centuries have fed their greed for wealth and power from the backs of the common man.

Under constitutional governments, rulers are elected by the majority of the people, not appointed. With this, the power of the common man emerges. Their majorities elect those who come from among their own ranks and only those who promise to protect the populous, not oppress them. Elections by the people, instead of appointments or conquests, bring the remarkable transformation of rulers who must now be servants of the people. To be elected, they must prove to the voters that they will defend the inalienable individual rights of the voters and no longer to be despots and oppressors of their liberties and their right to pursue their own happiness.

Over the ensuing decades, no American had the vision or courage to step forward to save this dying nation to correct these Constitutional contaminations—except one: Joseph Smith the prophet of the Restoration. With the full support of the Quorum of the Twelve, his 337 electioneering missionaries, the Council of Fifty and his 20,000 plus followers, he became a presidential candidate with a platform to end slavery and stop religious oppression for all creeds, sects and denominations. Joseph Smith was clear in his *Views* that he intended to repair the broken Constitution. He was the only man alive who possessed a personal knowledge that God would allow wrath and indignation to fall on America through the Civil War if these wrongs were not corrected—and they were not. Joseph Smith was murdered in the middle of his valiant quest to rescue this failing nation and the Constitution—because his mission was cut short by evil men, his worked ceased and the promised war came.

The Confederate Constitution

Sixteen years after the Prophet's martyrdom, the Confederacy embraced the two flaws in the Constitution; they celebrated them. They were the bedrock of their new unauthorized nation in the Promised Land. These adulterations were written just for them, giving them constitutional power to continue the brutality of slavery with the confidence that the federal government could not legally invade their states should they choose to remove additional civil and religious rights of their subjects.

They then sunk their dagger ever closer to heart of the Constitution by altering it even further, thereby wresting this government of the people, by the people and for the people, away from the people residing in the southern states, and giving it back to dictators. The people of the south did not elect the new rulers of the Confederacy; they were appointed by a small but powerful combination of wealthy aristocratic plantation owners. Many of their much-admired plantation mansions still stand today as monuments to their erstwhile glory.

The Lord's Declaration of Independence whose inspired signers appeared to President Wilford Woodruff to implore that their temple ordinances be done in the newly completed St. George Temple, was about to be officially discarded and trashed by the southern half of the United States. And the sacred U.S. Constitution was on the brink of collapse at their hands as well. One of the first official acts of those leading the rebellion by the southern states' Confederacy was to ditch the Declaration of Independence; they wanted no part of the just and holy principle of equality for all men and their pursuit of happiness—it was to be only for themselves as the dominant race.

These aristocrats boasted their feigned loyalty to the Constitution stating that they would continue to use the original document. Of course, they were delighted with the contaminations placed therein by their South Carolina founders. But they still needed to make a few additional changes to it. The simplest, yet most destructive alteration was the replacement of one word—*one word*. Instead of their preamble beginning with, "We the people", it was changed to say, "We the deputies."[9]

And there it was. With the change of one word, they destroyed the promise of peace and liberty for the common man in the South. And Satan had the fields to the north cultivated for his sophisms to take root in the Northern states in the coming years.

In the midst of the 1860 secession movement, Alexander H. Stephens, the new vice president to Jefferson Davis in the Confederate States, touted their grand achievement, declaring in a speech to an enthusiastic crowd in Savannah, Georgia, that their new confederate Constitution "has put to rest forever, all the agitating questions relating to… the proper status of the Negro in our form of civilization."[10] Then referring to those of the Founding Fathers of our nation who believed that slavery was morally, socially and politically wrong, he contended that *they* were the ones who were fundamentally wrong in their assessment of the Black race. That these inspired men should no longer be revered but maligned and forgotten along with their just and holy principles.

Stephens continued,

> They rested upon the assumption of the equality of the races.
> This was an error. Our new Government is founded upon the

---

9. The Constitution of the Confederate States of America

10. Charles W. Dew, *Apostles of Disunion*, University of Virginia, Charlottevile and London, 2001, p. 14

opposite idea; its foundations are laid, its cornerstone rests, upon the truth that the Negro is not equal to the white man; that slavery, subordination to the superior race, is his natural and moral condition.[11]

The great constitutional government in the Promised Land was about to perish from the earth by being turned back into the hands of dictators and tyrants who, over time, would have no use for the religious and civil liberties in the sacred Constitution or Declaration of Independence. In a few short decades Satan would be back in his truth-demolishing business.

Johnston's Army

In 1858, President James Buchanan ordered General Albert Sidney Johnston to Utah with infantry, cavalry and artillery. It was the largest troop concentration in the country at that time. And with Johnston's US Army of 3,500 camped south and west of Salt Lake City at Camp Floyd, general authorities in Utah's General Conferences during this period, spoke often on the continued relentless efforts of the adversary to destroy the Latter-day Saints. Their presence was deeply troubling to the Saints in Utah given their mistreatment by the governing bodies of the United States. In 1859 Elder Orson Hyde declared,

> "What is the real design of the Government in sending troops to Utah? This winter, or during this session of Congress, special legislation is contemplated; a stringent law against polygamy to be enacted; and the troops are sent here in advance of the passage of such an act to…strongly establish themselves in

11. Charles W. Dew, *Apostles of Disunion*, University of Virginia, Charlottevile and London, 2001, p. 14

these valleys and hold themselves in readiness to enforce that law when enacted. Then they would say, "Now, Mr. Mormon, we have got you!" Anything for a lawful pretense to raise a fuss with the "Mormons," to destroy them from the earth!" [12]

Referring to the United States, Brigham Young said,

"They lay their plans to accomplish such and such a work in so long a time, and then plan a movement to destroy the "Mormons." That is what they talk about and what is in their hearts, but they will be disappointed in it all." [13]

The Army contingent remained in Utah until President Lincoln called them back in 1861.

---

12. Orson Hyde, *Journal of Discourses* vol. 6, 11-18

13. Remarks by President BRIGHAM YOUNG, made in the Tabernacle, Great Salt Lake City, March 9, 1862. REPORTED BY G. D. WATT.

10

I Will Raise Up a Man

R EMEMBER, REMEMBER THAT it is not the work of God that is frustrated, but the work of men."[1]

With this scripture in mind, the very important statement noted earlier by Elder Dallin H. Oaks bears another look.

> It was a miracle that the Constitution could be drafted and ratified. It was the first written constitution in the world. Every nation in the world except six have adopted written constitutions, and the U.S. Constitution was a model for all of them.[2]

The constitutions that exist in most nations today were patterned after the American Constitution, so we can see why Lucifer went to such great lengths to destroy it. Over the decades since the Civil War, one by one, the people in these nations pressed for the adoption of their own heavenly gift of free government for themselves and their posterity. Each contributing to a worldwide upsurge in the protection of civil and religious rights—unprecedented in the history of the world. No man can claim responsibility for this unspeakable gift. Nothing but the Hand of God could have made such a providential impact for good in this world.

1. Doctrine and Covenants 3:3
2. The Ensign, February 1992

These Constitutions have opened the door to hundreds of thousands of missionaries to enter these countries and impart the message of the Restored Gospel, without fear of harassment or imprisonment or worse. Though wars and turmoil have raged, these constitutional governments literally protect the freedom of conscience and religious expression rather than oppress it.

What or who was it, that changed the disastrous course of this nation in this Civil War era? What turned Lucifer's near complete collapse of these American freedoms into a colossal reversal where civil and religious freedoms now blanket much of the modern world?

President Heber J. Grant was the seventh Prophet and President of the Church. Born in 1856, he was about ten years old when President Abraham Lincoln was assassinated and when the Civil War ended. As a Latter-day Saint, his was among the first generation of Mormons to escape the religious persecutions in the United States because his parents Jedediah and Caroline Grant, heeded the call to flee to the west to Mexican territory in the Rocky Mountains. On their trek west, the Grant's tiny daughter, Margaret took ill and died. She was buried in a hastily and tearfully dug grave by her young parents at some unknown place on the American plains. As arduous as was their forced exile from the United States, those Latter-day Saints who heeded the call to go westward would later be completely spared and insulated from the horrors of the Civil War.

> ...flee to the west, and this in consequence of that which is coming on the earth, and of secret combinations.[3] Ye hear of wars in foreign lands...but behold, they are nigh, even at your

---

3. Doctrine and Covenants 42:64

doors, and not many years hence ye shall hear of wars in your own lands.[4]

Raised Up and Inspired of God

President Heber J. Grant wrote an article to the Church membership in the February 1940 issue of the *Improvement Era*, commemorating the February 12, 1809 birth and accomplishments of Abraham Lincoln. Up until the time of the bicentennial of this nation in 1976, it was a common practice to honor George Washington and Abraham Lincoln during their birth month of February. Washington was one of those wise men raised up by God and who has aptly been called the father of the country; Lincoln guided this nation through the destructive, yet cleansing Civil War. But the reverence for these two great men has waned with each passing generation. In that message, President Grant made a significant declaration:

> Every Latter-day Saint believes that Abraham Lincoln was **raised up and inspired of God**, and that he reached the Presidency of the United States under the favor of our Heavenly Father. We honor Abraham Lincoln because we believe absolutely that God honored him and **raised him** to be the instrument in His hands of **saving the Constitution** and the Union[5] (emphasis added).

Any American can tell the story of Lincoln winning the Civil War, thereby freeing the slaves and preserving the Union. But how many embrace the understanding that Abraham Lincoln was raised up and inspired of God to save the Constitution, as President Grant informs

---

4.   Doctrine and Covenants 45:63

5.   Heber J. Grant, *"Lincoln and Law"* The Improvement Era, February, 1940

us in this message? How many Americans have considered that the Constitution was in jeopardy, as warned by Joseph Smith, Abraham Lincoln and Heber J. Grant with this message? How many understand that the Constitution's destruction was Lucifer's aim from the moment that it was designed by George Washington, Thomas Jefferson, John Adams, Benjamin Franklin and the rest of the wise men raised up for that purpose?.

Has there been any work of God that has not been opposed or distorted by Lucifer? But there were two very important and powerful Americans who understood this critical reality—that above all of the ills that contributed to the Civil War, the threat to the Constitution was the gravest of all dangers. One of those men was the Prophet Joseph Smith, and he was murdered in his courageous endeavor to redeem and repair the Constitution for future generations of the whole world.

The other man was President Abraham Lincoln.

In 1854, six years prior to becoming president, Lincoln found himself in a debate over slavery with Stephen A. Douglas. Lincoln rarely debated many of the popular issues of the day, and this day was no exception. On this day he was centered as he usually was on the principles of right over wrong, good versus evil. Lincoln reached the crux of his disagreement with Douglas by asserting that the core issue for permitting or excluding slavery depended upon "whether a Negro is or *is not* a man."[6] He said, "[Douglas] has no very vivid impression that the Negro is a human; and consequently has no idea that there can be any moral question in legislating about him."[7] But Lincoln argued that the Negro was very much a man and that the Declaration of Independence

6. Lincoln's State Fair Speech, October 5, 1854

7. Ibid.

teaches us that all men are created equal. Because the Negro is a man, there could be no moral right to enslave him. He told them that the institution of slavery was founded in the selfishness of man's nature.

The audience was moved by Lincoln's moral outrage as he lamented "the monstrous injustice of slavery."[8] "There can be no moral right in connection with one man's making a slave of another,"[9] he thundered. "Our revolutionary fathers"[10] knew that slavery was wrong, but for practical reasons they could not eradicate it at the time they organized the new government. "They did not allow the word "slavery" in the Constitution but permitted only indirect references to it."[11] Lincoln could not hide his indignation at Douglas's claim that he and the proslavery movement were merely acting in the spirit of the Founding Fathers by permitting self-government.

As Lincoln spoke of the framers of our Constitution, it was observed that, "he quivered with feeling and emotion" and "his feelings once or twice swelled within [him] and came near stifling his ability to speak."[12] By so doing he opened the audience's view to the magnitude of injury that American slavery would mean not just for this nation but for the entire world. The world's best hope depended on the continuation of a strong and free union of all states in America, united in purpose and resolve to uphold Constitutional liberties. "We are proclaiming ourselves political hypocrites before the world, "he exclaimed, "by thus fostering human slavery and proclaiming ourselves, at the same time, the

8. Lincoln, David Herbert Donald, p 176
9. Ibid., p 176
10. Ibid., p 176
11. Lincoln, David Herbert Donald, p 176
12. Ibid., p 176

sole friends of human freedom."[13] America had become the saddest of ironies.

A House Divided Against Itself Cannot Stand

Three years before the outbreak of the Civil War, he declared the following in his acclaimed, "house divided speech" to the Illinois Republican Convention. In it he spoke of his fear of an impending national crisis:

> Mr. President and Gentlemen of the Convention.
>
> If we could first know *where* we are, and *whither* we are tending, we could then better judge *what* to do, and *how* to do it.
>
> We are now far into the *fifth* year, since a policy was initiated, with the *avowed* object, and *confident* promise, of putting an end to slavery agitation. [The Kansas Nebraska Act of 1854]
>
> Under the operation of that policy, that agitation has not only, *not ceased*, but has *constantly augmented*.
>
> In *my* opinion, it *will not* cease, **until a *crisis* shall have been reached, and passed.** (Emphasis added)
>
> "A house divided against itself cannot stand."
>
> I believe this government cannot endure, permanently half *slave* and half *free*.[14]

After an eight-year absence from any political office, in 1858, Abraham Lincoln decided to run for the Illinois Senate seat held by incumbent Stephen A. Douglas. Their campaigns personified the great divi-

13. Lincoln's State Fair Speech, October 5, 1854
14. Ibid. 15.

sion that existed in the land regarding the issues of slavery. Lincoln had a sense that some across the nation might show an interest in take a passing note to a strong challenge to the powerful Stephen A. Douglas, which he felt he could give. As it turned out, people throughout the nation followed their race and read their seven debates that were published in newspapers around the country. Even today the Lincoln and Douglas debates are studied and admired. Douglas was the heavy favorite to retain his seat in Congress, in fact he was considered to be the most powerful man in the U.S. and the certain victor in the upcoming 1860 presidential race.

The strength of Lincoln's challenge to Douglas was not fueled by ambition; he did not aspire to the office for personal reasons. He was driven by fear for this declining nation, its disregard for law and the inalienable rights of all men and women. For more than two decades since his Lyceum speech and Dr. Peter Aker's stunning prophecies, he anxiously observed one incident after another that drew this nation deeper toward a dangerous and profound national crisis, and Stephen A. Douglas' pro-slavery policies were at the tip of that lethal spear. Lincoln saw no one in America who seemed to perceive these dangers as he did; no one was effectively fighting this much larger enemy who was intent upon the demise of all Constitutional freedoms. Abraham Lincoln's mission had become Joseph Smith's mission, only two decades later, to save this "last best hope of earth" as Lincoln referred to it.

So remarkably, this unremarkable former Congressman took on the establishment by grasping the opportunity that lay before him to oppose Douglas. This political challenge would serve as a forum from which to begin his defense of this declining nation through these debates. It was a personal and solitary crusade that placed Abraham Lincoln on the most extraordinary and unlikely ascension to the White House in all our history. The power of his message was embraced by hundreds of thousands across the country. Through these debates, the name of Abraham Lincoln became associated with the eradication of the epidemic evils of slavery and lawlessness in American and for the return to our original righteous foundations, placed there by the Lord through the Founding Fathers.

And yet, Lincoln was still a reluctant hero. In his final debate with Douglas, Lincoln revealed his deepest sentiments of aversion towards politics and position. He meekly revealed to a capacity crowd that,

> Ambition has been ascribed to me. God knows how sincerely I have prayed from the first that this field of ambition might not be opened. But today, could the whole slavery question [be] replaced with unyielding hostility to the spread of it...I would...gladly agree that Judge Douglas should never be out, and I never be in, an office, so long as we both or either, live.[15]

After the results of the election retained Stephen A. Douglas in his Senate seat, Lincoln wrote to his friend Anson Henry,

> I am glad I made the late race. It gave me a hearing on the great and durable question of the ages, which I could have had no other way; and though now I sink out of view, and shall be forgotten, I believe I have made some marks which will tell for the cause of civil liberty long after I am gone.[16]

---

15. Phillip L. Ostergard, *The Inspired Wisdom of Abraham Lincoln,* Tyndale House Publishers, Inc., Carol Stream, Illinois, 2008, p. 98
16. Ibid., p. 99

The next year, though out of the public eye, his thoughts remained on this subject. He wrote to Henry Pierce on April 6th, 1859 saying,

This is a world of compensations; and he who would be no slave must consent to have no slave. Those who deny freedom to others, deserve it not for themselves; and, under a just God cannot long retain it.[17]

I Tremble for My Country

In September of that same year he gave a speech in Columbus, Ohio, quoting the great founding father, raised up by God, Thomas Jefferson who said,… "I tremble for my country when I remember that God is just!" Then Lincoln continued with the same message that he propounded as a young man in the Lyceum speech, and the same Prophetic warnings uttered by the Prophet Joseph Smith.

There was danger to this country—danger of the avenging justice of God in that little unimportant [slavery] question of Judge Douglas. He supposed that there was a question of God's eternal justice wrapped up in the enslaving of any race of men or any man, and that those who did so braved the Arm of Jehovah –that when a nation thus dared the Almighty, every friend of that nation had cause to dread His wrath. Choose ye between Jefferson and Douglas as to what is the true view of this element among us.[18]

17. Phillip L. Ostergard, *The Inspired Wisdom of Abraham Lincoln,* Tyndale House Publishers, Inc., Carol Stream, Illinois, 2008, p. 9
18. Phillip L. Ostergard, *The Inspired Wisdom of Abraham Lincoln,* Tyndale House Publishers, Inc., Carol Stream, Illinois, 2008, p. 99

These highly principled and impassioned statements revealed his fear of, and distain for the evils of slavery and lawlessness. They revealed his reverence for the Almighty God, the Declaration of Independence and the Constitution. His messaging, which was more prophet-like than political, left a dramatic imprint on the minds and hearts of many people across America.

1860 Presidential Election

In January 1860, less than a year before his election to the Presidency, his thoughts and energies were beginning to accept the more peaceful realm of work and family in Springfield and a mental and emotional retirement from politics. While slipping back into his life of anonymity, candidates were lining up support for their runs for the 1860 presidential primaries. But this respite from the rigors of public life was about to be shattered with a most unexpected letter that arrived at Lincoln's Springfield home on Jackson Street from New York City.

It was an invitation to speak at the renowned Plymouth Church, led by the highly respected Henry Ward Beecher. To be invited to the elite audience of influential New Yorkers was unanticipated and historically pivotal, and it confirmed the power of his messaging in the Lincoln and Douglas debates. The prominent elite of New York had to see for themselves, this curious and gangly prairie lawyer from whose lips flowed such stirring truths. Soon after his acceptance, the location was changed to the Cooper Union Institute where some fifteen hundred braved the cold of that February 27th night and packed the hall to see the man who was about to become the American Moses named Abraham.

As he stood before the discriminating audience, their doubts appeared to be confirmed. His hair was not fully combed, his suit a bit rumpled (obviously Mary did not make the trip with him) and his high-pitched voice with the Hoosier twang was far from the sophistication that they admired in each other. But as his initial uneasiness subsided, and the truths and pure intelligence began to echo throughout the hall, their doubts melted and their approval crescendoed to the height of elation.

Like Joseph Smith's political "Views," his message centered upon the Founding Fathers and their world changing Declaration of Independence and U. S. Constitution. He spoke as he had dozens of times before of the epic truth that all men are created by God and stand equal in his sight. With deep emotion, he propounded that the vast majority of these founders intended that the black slave was included in this declaration of equality. To punctuate this point he named each of the thirty-nine signers of US Constitution and how each one voted on the matter of restricting slavery. With this he established the compelling fact that all except three of the Constitutional delegates wanted a provision in the Constitution to end slavery in America. An overwhelming endorsement by the Founding Fathers of the fact that slavery was an evil of the Adversary, a crippling cancer to the freedoms they endeavored to establish.

Lincoln concluded his Cooper Union address with these inspiring words,

> Let us be diverted by none of those sophistical contrivances wherewith we are so industriously plied and belabored—contrivances such as groping for middle ground between the right and the wrong…reversing the divine rule, and calling, not the sinners, but the righteous to repentance![19]

19. Phillip L. Ostergard, *The Inspired Wisdom of Abraham Lincoln,* Tyndale House Publishers, Inc., Carol Stream, Illinois, 2008, p. 205

With the crowd exploding in loud applause and approval, he continued,

> Neither let us be slandered from our duty by false accusations against us, nor frightened from it by menaces of destruction to the Government…

> Let us have faith that right makes might, and in that faith, Let us, to the end, dare to do our duty as we understand it![20]

When he closed, the capacity crowd leaped as one to its feet, amidst more applause, punctuated with hat and handkerchief waving. Noah Brooks of the *New York Tribune,* exclaimed, "He's the greatest man since St. Paul." A Harvard student told his father, "It was the best speech I ever heard."[21] The following day, four New York papers printed the speech in its entirety. It was immediately published in pamphlet form and issued as a Republican tract in newspapers from New York, Chicago, Albany and Detroit. In all, it was a superb political development for the unannounced presidential candidate.

The dramatic level of enthusiastic approval in New York somewhat surprised him, and he was gratified that his moral message of right versus wrong would be so well accepted. But before he could make his return to the train station for his journey back to Springfield, requests for him to speak poured in from Rhode Island, New Hampshire and Connecticut. To these unexpected audiences he gave this same general message and received a similar degree of acceptance. All of his impassioned pleas for a righteous grass roots defense of truth and Constitutional freedoms

20. Ibid., p. 205, 206
21. Lincoln, David Herbert Donald, p 239

were published in newspapers across the nation. Once again, the name of Abraham Lincoln was on the lips of millions of Americans.

On March 4th, he wrote a letter to his wife, Mary in Springfield saying,

> I have been unable to escape this toil. If I had foreseen it, I think I would not have come east at all. The speech at New York…went off passably well and gave me no trouble whatever. The difficulty was to make nine others, before reading audiences who had already seen all my ideas in print.[22]

Lincoln for President

His regret was to no avail. His Cooper Union Speech catapulted him into the Republican nomination for President of the United States. Lincoln would run against three other Presidential candidates, fellow Illinoisan Stephen A. Douglas and former Vice-President John C. Breckenridge from Kentucky. Both from the split-apart Democratic Party—the result of the pro-secession radicals' calculated move earlier that year, at the Democratic Convention in South Carolina, to split the Party and force a Republican win. The aim of this secret combination was to create a crisis. They calculated that an election of the first Republican president who embraced antislavery sentiments, no matter who he might be, would raise the clarion call of rebellion the South. It worked. The fourth candidate was John Bell. Lincoln would remain on the sidelines pledging to make no political speeches during the campaign, saying only that if elected he would procure "Justice and fairness to all."[23] His primary

22. Phillip L. Ostergard, *The Inspired Wisdom of Abraham Lincoln,* Tyndale House Publishers, Inc., Carol Stream, Illinois, 2008, p. 207

23. Lincoln, David Herbert Donald, p 254

opponent, Stephen A. Douglas ignored tradition and unabashedly campaigned to promote himself in the race.

Just weeks before the presidential election of 1860, Lincoln was certain that political signs indicated that he would be the surprise victor and become the next president of the United States. State elections took place one month prior to the November 6th presidential election, and all eyes were on these important results. The Republicans had conducted a brilliant campaign resulting in several historically Democratic states voting Republican, boding well for Lincoln in November. Following the state returns Lincoln wrote to his former opponent on the Republican ticket, William Seward, and said, "It now really looks as if the Government is about to fall into our hands. Pennsylvania, Ohio, and Indiana have surpassed all expectations."[24]

The state of Illinois had offered him an office in the State House in Springfield to conduct his campaign. His office was next door to Newton Bateman's, the Illinois State School Superintendent. Between the two rooms there was an inner door, which Lincoln preferred to remain open, for the sake of a better circulation of air; and through this door the two became very close during his brief time there.

Newton recorded a stirring conversation that Lincoln had with him that bears consideration. Lincoln invited Bateman to his office to review a recent straw poll that had been undertaken in Springfield about the upcoming presidential election. Lincoln was particularly interested in how the ministers in his community intended to vote. Newton records,

> In that manner they went through the book, and then he
> closed it and sat silently and for some minutes. At length he
> turned to me with a face full of sadness, and said: 'Here are

24. Ibid., p 255

twenty-three, ministers, of different denominations, and all of them are against me but three; and here are a great many prominent members of the churches, a very large majority of whom are against me. Mr. Bateman, I am not a Christian— God knows I would be one—but I have carefully read the Bible, and I do not so understand this book'; and he drew from his bosom a pocket New Testament. 'These men well know,' he continued, 'that I am for freedom in the territories, freedom everywhere as far as the Constitution and laws will permit, and that my opponents are for slavery. They know this, and yet, with this book in their hands, in the light of which human bondage cannot live a moment, they are going to vote against me. I do not understand it at all.'

Here Mr. Lincoln paused for long minutes, his features surcharged with emotion. Then he rose and walked up and down the room in the effort to retain or regain his self-possession. Stopping at last, he said, with a trembling voice and his cheeks wet with tears: "'I know there is a God, and that He hates injustice and slavery. I see the storm coming, and I know that His hand is in it. If He has a place and work for me—and I think He has—I believe I am ready. I am nothing, but truth is everything. I know I am right because I know that liberty is right, for Christ teaches it, and Christ is God. I have told them that a house divided against itself cannot stand, and Christ and reason say the same; and they will find it so. Douglas don't care whether slavery is voted up or voted down, but God cares, and humanity cares, and I care; and with God's help I shall not fail. I may not see the end; but it will come, and I shall be vindicated; and these men will find that they have not read their Bibles aright."

Much of this was uttered as if he were speaking to himself, and with a sad and earnest solemnity of manner impossible to be described. After a pause, he resumed: "Doesn't it appear strange that men can ignore the moral aspects of this contest? A revelation could not make it plainer to me that slavery or the government must be destroyed. The future would be something awful, as I look at it, but for this rock on which I stand [alluding to the Testament which he still held in his hand] especially with the knowledge of how these ministers are going to vote. It seems as if God had borne with this thing [slavery] until the very teachers of religion have come to defend it from the Bible, and to claim for it a divine character and sanction; and now the cup of iniquity is full, and the vials of wrath will be poured out.[25]

The truth is this: With this nation's cup of iniquity full to overflowing, the vials of wrath were less than a year from being poured out upon it. Those ministers had not read their Bibles aright, Lincoln did not live to see the end, but after an arduous four-year ordeal in the White House he was vindicated—and glorified. He was right on all counts.

Huge Lincoln rallies were taking place throughout the North, conducted by his campaign committee and fellow Republicans, but all in his absence. Through the entire campaign Lincoln remained in Springfield. In hindsight, his silence probably became his best offence because it gave his opponents little to criticize. Outside of Springfield, the

25. Newton Bateman, *Abraham Lincoln*, p. 35.

northern half of the nation wanted to know about this little known candidate and Lincoln was flooded with telegrams, letters, photographers, and reporters. Few in the South had interest in him. Nearly 200,000 autobiographical sketches of Lincoln's life were printed and distributed. People were intrigued with his humble beginnings and the fact that he was a self-made man.

On Election Day Lincoln joined the Republicans in the capitol to hear the returns as they arrived by telegraph. After years of success and influence in Illinois, Stephen A. Douglas also watched with his Democratic supporters, as his home state of Illinois went Republican and backed Lincoln, as did Indiana and a number of other Western states. But the critical returns would be those from the Eastern States. By ten o'clock word arrived that Pennsylvania had surprisingly voted Republican. It wasn't until two o'clock that word finally arrived that the important state of New York also went Republican, sealing the election for Lincoln. Abraham Lincoln, the Rail Splitter and Self-Made Man, would be the next President of the United States. He won it ominously, without a single vote from ten of the Southern States. Lincoln recalled, "I went home, but not to get much sleep for I then felt as I never had before, the responsibility that was upon me."[26] Days later the final tally registered 180 electoral votes for Lincoln, 72 for Breckenridge, 39 for Bell, and 12 for Stephen A. Douglas.

President Abraham Lincoln

On his way to Washington by train, the President-Elect reluctantly made a number of brief speeches. One very noteworthy speech in New Jersey revealed that he had a consuming sense and conviction that God

26. Lincoln, David Herbert Donald, p 256

created this nation for some higher purpose. As the powers of good and those of evil were colliding in this country in the mid 1800s, evil was gaining significant ground over the good. He believed that this political and moral drift from the original intentions of the Founding Fathers had angered the Living God, as Lincoln often referred to Him. After becoming President, he frequently declared that the Civil War was the Almighty's judgment for the nation's sins. In this message just days before his inauguration, Lincoln took occasion to once again speak reverently of the inspired group of the Founding Fathers. It will be read in two parts.

> I recollect thinking then, boy even though I was, that there must have been something more than common that those men struggled for. I am exceedingly anxious that that thing which they struggled for; that something even more than National Independence; that something that held great promise to all the people of the world to all time to come…"[27]

We must stop in the middle of this important Lincoln declaration to ponder on just what he was referring to in speaking of an entity that was more than common, more than National Independence, "that something that held great promise to all people of the world," not just in his time but for all future time. What could it have been that was on such a grand and wondrous scale as to profit people of the entire world for all time to come?

Was it the future constitutions in the world? Likely not, because it was something more astounding than even national independence. Let it be known and declared to all the world that, that *something* of great promise to the world was the restoration of all things by the holy

27. Roy Basler, Editor, Collected Works of Abraham Lincoln, vol. IV, p .23

Hand of God! That the redemption of mankind might continue its decreed course through the Son of God, the Savior of the World, even Jesus Christ! That the world might make its preparation for His coming again, this time in glory "and all the holy angels with him,"[28] to accept his rightful place on His earthly throne, as King of Kings and Lord of Lords!

And as a forerunner to this great revelation in the latter days of this earth's existence, constitutional governments, which after Lincoln's martyrdom would, as he and Joseph Smith foresaw, begin to cover the globe. These free governments have offered their citizens, like those of the United States, the same liberty to worship Almighty God "according to the dictates of [their] own conscience."[29] These constitutions throughout the world have served as a powerful barrier to Lucifer's blinding bondage of centuries past, much like the protective hedge built around the nobleman's vineyard in the parable of the redemption of Zion given in D&C 101:44-62. Because of these governments of the people and by the people, millions coming from nearly every nation and tongue have used this liberty to hear and then embrace the message of the restored gospel, to come follow Jesus Christ, repent of their sins, and be baptized into his earthly kingdom through the restored power and authority from God.

Continuing with President Lincoln's important statement:

I am exceedingly anxious that this Union, the Constitution, and the liberties of the people shall be perpetuated in accordance with the original idea for which the struggle was made, and I shall be most happy indeed if I shall be an humble in-

---

28. The Holy Bible, Matthew 25:31
29. Article of Faith, #11, *The Pearl of Great Price* p. 60

strument in the hands of the Almighty, and of this, his almost chosen people, for perpetuating the object of that great struggle.[30]

God's Humble Instrument

Was Abraham Lincoln referring to the restored gospel in this statement about "something that held great promise to all people of the world?" He did not elaborate. But it must be conceded that he took to the White House more knowledge of the Latter-day Saints and their doctrine than any other President before or since. To be sure, he was very aware of the Prophet Joseph Smith and the Latter-day Saints who lived in his home state of Illinois for six years. Lincoln read hundreds of newspaper articles about the Prophet of the Restoration and his Latter-day Saints; he voted for their Nauvoo Charter and debated their issues as a Legislator in the State of Illinois while they resided there. Records indicate that he had a number of Mormon friends, many who were among the estimated 150 members of the Springfield, Illinois branch of the Church during the early 1840s. [31]

Lincoln knew of Joseph Smith's candidacy for President of the United States in 1844 and knew of his 12-page *Views* giving him an understanding of Joseph Smith's political platform. It is probable that Abraham Lincoln read Joseph Smith's twelve-page political pamphlet or *Views* with interest in 1844. It was personally delivered to the newspapers in Springfield, Illinois, by electioneering missionaries. Lincoln spent much time at the newspaper office of his editor friend, Simeon

30. Roy Basler, Editor, Collected Works of Abraham Lincoln, vol. IV, p .23

31. Ron L. Andersen, *Abraham Lincoln and Joseph Smith, How Two Contemporaries Changed the Face of American History,* Plain Sight Publishing, an Imprint of Cedar Fort, Inc., Springfield, Utah, pp. 121-123

Francis of the *Sangamon Journal,* which quoted favorably from Joseph Smith's "Views" in its April 4, 1844 issue. It is quite certain that Lincoln would have agreed with much of General Smith's political positions.

Lincoln's political platform during his presidency was extraordinarily similar to the martyred Prophet's views on the government and how to repair it. In just the first paragraph of the *Views* document, Lincoln would have observed that Joseph Smith embraced the same position as he: that all are equal in the sight of God, a position that was not widely accepted in America. Seventeen years later he took those views with him to the White House as President.

In the first paragraph of his *Views,* Joseph Smith made an interesting statement, "I ever feel a double anxiety for the happiness of all men, both in time and eternity." This phrase, time and eternity is very much a Latter-day Saint term and one that President Lincoln used at least *twice* during his Presidency. It is very likely that he learned it from reading the *Views* or through some conversation with a Springfield Mormon acquaintance, of which he had many. One of those times was during his second State of the Union address in 1862 in which he said, "In times like the present, men should utter nothing for which they would not willingly be responsible through time and eternity."[32] The other occurred during his run for re-election in 1864. Some constituents had warned him that if he were serious about winning the election, he would rescind his highly controversial Emancipation Proclamation. To one he responded that although he may be a slow walker, he did not walk backwards. And to another he resolutely replied that he would be damned in time and eternity should he ever attempt to rescind what he believed God had guided him to do.

32. Abraham Lincoln, Second State of the Union Address (1 December 1862)

But the most compelling element of Lincoln's awareness of the doctrine of The Church of Jesus Christ of Latter-day Saints is the fact that he had in his possession, in the White House, the *Book of Mormon*. He didn't stumble upon it; he requested it. This sacred book, foreseen by and written in part by the Prophet Nephi himself, as having the power to inspire millions to believe in the great restoration of all things in the last days, resided in the White House during some of this nation's darkest days, in the possession of the President of the United States, a man of great faith and power, for eight months.

Some months after becoming President, for an unexplained reason he sent an aide to the Library of Congress in November of 1861, to bring to him books about the Mormons. The aide signed Lincoln's name to the register for having checked-out three books on the Mormons. Two of these books were written by enemies of the Church and were critical of the Mormons; these books were returned just a few days later, but an additional book on the same subject was brought to him.

This additional one is of interest; it was a rare book for that time because its author was not a Latter-day Saint but he made a laudable effort to address the facts objectively and fairly and he had many reliable sources for his information. Charles MacKay, from England wrote the book in 1851; it is entitled, *The Mormons or Latter-day Saints with Memoirs of the Life and Death of Joseph Smith, the American Mahomet*. If Lincoln read just the opening paragraph in MacKay's book, and he likely did, he would have read this:

The Mormons have thriven amid oppression of the most cruel and pertinacious kind; they have conquered the most astonishing difficulties; they have triumphed over the most vindictive enemies, and over the most unrelenting persecution; and from the blood of their martyrs have sprung the courage, the zeal, and the success of the survivors. They can boast not only an admirable and complete organization, but the possession of worldly wealth, influence, and power. Their progress within the last seven years has been rapid to a degree unparalleled in the history of any other sect of religionists. The remarkable career of Joseph Smith, the Prophet of the Mormons, and the story of the rise of the sect which he founded, is one of the most curious episodes in the modern history of the world.[33]

Even more striking than this passage was in the following paragraph where MacKay included his friend, Apostle Orson Pratt's beautiful version of the first vision. And while giving the account of the boy Joseph conversing with God the Father and His Son, Jesus Christ in the grove near his home, Pratt wrote:

He was also informed upon the subjects which had for some time previously agitated his mind—namely, that all of the religious denominations were believing in incorrect doctrines, and consequently that none of them was acknowledged of God as his church and kingdom. And he was expressly commanded to go not after them.[34]

Consider Lincoln's lifelong religious conflict with the organized religions of his day as he read this striking confirmation of his own personal belief about the denominations of his day. This must have been read with great wonder by Lincoln, who, though longing for years to belong

33. Charles MacKay, *The Mormons: or Latter-day Saints. With Memoirs of The Life and Death of Joseph Smith, The "AMERICAN MAHOMET"*, London, Office of the National Illustrated Library, 1851, p. 16

34. Ibid., p. 18

to a congregation of his same faith, simply could not align himself with any of the Protestant religions because he understood them to misinterpret the doctrines in the Bible. And this would have been found on just the fourth page of MacKay's book.

The third book originally checked out on that first day was the *Book of Mormon* and that book President Lincoln retained in his possession for eight months.[35] He personally returned the *Book of Mormon* in July of 1862 and the authentic signature, *A. Lincoln*, as he commonly signed his name, still resides to this day in the register of the Library of Congress for having returned the great book.

---

35. Borrower's Ledger 1861-1863, 114, Archives of the Library of Congress, Library of Congress, Washington, DC.

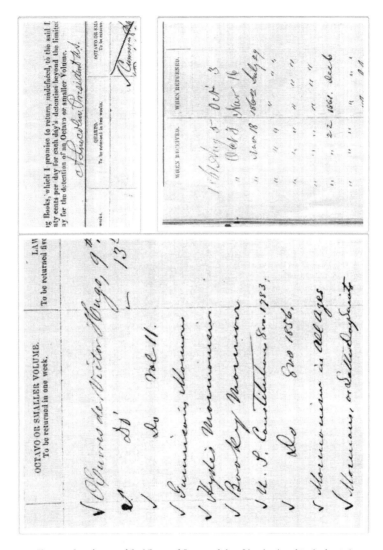

Close up photo images of the Library of Congress ledger Lincoln signed to check out the Book of Mormon and other books related to the Church. He kept the Book of Mormon for eight months. Photos provided courtesy of the Library of Congress.

[Borrows from Library of Congress: "Oeuvres de Victor Hugo, vol. 11." Additional books sent to White House are Gunnison's "Mormons," Hyde's "Mormonism," and "Book of Mormon." The Book of Mormon; an Account Taken by the Hand of Mormon from the Plates of Nephi. By Joseph Smith Jr., Palmyra, N.Y., 1830.]

How heartened he must have felt when he read Book of Mormon scriptures like,

> [The Lord] inviteth them all to come unto him and partake of his goodness; and he denieth none that come unto him, black and white, bond and free, male and female; and he rememberth the heathen; and all are alike unto God, both Jew and Gentile.[36]

This would have been a moving affirmation for Lincoln, which declared that he just may have been closer to eternal truth than many of his friends or family ever credited him for.

Re-election

In 1864 Lincoln was running for re-election; the American people were so tired of the carnage of war that many, including him were doubtful that he would be elected. The Democratic candidate George McClellan, was gaining ground on his campaign of "Peace at Any Price." The Northern Democrats promised to negotiate an immediate peace with the South and thus put an end to the curse of war. That meant that truth and liberty would be compromised yet again. Remarkably they were willing to give the South their slaves, they were willing to surrender and divide the nation, and thereby end all that Lincoln had been so determined to do in preserving the Constitution. It is troubling that so many Americans in the North did not see the greater good being pursued by President Lincoln. The gates of hell were being offered yet another opportunity to prevail over heavenly good in this election.

Unexpectedly, it was General William Tecumseh Sherman who would make a dramatic move to change the minds of the citizens, both

---

36. II Nephi 26:33

North and South. He had a battle plan that both General U.S. Grant and Lincoln doubted. He proposed that his army of 62,000 men drive south to take the city of Atlanta, the center for supplying the Confederate Army. General Sherman believed that if successful, he could so cripple the struggling Confederate army and bring the long war to an end in place of another year or more of battlefield body counts on both sides. By going through to the heart and strength of the South he would have to disconnect himself and his army from all Union supply and reinforcement lines and would be without communications to the North for weeks at a time.

At length, Lincoln and Grant conceded and Sherman began his unprecedented assault. With no way to be re-supplied, his army would live off the farms, stock and stores in their path. This army supply path was at times eighty miles wide. His soldiers were ordered to forage liberally but under the following conditions: they were forbidden to enter houses, they could take what they found in the open, crops, livestock, gardens. They were not to pillage poor families, but it was open season on the wealthy southern aristocrats whom they could plunder at will as just retribution for their rebellion. Any plantation mansion in their path was burned to the ground but no civilian was to be injured or harmed. Along the way they destroyed bridges, railroads, supply roads, factories and cotton bales, anything that might contribute to the Southern fighting machine.

As Sherman's Army advanced towards its destination, it met stiff resistance from the Confederate army but prevailed. On November 15, 1864, they entered Atlanta and set ablaze their rail depot, factories, warehouses of ammunition and weapons, cotton bales, and any other industry that was being run to supply the Confederate army. When news of this grand achievement reached newspapers in the North, it so heartened the populace that many could finally see that Lincoln's policies were increasingly bearing fruit and they rallied behind him to give him a second term as President. The news of the fall of Atlanta was extremely discouraging for the South and many lost hope of ever winning the war.

Sherman continued his march southward to Savannah and took the city without a fight. On December 22, 1864, he sent President Lincoln a telegram saying "I beg to present you as a Christmas gift the city of Savannah with 150 heavy guns and plenty of ammunition and also about 25,000 bales of cotton."[37] He then turned his course northward and sacked the city of Columbus, South Carolina, the birthplace of the rebellion, and then Raleigh, North Carolina. As he hoped, it was a debilitating blow to the Southern fighting forces.

From the beginning he believed that his success would be the most humane way to eradicate the South's ability to resist by cutting off man-ufacturing, supplies and transportation to the army. It would also make "the civilians so miserable as to break the morale of Confederates at home and in the field."[38] He spoke often of his impression that after nearly four years of hatred for the North and vice versa, it was time to make war so terrible that the rebels would never again take up arms. He believed that the entire South bore a collective responsibility.

General Sherman was right. His successful campaign delivered a crippling blow to the Southern resolve to continue their devastating re-bellion. The scope and magnitude of Almighty God's promised, "wrath, indignation and chastening hand" over the lawless persecutions of His

---

37. Burke Davis, *Sherman's March*, Random House, Inc., New York,1980 p. 118
38. Ibid., p. 10

Saints in His Promised Land and the disregard for, and the contaminations that were tolerated in His sacred Constitution are stunning. Yet, as Lincoln declared in his Second Inaugural Address, these Civil War judgments of God "are true and righteous altogether."

The people of the North devoured news of Sherman's march with elation. His success created a dramatic turn of public support for their great President. Election Day, November 8, 1864, finally arrived with the Republicans garnering a decidedly strong victory carrying every state but New Jersey, Delaware and Kentucky, the birth State of both Abraham and Mary. Abraham Lincoln was re-elected to serve four more years as President of the United States with a resounding margin of 221 electoral votes to 21 for McClellan. Lincoln was particularly pleased with the margin of votes by the soldiers in the field: 116,887 for Lincoln and 33,748 for former General McClellan.

Lincoln gained his re-election in November 1864. Perceiving the Southern rebellion's certain collapse to be just weeks away, President Lincoln was now prepared to do the unthinkable—unthinkable for the past two-hundred and fifty years. He had set himself firmly on the path, which the Great God in Heaven had opened, to convince Congress to pass the Thirteenth Amendment that would end slavery forever. Its success would throw out the three-fifths clause from the Constitution, repairing one of the flaws that had encumbered it since its creation.

Recapitulation

Before describing the dramatic events that took place during the month of January 1865, a reminder first of the epic magnitude of what Abraham Lincoln was about to undertake.

As depicted in earlier chapters, all of the history of God's preparations for this last dispensation might be accurately capsulated into Lucifer's fight against God—agency over bondage. Through the lion's share
of history Lucifer has reigned with blood, horror and evil in every cor-
ner of the world and in every dispensation of time. With the awakening
of heavenly light descending in each successive dispensation the won-
ders of God and His truths were manifest in remarkable degrees, but
each eventually ended with the evils of the adversary prevailing against
the seekers of light and truth.

God has revealed that in the last dispensation, the Dispensation of
the Fullness of Times Lucifer would not, in the end, prevail. Nephi's
great vision of The Almighty's preparations and workings for the Promised Land is a vision of that centuries-long preparation. Important stages
in that progression were shown to the young Prophet that he might
record it in the Book of Mormon for all to see and know the marvelous
workings of the Lord Jesus Christ.

Nephi saw Lucifer's evil in the torture and murder of the Gentile
Saints under Satan's captivity in Europe. These faithful Saints were inspired by the Holy Ghost to follow Christopher Columbus to the Promised Land, a man of deep and unwavering faith. Here, with Bible in
hand, these people received the delicious taste of freedom to worship as
they pleased. They battled for their freedom against the mother country
in the Revolutionary War where, under the power of God they prevailed
with a miraculous victory and with their independence. It was at this
same time that the Lord had placed great men in America, men whom
he raised up for the purpose to establish a government such as had never
been known.

God gave additional revelations to Joseph Smith extending this on-going process of His holy workings. He revealed that he would raise up men to establish the Constitution in D&C 101. He also revealed that because the Saints would be persecuted, he would bring judgments in the form of war "beginning with the rebellion in South Carolina" in D&C 87.

This government would have a constitution, one that guaranteed that the voice of the people would determine the laws and the leaders who would govern them. There would be no kings or dictators in this Promised Land. This new model of government would be the defining hallmark of these blessed Gentiles. Free-minded people around the globe would admire this government and they in turn would adopt their own constitutions of civil and religious freedom. These people above all, wanted to guarantee their freedom to worship the Almighty God according to dictates of their own conscience. It was this right that was placed as the very first freedom to be protected in the Bill of Rights in the United States Constitution.

This Constitution proved to be a debilitating stumbling block for the great deceiver of nations and people. Yet Lucifer managed to infiltrate this sacred document with his two insidious parasites: slavery would be protected and the power of the Federal government to protect the sacred freedoms would be restricted. With these weapons in hand in January 1865, he was at the threshold of destroying these marvelous endowments from God. In Washington, the halls of Congress in January 1865 became an epic battlefield between good and evil. If Lincoln succeeded, these freedoms would prevail. If he did not, they were at risk of all being lost; the power and potential of the US Constitution and the dozens of other constitutions that would cover the earth simply would not be.

The Thirteenth Amendment

In December 1864, Lincoln shocked his Cabinet by revealing his intention to press the House of Representatives to once again vote on the passage of an amendment to the Constitution to end slavery. Earlier in 1864, the Senate passed this bill but it failed in the House. There seemed to be no logical reason for Lincoln to press for this. Although never expressed by Lincoln there was a very compelling reason to move at that time and do so with earnest—Lincoln would be dead within three months. Lincoln often expressed to friends that he was certain that he would not survive his Presidency. In the coming weeks he would have a dream where he saw himself lying in state in the East Room of the White House. This dream was so compelling to him that he felt he had to tell Mary and other close associates. It's not known if the next president would have possessed the same vision as Lincoln on this monumental matter.

His Cabinet pressed back hard when asked to support him in this great cause that they could not see. Initial estimates indicated that he would fall far short of the majority needed, many Democrats would have to side with the Republicans and these were the same Democrats who had voted against it just months earlier, killing the bill. Why not wait until the war is over and the new Republican Senators and Congressmen in their seats? It made no sense to them. There were some in his own Republican party who were disappointed that it was Lincoln still in office and not another Republican, receiving Lincoln's "nonsense" with disdain. Yet every Republican vote was needed for the amendment to hold any hope of success.

Lincoln, who through his Presidency had been criticized for his deliberate pace in his approach to the many issues he faced over the previous term, was different with this one. He was resolute and determined that doubters would not prevail to derail him from this momentous opportunity. President Lincoln was powerful in a dramatic way through this process, possessing what could be identified as being moved and powered of the Almighty God.

He explained to his mostly doubtful Cabinet his reasons for this momentous step to be done without delay. He reminded his Cabinet that even with winning the war, the Constitution still allowed for slavery. He explained that the Emancipation Proclamation made two years previously was a war measure and may not be binding after the war. The Constitution gives the President authority to act outside the Constitution in undefined ways during the time of war. Seizing on this Constitutional authority, he issued the proclamation to free the slaves only in the rebelling states as a wartime measure. His intent was to arm the slaves and allow them to fight for their own freedom. Some 180,000 of these brave men volunteered to join the Union army and fought bravely, turning the tide of the war to the Union's favor. Some 33,000 free Blacks and former slaves gave their lives for their country, proving Lincoln's declaration that "in giving freedom to the slave, we assure freedom to the free."[39]

Lincoln continued, asking his Cabinet to consider the fate of the Emancipation Proclamation, reminding them that a challenge to its Constitutionality could be made that since the war is ended and the rebelling states are no longer rebelling, it could be ruled null and void. Four million slaves might be taken back into slavery.

---

39. Ronald C. White, Jr. *The Eloquent President*, Random House, New York, 2005, p, 170

With growing intensity Lincoln explained that at the war's end these rebel soldiers and officers would soon be allowed to return to their homes and take up their state and local political offices. By so doing, nothing could be done to stop a state from calling back the blacks into servitude. The Constitution still was in force saying that the black man counts three-fifths of a person in filling the seats in the US House of Representatives. Slavery was still legal. Nothing would be changed. If they did not act now in repairing the Constitution and ending slavery with a Constitutional amendment, all of the grief and carnage of this war would be for naught. This nation would go on with nothing gained from the civil war except Union. The slaves were free but could with relative ease be called back into servitude and bondage. Lucifer still had his hand in the Constitution.

With Lincoln's re-election the Republicans also gained 40 seats in both houses. Lincoln instructed William Seward to orchestrate a campaign focused on the 40 Democrats who would soon be returning home to encourage them to ponder on the immensity of this occasion and to please vote their conscience in these their final days in office. Lincoln personally called on many of those opposed to his amendment and in gracious humility supplicated their support. Just two days before the January 31st vote they had made a dramatic advance securing all of the required Democratic votes except two. Lincoln continued to encourage them and express his optimism that the bill would pass.

John B. Alley was in attendance at the tense meeting and wrote, "Two members of the House were sent for and Mr. Lincoln said that those two votes must be procured. When asked, 'How?' To the surprise of all, Lincoln thundered,

> I am President of the United States, clothed with great power.
> The abolition of slavery by constitutional provision settles

the fate, for all coming time, not only of the millions now in bondage, but of the unborn millions to come—a measure of such importance that those two votes must be procured. I leave it to you to determine how it shall be done; but remember that I am President of the United States, clothed with immense power, and I expect you to procure those votes.[40]

Mark January 31, 1865, as one of the most important days in modern history.

At noon on this day the galleries of the House of Representatives were full to overflowing. A group of Congressmen escorted a number of Black men and women into the gallery to observe the historic event. The atmosphere was electric. Would the two votes be found? Carl Sandburg described the voting.

The Yeas and Nays are ordered. Alley, Allison, Anderson and so on. These are all Republicans, their Yeas expected. Comes the name of James E. English, a Connecticut Democrat. He shouts "Aye!" A long roll of applause bursts from the gallery and Republican House members. The speaker hammers his gavel. The tumult goes down. Again the voice of the clerk can be heard. For the Republican Ayes as the roll call goes on, there is quiet. But with each Democrat shouting his vocal Aye at the calling of his name there is tumult of hand clapping, cheers, laughter, the noisemaking of pent-up emotion let loose. Eleven Democrats answer Aye.

Swift pencils add up the lists. The clerk whispers to the Speaker who announces that the question is decided in the

40. Carl Sandburg, *Abraham Lincoln, The Prairie Years and the War Years,* Harcourt, Brace & World, Inc. New York, 1954, p. 644

affirmative—Yeas 119, Nays 56, 8 not voting. And said the Congressional Globe: "...the two thirds required by the Constitution of the United States having voted in favor thereof, the joint resolution was passed."[41]

The cheering, elation, tears, hugs and backslapping went on and on inside the Capital. People were seen running in all directions with the news. Cannon fire was soon heard thundering a 100-gun salute for the monumental victory.

The Thirteenth Amendment to the Constitution passed by a margin of three votes. Eight Democrats did not attend the session. Another miracle; so very similar to the miracle of Constitutional Convention where the Constitution was formed in 1787. The Senate had earlier voted in favor of the Amendment so the deal was done. The next day Lincoln's home state of Illinois rewarded him by being the first state to ratify the amendment. Three-fourths of the states would need to do the same to amend the Constitution and these were also procured.

Just as the passing of the Constitution has been deemed a miracle, yet another manifestation of God's power was received on January 31, 1865. Until that day Satan was just two votes away from absolute domination once again on the earth. Three votes in the remarkable Constitutional process ended his domination. It was a dramatic end to his four hundred year scheme of wielding his ugly weapon of slavery to combat and upset the Lord's sacred Constitution. He failed. Good prevailed over evil. And who superintended this extraordinary moment for the ages? It was God's humble instrument, Abraham Lincoln.

41. Ibid., p. 645

11

A New Birth of Freedom

A FTER ENDURING FOUR years of mental and emotional anguish while the nation was torn by the war, Lincoln was blessed to see the first fruits emerge from the great chastisement of war in an unexpected yet monumental development for this now humbled nation. In that fateful 30 days of January 1865, he worked skillfully with the opposing Democrats and recalcitrant Republicans in Congress for the ratification of the Thirteenth Amendment to the United States Constitution that would officially abolish and prohibit slavery. Here is the simple language of the Thirteenth Amendment that saved the world untold corruption and evil.

> **Section 1.** Neither slavery nor involuntary servitude, except as punishment for crime whereof the party shall have been duly convicted, shall exist in the United States, or any place subject to its jurisdiction.

> **Section 2.** Congress shall have power to enforce this article by appropriate legislation.

This amendment would slam shut the door that the Constitution's destructive three-fifths ruling had propped open for the expansion of slavery in America for some "four score and seven years" since its creation. Lincoln had longed for its legal removal, and now the war provided the unexpected opportunity. And then with guarded elation, Lincoln would observe over the months of February, until his assassination in April, how one by one, twenty-seven of the thirty-six states—the needed three fourths majority—ratified the new Amendment to end slavery forever in this nation. All other states would eventually ratify the amendment, with the last state doing so quite recently: Mississippi ratified the amendment in March 1995. At the news of the Amendment's passing, African Americans assembled in large groups where they clapped and sang, "Sound the loud timbrel o'er Egypt's dark sea, Jehovah has triumphed, His people are free."[1]

The Thirteenth Amendment would be the first fruit to emerge from the great national cleansing. There would be additional, highly significant harvests from the Almighty's refining and the softened hearts of the now chastened American people. This was demonstrated by the votes of their representatives to end slavery forever in the United States, something that was unthinkable before the war. From the White House, Lincoln pronounced the amendment "a great moral victory."[2] Then pointing toward the Potomac River and his brothers in the South he said, "If the people over the river had behaved themselves, I could not have done what I did."[3]

Second Inauguration

Indeed the war was the catalyst for a series of dramatic national transformations. The Thirteenth Amendment would be a crowning

1. With Malice Toward None, Stephen B. Oates, p 405
2. Ibid., p 405
3. Ibid., p 405

and lasting achievement in any President's legacy, but there were several more "great moral victories" just on the horizon that the Almighty God and His "humble instrument" would unfold; a horizon that Lincoln would not live to see.

As Inauguration Day approached for Lincoln's second term, a friend observed that he "looked badly and felt badly." To his long-time friend, Joshua Speed, Lincoln admitted, "I am very unwell," my feet and hands are always cold—I suppose I ought to be in bed."[4] Still on March 4, Lincoln climbed into the carriage that would take him on the traditional ride on Pennsylvania Avenue, lined with waving crowds and playing bands, to the Capitol where he would give his second inaugural address and be sworn in for four more years. Having rained in the days prior, Washington was awash with mud that was particularly troublesome for the women and their fine dresses. Noah Brooks observed that these women were in a "most wretched, wretched plight" with the mud.

Inauguration day was again wet, cold, windy, and gray as Lincoln stood under the recently completed Capitol Dome that had been years in the building, delayed by the war. This new Dome towering over the tired President was a fitting symbol of the continuing grand and harrowing process of nation-building, started four score and nine years earlier.

The process, initially sabotaged by the powers of darkness would finally be set in motion as it was originally intended, with the inalienable rights for all men guaranteed by the United States Constitution and protected by a strong and righteous central government of the now *reunited* states.

Lincoln stood before the Washington crowd, at the threshold of the most critical test of self-governance, an experiment initiated by the faith

4. Ibid., p 409

and courage of the Founding Fathers to determine whether such a re-public can long endure. The cleansing that was now concluding would ensure that this "government of the people, by the people, and for the people shall not perish from the earth,"[5] as it so nearly did.

There may have been another highly significant manifestation that cold dreary morning. The moment Lincoln took the podium, the clouds parted and the brilliant sunlight shone on him and the large crowd for a brief moment. After his short yet powerful address, Lincoln asked his trusted friend Noah Brooks, "Did you notice that sunburst? It made my heart jump."[6] The sunburst was either a fortuitous coincidence or Lin-coln just may have perceived the Hand of God, confirming His humble and unwavering servant who had only 42 days remaining in this earthly realm.

In the days preceding the second inauguration an unusual mix of people streamed into Washington to observe the historic event. At this inauguration most of the estimated forty to forty-five thousand present that day carried the hurt of a lost or wounded soldier in their hearts. There were many more Black faces in the crowd than at any other in-auguration, African Americans who came to hear the words of "Father Abraham," their deliverer; and who, though now free, were beginning to experience a new resentment from whites for having won their free-dom at such a devastating cost.

There were thousands of soldiers present as well, most from some forty hospitals in the Washington area, and many of these soldiers were sad and pain-racked amputees. Others bore the disfigurement of head injuries from bullet or shrapnel that would be theirs to endure for the

5. Gettysburg Address, Abraham Lincoln
6. With Malice Toward None, Stephen B. Oates, p 411

rest of their lives. Many sensed a heightened hope, as signs indicated the Confederate military was rapidly collapsing and the war nearing an end.

Still others bore a boiling hatred and resentment for the North and especially for Abraham Lincoln and the terrible injustice that, in their minds he had inflicted on the South. One such stood in the crowd some thirty-five feet behind and above Lincoln as he delivered the greatest sermon of his Presidency. John Wilkes Booth stared down intently on the president as his mind fabricated delusional plans to accomplish what so many had failed to do. And, like the first inauguration, there were sharpshooters on the tops of buildings and police and military at the ready to ward off what all knew was a heightened reality—that, more than ever, there were now those who sought to take the life of Lincoln.

President Lincoln's address consisted of only 703 words, the second shortest inaugural address to be given. George Washington's was the shortest when no tradition was yet in place for newly elected Presidents. Lincoln's message consisted of just four paragraphs in which Lincoln referred to God fourteen times, quoted the Bible four times and invoked prayer three times. Nothing would be said of his astonishing accomplishments of the past four years. As was his pattern, he spoke little of politics, preferring to speak of the greatness of the Almighty whom he so faithfully served and so deeply loved.

He used personal pronouns only twice, *I* and *myself*, in the first paragraph, and not again. Because we approach the Second Inaugural through the larger lens of his previous speeches, there should be no surprise at this. He rarely spoke of himself; he did not use one personal pronoun in the Gettysburg Address. From the outset of the address, all of his sentiments are directed away from himself."[7]

---

7. The Eloquent President, Ronald C. White, Jr., p 286

In what could have been the greatest victory speech in American history, Lincoln says nothing of conquest. Instead of speaking of himself and his great triumph, instead of reviling the guilty in the South and the vociferous detractors in the North, all of which would have been met with resounding approbation by the crowd, his intent and delivery was quite apart from expected political discourse. He used this occasion, not to speak of himself, but to speak of God by declaring to the nation and to the world, of the great national deliverance from sure destruction and chaos, which was now concluding. His purpose was to instruct the people of America that this monumental deliverance was not done by him, or by the superiority of the Union military, but by the Living God. And to clearly declare that the horrific castigation of the Civil War, which was finally coming to a close, was the just and deserved chastening of the Almighty God for the sins of a highly blessed people gone astray.

Unlike so many political speeches that are organized and reviewed by a team of speech writers, Lincoln developed his alone, and who can doubt that it was done with open Bible and fervent prayer asking his trusted God for guidance and for His approbation of its contents. He began his address with an introduction and a very brief overview of the events of the past four years. In his second paragraph he moves toward the heart of his message by meekly declaring:

> On the occasion corresponding to this four years ago, all thoughts were anxiously directed to an impending civil war. All dreaded it—all sought to avert it. While the inaugural address was being delivered from this place, devoted altogether to saving the Union without war, insurgent agents were in the city seeking to destroy it without war—seeking to dissolve the Union, and divide effects, by negotiation. Both parties

deprecated war; but one of them would make war rather than let the nation survive; and the other would accept war rather than let it perish. And the war came.[8]

In his book, *Lincoln's Virtues,* William Lee Miller observes,

[Lincoln] would not stoke the fires of national self-righteousness. His interpretation of America's role in the world...would stand as something of a corrective to blatant national egoism and self-deception. President Lincoln would not insist, as President Polk had insisted [with the War with Mexico], that the other side in his war was altogether and absolutely to blame for the war's beginning and for its continuance—even though some might say that President Lincoln would have far more justification for doing so than had President Polk. Lincoln would not reiterate the South's guilt; he would recommend amnesty toward the Confederate leaders and generosity to the Southern people; he would say that neither side wanted war, and would describe the beginning impersonally: 'And the war came.'[9]

"The people who begin a war," says Ronald C. White, Jr., "almost always do so with the sense that they are in charge. Lincoln, looking back with the hindsight of four years, is suggesting that the generals, the soldiers, and the commander-in-chief were not completely in control

---

8. The Eloquent President, Ronald C. White, Jr., p 289

9. Lincoln's Virtues, William Lee Miller, p 191

of the war."[10] In paragraph three, Lincoln would "situate slavery as an inclusive problem that was the responsibility of the whole nation."[11]

> One eighth of the whole population were colored slaves, not distributed generally over the Union, but localized generally in the Southern part of it. These slaves constituted a peculiar and powerful interest. All knew that this interest was somehow the cause of the war. To strengthen, to perpetuate, and extend this interest was the object for which the insurgents would rend the Union, even by war; while the government claimed no right to do more than to restrict the territorial enlargement of it. Neither party expected for the war, the magnitude, or the duration, which it has already attained. Neither anticipated that the cause of the conflict might cease with, or even before, the conflict itself should cease. Each looked for an easier triumph, and a result less fundamental and astounding.[12]

Explains Ronald C. White, Jr., "No one knew it, but Lincoln was preparing his audience to hear about God's purposes by rehearsing the finitude of human purposes."[13]

Lincoln continued:

Both read the same Bible, and pray to the same God; and each invokes His aid against the other. It may seem strange that any man should dare to ask a just God's assistance in wringing their bread from the sweat of other men's faces; but let us

10. The Eloquent President, Ronald C. White, Jr., p 289
11. Ibid., p 289
12. Ibid., p 289
13. The Eloquent President, Ronald C. White, Jr., p 291

judge not that we be not judged. The prayers of both could not be answered; that of neither has been answered fully.[14]

Again, Mr. White notes, "Speaking to an audience so ready to judge, Lincoln invoked the authority of Jesus in the New Testament to restrain an all too human impulse."[15]

The audience does not know it yet, but in this transitional section Lincoln is about to "connect human purposes, with their tendency toward pretentiousness, to what will emerge as the central theme in this address, the purposes of God."[16] William Lee Miller said, "President Lincoln, with the strongest of motives to do so, would not claim that God has marked out a superior role for … his side in the war. In the Second Inaugural he would say that, "the Almighty has His own purposes," meaning exactly that [God's] purposes were larger than those of either side, including his own."[17]

> The Almighty has His own purposes. "Woe unto the world because of offenses! For it must needs be that offenses come; but woe to that man by whom the offense cometh!" If we shall suppose that American Slavery is one of those offences which, in the providence of God, must needs come, but which, having continued through His appointed time, He now wills to remove, and that He gives to both North and South, this terrible war, as the woe due to those by whom the offense came, shall we discern therein any departure from those divine at-

14. Ibid., p 290

15. Ibid., p 290

16. Ibid., p 290

17. Lincoln's Virtues, William Lee Miller, p 191

tributes which the believers in a Living God always ascribe to Him?[18]

White explains, "Lincoln arrived at the architectural center of his address. After chronicling a variety of purposes and intentions, Lincoln presented his own meaning of the war, to be found in the purposes of God."[19] To describe these purposes, he wisely chooses the words of Jesus Christ himself, found in Matthew 18:7, to remind them that since the beginning of time, the Great Jehovah has allowed woe to come to the rebellious and impenitent as a fitting process of redemption.

The terrible woe endured at this time is no departure from His eternal ways. Lincoln's reference to American Slavery rather than Southern slavery is significant. While it was the slave-owning insurgents in the South who triggered the Civil War, for many decades earlier the slave trade (the capturing, shipping, and selling of Africans) was centered in New England. The trading of slaves, though abolished earlier in the nineteenth century, was very much a part of the two and one half centuries of the "peculiar institution," a long overdue debt that had come due for those in the North as well.

Unexpectedly to everyone, Lincoln was ready to close and he would do it as was his pattern by expressing words of kindness, and reconciliation, but they would include the reality and righteousness of God's judgments, that this war would end only when God felt that the "uttermost farthing" had been paid to fulfill the demands of justice. He would use words from his beloved Psalms, the nineteenth chapter and ninth verse to proclaim as he so often had before, that the works of God and

---

18. The Eloquent President, Ronald C. White, Jr., p 293
19. Ibid., p 293

His judgments could never be abrogated in the centuries preceding, nor in the present, by mortal man.

> Fondly do we hope—fervently do we pray—that this mighty scourge of war may speedily pass away. Yet, if God wills that it continue, until all the wealth piled by the bond-man's two hundred and fifty years of unrequited toil shall be sunk, and until every drop of blood drawn with the lash, shall be paid by another drawn by the sword, as was said three-thousand years ago, so still it must be said, "the judgments of the Lord, are true and righteous altogether."[20]

Jesus said, "For out the abundance of the heart, the mouth speaketh."[21] Lincoln had just spoken from his guileless heart and would now close with another expression of the abundance of quite possibly, the purest heart of any mortal man or woman with these enduring words:

> With malice toward none; with charity for all; with firmness in the right, as God gives us to see the right, let us strive on to finish the work we are in; to bind up the nation's wounds, to care for him who shall have borne the battle, and for his widow, and the orphan—to do all which may achieve and cherish a just, and a lasting peace, among ourselves, and with all nations.[22]

In seven minutes, even as people were still arriving, it was over. He bowed solemnly to the applauding crowd, turned to his former Cabinet member, Salmon P. Chase, to be sworn in as President for four more years. Lincoln had appointed Chase a few months earlier as Chief

20. Ibid., p 298
21. The Holy Bible, Matthew 12:34
22. The Eloquent President, Ronald C. White, Jr., p 301

Justice of the Supreme Court, at the passing of Roger B. Taney, author of the disgracing and damning Dred Scott decision. Lincoln told the new Justice that he hoped he would understand that "the function of courts is to decide cases—not principles."[23] Chase was the same who opposed Lincoln in his second run for the Republican nomination and who was involved during that election in questionable tactics against Lincoln. But again, there was no room for resentment or retribution in the heart of Lincoln, as it was filled only and always with forgiveness. And he knew that Chase, in spite of his disloyal ambition, was an ardent defender of equality for all and the best choice for such a critical office. Placing his hand on a Bible, this time opened to the fifth chapter of Isaiah, he took the solemn oath of office ending with an emphatic "so help me God," and then reverently bowed again and kissed the Holy Book. Chase noted that his kiss was placed on the verses 25 and 26.

Verse 25

Therefore is the anger of the Lord kindled against his people, and he hath stretched forth his hand against them, and hath smitten them: and the hills did tremble and their carcasses were torn in the midst of the streets. For all this his anger is not turned away, but his hand is stretched out still.

Verse 26

And he will lift up an ensign to the nations from far, and will hiss unto them from the ends of the earth, and behold they shall come with speed swiftly.

---

23. Lincoln, David Herbert Donald, p 551

The address was to the people whom he had so humbly and diligently served. The oath taken with his hand over the compelling words of the prophet Isaiah, and the kiss on Chapter five, seemed to be his personal yet public oblation to his beloved God and Redeemer.

A few days later, Lincoln responded to a congratulatory letter from a friend, New York politician, Thurlow Weed, in which Lincoln said of the address, "I expect the latter to wear well—perhaps better than anything I have produced."[24] Of course, millions for nearly a century have read and will continue to read the words of this address emblazoned on the wall of the inspiring Lincoln Memorial in Washington, D.C.; this message has, indeed, worn well. He continued in the letter to his friend,

> I believe it [the address] is not immediately popular. Men are not flattered by being shown that there has been a difference of purpose between the Almighty and them. To deny it, however, in this case, is to deny that there is a God governing the world. It is a truth that I thought needed to be told.[25]

In fact the speech was only interrupted a couple of times with mild applause. It was far from the expected and traditional political speech. What could have been one of the most rousing victory speeches in history, this speech had, in fact, no words of jubilation, conquest or political rhetoric. Lincoln had no interest in instilling triumphant elation in the hearts of the large crowd nor in the nation overall.

His aim was quite the opposite: He hoped to instill contrition, and penitent hearts that in such a condition, "the better angels" of their natures, become so much more easily inclined to their merciful Heavenly

---

24. The Eloquent President, Ronald C. White, Jr., p 303
25. Ibid., p 303

Father in humble repentance and adoration.[26] The eloquent and defiant voice of Black America, Fredrick Douglass, now a respected friend of the President noted in his diary, "The whole proceeding was wonderfully quiet, earnest, and solemn. The address sounded more like a sermon than a state paper."[27] Indeed, the President of the United States did not address them as a politician; this President rarely did. Instead, he addressed them as a mouthpiece of, using his term, the "Living God."

The War Comes to an End

The following month on April 6th, General Ulysses S. Grant began his massive and relentless assault on Robert E. Lee's starving Army entrenched near Petersburg, Virginia; General Lee's Army fought bravely as they so often had. But General Grant was equally tenacious, much better equipped. After the intense and deadly three day battle, Lee surrendered to Grant. On the day of the receipt of the news of Robert E. Lee's surrender to Grant, Lincoln called his Cabinet together.

> ...the Cabinet meeting was held an hour earlier than usual. Neither the President nor any member was able, for a time, to give utterance to his feelings. At the suggestion of Mr. Lincoln all dropped to their knees, and offered, in silence and in tears, their humble and heartfelt acknowledgments to the Almighty for the triumph He had granted to the national cause.[28]

A couple of days later, on Good Friday, April 14th, Lincoln began his final day in mortality with breakfast in company of Mary and their oldest son, Captain Robert Todd Lincoln, who had just arrived from

---

26. Abraham Lincoln's First Inaugural Address (EP 62)
27. The Eloquent President, Ronald C. White, Jr., p 301
28. William Jackson Johnstone, *The Christian*, New York, Eaton & Mains, 1913, p. 179

his military service as an aid for General Grant at Appomattox. The Lincoln's were joyful to see their son again, and deeply relieved that he had escaped harm in the conflict. Robert was able to inform his father on many details of Lee's surrender since Robert spent that momentous day on the porch of the Appomattox Farm House in which Grant and Lee met.

They also had a pleasant discussion in which the loving father advised his son regarding the future plans in Robert's career. Their trusted and beloved White House resident, and Mary's official dress maker, Elizabeth Keckley, observed, "His [Lincoln's] face was more cheerful than [she] had seen it for a long while."[29] Lincoln was in high spirits; this Good Friday was certainly one of the happiest days of Lincoln's presidency, and possibly his life.

Later that morning his final Cabinet meeting was convened, to which General Grant had been invited to report on the surrender at Appomattox. Lincoln's friend, Joshua Speed, remarked that he did not recall seeing Lincoln so vibrant and alive. Lincoln's Secretary of War, Edwin Stanton, said Lincoln that day was "grander, graver, more thoroughly up to the occasion than he had ever seen him."[30] He also said that Lincoln "spoke very kindly of General Lee and others of the Confederacy," exhibiting "in marked degree the kindness and humanity of his disposition, and the tender and forgiving spirit that so eminently distinguished him."[31]

This Cabinet meeting, devoid of the despairing bad news that had been ever present in the past four years, added to Lincoln's contentment Fredrick W. Seward, who was attending in place of his injured father,

29. Team of Rivals, Doris Kearns Goodwin, p 731
30. Lincoln, David Herbert Donald, p 591
31. Team of Rivals, Doris Kearns Goodwin, p 732

William, recorded that all members present expressed, "kindly feelings toward the vanquished, and [a] hearty desire to restore peace and safety at the South, with as little harm as possible to the feelings or property of the inhabitants."[32] Such sentiments for their former enemies by his Cabinet reflected that Lincoln's approach of forgiveness and charity, so consistent with the principles Lincoln had repeatedly read of the Savior in the New Testament, was taking hold.

He told them that he considered it "providential that this great rebellion was crushed just as Congress had adjourned" allowing him and his Cabinet to move ahead with their reunification campaign based on the foundation of "malice toward none and charity for all."[33] "We could do more without them than with them,"[34] and then added, "There were men in Congress who, if their motives were good, were nevertheless impracticable, and who possessed feelings of hate and vindictiveness in which he did not sympathize and could not participate."[35]

The Dream

In this final Cabinet meeting Lincoln expressed his hope that Grant would have news of Confederate General Joe Johnston's surrender to General Sherman in the South. Grant regretfully informed the President that such news had not arrived, to which Lincoln calmly expressed his certainty that it would soon come "for he had last night the usual dream which he had preceding nearly every great and important event

32. Ibid., p 731
33. Team of Rivals, Doris Kearns Goodwin, p 732
34. Lincoln, David Herbert Donald, p 592
35. Team of Rivals, Doris Kearns Goodwin, p 732

of the War."[36] Secretary of the Navy, Gideon Welles, then asked Lincoln to describe the dream.

Turning to Welles he said that it involved the navy's "element, the water—that he seemed to be in some singular, indescribable vessel, and that he was moving with great rapidity towards an indefinite shore; that he had this dream preceding Sumter, Bull Run, Antietam, Gettysburg, Stone River, Vicksburg, Wilmington, etc."[37] Grant responded by saying that not all of those battles resulted in Union victories, to which Lincoln explained that good news always followed this dream and he was confident that Johnston would surrender (which he did a few days after).

By now his Cabinet was accustomed to hearing Lincoln express sentiments and make decisions based on spiritual impressions of divine guidance that followed his prayers of supplication to the living God and from his dreams. In light of this firmly held belief, we must consider the condition of Lincoln's mind and of his spirit in these last few hours of his life. For four years he had "talked to God" regarding the nation's crisis, and he had yearned that He [God] would reveal His will to him throughout the war, and for years Lincoln felt that God had, in various ways, guided his decisions and actions.

It can be safely advocated that few men on earth had drawn closer to God during that time than had Lincoln. He made a number of key Presidential decisions during this nation's greatest crisis based upon his unwavering intent to do God's will. Not that of Congress, neither his Cabinet, nor public opinion. These recurring dreams of him standing alone on the high-speed aquatic vessel racing toward the shore could certainly be coincidental and meaningless happenings. But it is clear

---

36. Ibid., p 732
37. Ibid., p 731

that Lincoln did not see them as such; on the contrary, he placed a high degree of confidence in their reliability as personal affirmations that God's hand was guiding this great national transformation.

But if they were communications from the Lord to His humble instrument, as God had historically done with his chosen servants many times before, why had this dream occurred with defeats as well as victories, as pointed out by General Grant? We may never know the answer, but Lincoln often expressed his belief that God had his own purposes in the war and that such purpose might be beyond preserving the Union and freeing the slaves. One such additional purpose, again as declared by Lincoln, was the humbling and punishing of the wayward people of the United States. In which case each bloody battle, whether won by the Union or the South, certainly contributed to the chastening contrition, the rising of the "better angels" of their natures, on the part of Gentile Christian America that resided on that "indefinite shore."[38] This state of penitence, which was now pervasive throughout America, would pave the way for the people's humble acceptance of the greatest social and moral transformation in this nation's history that followed the war and Lincoln's assassination.

The troubled Mary Lincoln, who at times had been masterful as First Lady and at other times an embarrassment, was a full benefactor of Lincoln's cheerful final day. She told Francis Carpenter, "She had never seen him so cheerful" and that "his manner was even playful." She said, "At three o'clock, in the afternoon, he drove out with me in the open carriage, in starting, I asked him, if any one, should accompany us, he immediately replied—'No—I prefer to ride by ourselves today.' During the drive he was so gay, that I said to him, laughingly, 'Dear Husband, you almost

38. Team of Rivals, Doris Kearns Goodwin, p 731

startle me by your great cheerfulness,' he replied, 'and well I may feel so, Mary, I consider *this* day the war, has come to a close—and then added, 'We must *both*, be more cheerful in the future—between the war & the loss of our darling Willie—we have both, been very miserable.'"[39]

On this their last afternoon together, Lincoln spoke of their happy and sad days in Springfield, "and recollections of his early days, his little brown cottage, the law office, the court room, the green bag for his briefs and law papers, his adventures when riding the circuit."[40] They made plans for the end of the next term to travel to Europe, to the Holy Land, over the Rocky Mountains to California and then back to Springfield to live out their final days.

Ford's Theater

As the carriage was nearing their return to the White House, Lincoln saw that a group of old friends, who had come to the White House to visit, were now leaving. He called out to them to return and he spent the late afternoon with these treasured friends. Soon he was called to an early dinner to allow for their 8 o'clock arrival at Ford's Theater to see the celebrated actress Laura Keene in *Our American Cousin.* Again one of these last visitors recorded that Lincoln had never seemed "more hopeful and buoyant concerning the condition of the country. He was full of fun and anecdotes, feeling especially jubilant at the prospects before us."[41]

After dinner, Lincoln, accompanied by detective Crook, made one last walk across the street to the War Department office for any telegraphed news of surrender by Johnston. There was none. But unbe-

39. Team of Rivals, Doris Kearns Goodwin, p 733
40. Ibid., p 733
41. Team of Rivals, Doris Kearns Goodwin, p 734

knownst to Lincoln, Generals Sherman and Johnston had, on that same Good Friday, held their first meeting for a negotiated surrender that would be completed a few days later. Sherman had been influenced by Lincoln's persistence in establishing forgiveness and reconciliation for the South when he met with Generals Sherman and Grant in his visit just two weeks earlier at City Point.

Sherman was also aware of General Grant's Lincoln-influenced magnanimously merciful terms of surrender with General Lee, and he offered similar terms to Johnston. Lincoln's oft seen dream of the night before had again portended the good fortune for which he had hoped and prayed. As they walked back to the waiting carriage, detective Crook "almost begged" Lincoln to change his plans to attend the theater and remain safely in the White House.[42] But Lincoln was determined to go. At which point, Crook asked to stay on as an extra guard. "No, Lincoln replied, "You've had a long hard day's work, and must go home." "They parted at the portico of the White House, Lincoln calling out good-bye as he started up the steps."[43] Crook was left feeling uneasy at the seeming finality inflected in Lincoln's farewell.

Lincoln's marshal and personal protector, Ward Hill Lamon, had been sent days earlier on an assignment to Virginia, but before leaving, he begged the President, "Promise me you will not go out at night while I am gone, particularly to the theater."[44] Despite all the concern, Lincoln rarely appeared to be preoccupied with his own safety.

Curtain time at Ford's was eight o'clock but it was after eight when the Lincoln's left the White House where Lincoln said to his friend, Schuyler Colfax, words that transcended beyond the short carriage ride to the the-

---

42. With Malice Toward None, Stephen B. Oates, p 429

43. Ibid., p 429

44. Lincoln, David Herbert Donald, p 594

ater to the approaching end of his unequaled mortal life, "I suppose it is time to go, though I would rather stay."[45] After picking up their guests, the Lincoln carriage drove down Tenth Street, which was still illuminated in celebration of the Union victory, to Ford's Theater. By the time they arrived, the play was well into the first act as anxious spectators kept looking expectantly up to the president's box for his arrival. The moment they entered the theater a signal was given at which the actors paused and the orchestra broke into a resounding "Hail to the Chief" anthem. The audience rose to their feet in loud applause and cheers for their President.

One spectator remembered, "The President stepped to the box rail and acknowledged the applause with dignified bows and never-to-be-forgotten smiles."[46] Sitting in a rocking chair, which had thoughtfully been provided by an admirer, Lincoln sat by his wife Mary for over an hour, entertained by the performance and clearly enjoying each other's company. "When actors scored hits, Mary applauded, but her husband simply laughed heartily. A man in the orchestra observed that Mrs. Lincoln often called the President's attention to actions on the stage and 'seemed to take great pleasure in witnessing his enjoyment.' Seated so close to her husband that she nestled against him, she whispered: 'what will Miss Harris think of my hanging on to you so?' With a smile he replied: 'She won't think any thing about it.'"[47]

John Wilkes Booth entered the theater around 9:00 p.m. and listened from the foyer to the play that he knew by heart to determine that it was playing on schedule, then left to saddle his rented horse in the stable behind the theater. He then led the horse to the rear alley entrance to the theater and left it with a stagehand with instruction to

45. Team of Rivals, Doris Kearns Goodwin, p 734
46. Lincoln, David Herbert Donald, p 595
47. Lincoln, David Herbert Donald, p 595

hold it for ten to fifteen minutes. There was time for one more drink, so walking in the passage way under the stage and listening to the players acting overhead, he crossed to the front of the theater to the Star Saloon next door and at around 10:00 p.m. he ordered a whiskey and drank it alone. Slapping some coins on the table, he left the saloon, turning right to the Ford's Theater entrance just a few feet away. He still had a few minutes so he tarried in the lobby and listened to determine the play's progress. Soon he ascended the curving staircase.

The guard who was stationed with the footman at the presidential box entrance momentarily left his post leaving the footman alone to guard the entrance. At about 10:12, the impeccably dressed John Wilkes Booth walked up to the footman presented him his card and chatted briefly with him. In a moment the footman allowed the well-known actor entrance to the box. Once inside, Booth waited unseen in the vestibule, for two of the actors to exit, leaving the stage with only one actor; he wanted as much of the stage as possible for himself. Booth knew that the lone actor's upcoming line would bring a wave of laughter. Just as the audience burst into an arousing laugh, Booth raised his pistol and at a distance of about two feet from the President, fired a single bullet that entered the back and left of Lincoln's skull.

President Abraham Lincoln's head fell forward; bleeding and unconscious he remained in the chair as if he were asleep. The young Major Rathbone seated at the side of the Lincoln's lunged toward the assassin but Booth was prepared with his sharpened hunting knife and cut a long and deep wound from the elbow to nearly the shoulder of Rathbone, leaving him bleeding profusely. Booth pushed him aside and then vaulted over the rail of the box to the stage. The audience was confused; were they being treated to an unscripted surprise? The shot was muffled by the heavy laughter, and the familiar site of John Wilkes Booth leaping to the stage was not unexpected, as dramatic leaping entrances from heights of ten to twelve feet had been one of Booth's signature renditions in earlier plays.

But with Booth's melodramatic shout from the stage of *"Sic semper tyrannis"* ("Thus always to tyrants"—the motto of the state of Virginia), "The South is avenged!" with his bloody dagger raised in the air. Mary Lincoln screamed, "They have shot the president! They have shot the president!" as the blue gray smoke from the gunshot rose from the presidential box. The audience quickly realized that their mirthful evening had just become the most singularly tragic moment of this nation's history.[48] Booth's relished leap to the stage in front of the startled audience did not turn out as he planned. His spur caught on one of the draped flags over the box railing and possibly contributed to him breaking his left leg near the ankle with the awkward landing some twelve feet below. Booth hobbled to the alley and his waiting horse and galloped undetected out of the city.

The would-be hero, John Wilkes Booth was hunted down and unceremoniously shot and killed twelve days later while hiding in a barn. Booth would live long enough to realize that the well-informed in the South did not regard his assassination of President Lincoln as a welcome nor heroic occurrence, but rather quite the opposite; the Confederacy's defeat was so completely devastating and the North's rising clamor for vengeance so wide spread, that Southern leaders saw Lincoln's compassion and magnanimity as the one great source of safety to which they could cling. John Wilkes Booth had killed that best friend the South now had. He would become a hero to no one.

---

48. Manhunt, James Swanson, p 19

12

Lucifer Is Not Done Yet

As THE WAR came to a close, there remained a dramatic and significant question to be addressed—one that had consumed much of Abraham Lincoln's final year in office, it haunted him, kept him awake at night, and etched lines of worry deep in his face before his passing. How would the two separate political, social, and cultural entities that had been bitter military enemies just days before, be reunited as one nation. And how would they now include four million uneducated, penniless and property-less freed slaves as fellow citizens? There is "no greater [task] before us," Lincoln bluntly told his Cabinet, or for that matter, before "any future Cabinet."[1]

The Fourteenth Amendment

As Lincoln had feared, the adjustment to freedom was a bitter pill for some in the South. They resented the efforts to educate and establish the now-freed Blacks still in the southern states. Many social advocates, Black and White laboring to lift the beleaguered race were murdered and these indignant Southern radicals threatened and terrorized others.

1. Jay Winik, *April 1865, The Month That Saved America,* Perennial, An Imprint of HarperCollins Publishers, 2001, Intro., p xii

In fact the Ku Klux Klan was organized in the year following the end of the war for that very purpose. This widespread and indiscriminate violence in the South pushed the Federal government to do what Joseph Smith had vowed to do if elected President back in 1844. They passed and ratified the Fourteenth Amendment in 1868. With this amendment to the Constitution, the Federal Government no longer would or could lay back in passivity while citizens of the states were being deprived of their inalienable rights, as with the Latter-day Saints two decades earlier.

The Fourteenth Amendment also offered citizenship to the four million freed slaves and their American born posterity, holding states accountable to obey the Constitution. There can be no question that Lincoln would have embraced the passing of this amendment had he lived. In fact it would likely have been passed long before 1868 had he lived. He had long desired that measures be taken that would control and prosecute the violent mob lawlessness that pervaded pre-war America and was again emerging in the post-war southern states against the unfortunate freed-Blacks. The amendment states:

> All persons born or naturalized in the United States, and subject to the jurisdiction thereof, are citizens of the United States and of the State wherein they reside. No State shall make or enforce any law which shall abridge the privileges or immunities of citizens of the United States; nor shall any State deprive any person of life, liberty, or property, without due process of law; nor deny to any person within its jurisdiction the equal protection of the laws....

This amendment to the Constitution repaired the damage done by a half-dozen uninspired Constitutional Convention delegates who had demanded that states not be held accountable to it in the original drafting of the Constitution in 1787. The injury done by these short-sighted delegates is incalculable. Again, it must be said that had Joseph Smith been elected President and supported in his righteous objectives, he would have ended slavery peacefully by purchasing the slaves from the owners, who bought them, a strategy strongly embraced by Abraham Lincoln, but flatly refused by the populace during his administration.

Joseph Smith would also have made the States responsible to protect the privileges and liberties in the Constitution to their citizens. He would have made the Federal Government accountable to press recalcitrant states into submission to the law who allowed oppression of their citizens, as was the case with the Mormons in Missouri and Illinois in the 1830s and 40s. So much suffering and destruction could have been avoided had righteousness been the rule.

Some Great Good to Follow

In a letter to Eliza P. Gurney, written seven months before his assassination, Lincoln expressed his faith that in spite of the daunting challenges faced, great things would result from the terrible conflict of the Civil War,

We hoped for a happy termination of this terrible war long before this; but God knows best, and has ruled otherwise…we must work earnestly in the best light He gives us, trusting that so working still conduces to the great ends He ordains. *Surely He intends some great good to follow this mighty convulsion*, [italics added] which no mortal could make, and no mortal could stay.[2]

---

2. David Herbert Donald, *Lincoln*, Touchstone, New York, 1995, pp. 514,515

There would be many "great ends" that followed the awful chastisement of America, following Lincoln's death. Over time, the United
States would eventually emerge from the Civil War, *finally* as *United*
States; the states' rights overreach was extinguished. The power of war
would create a humble submissiveness in hearts of many Americans,
giving rise to the emergence of "their better angels."[3] And finally, once
and for all, the people were ready to accept that they were one nation
under God and indivisible. With emancipation came the heretofore-
unthinkable Thirteenth Amendment to the Constitution, removing forever the three-fifths clause in the Constitution that led to decades of the
slave States' unbalanced domination in halls of Congress.

William Lee Miller sums up Abraham Lincoln's extraordinary han-
dling of this national transformation:

And when American slavery would finally be ended, it would be
done altogether within the Constitution and the law, by the Thirteenth
Amendment to the Constitution, recommended to the Republican
Convention of 1864 by President Lincoln, finally passed by the Thirty-
eighth Congress under the urging and through the political maneuver-
ing of President Lincoln, joyfully signed by President Lincoln after Congress passed it (although Presidents don't need to sign amendments),
ratified by three-fourths of the states after he was dead, and thus made a
part of the Constitution, ending slavery forever—*constitutionally* ended,
under the law, with the Union intact.[4]

Because of the war, this Constitution, with the second flaw repaired
by the Fourteenth Amendment, was now able to emerge unfettered,
as originally intended by our inspired Founding Fathers. This nation

---

3. Abraham Lincoln, *First Inaugural Address*, March 4, 1861

4. William Lee Miller, Lincoln's Virtues, Vintage Books, New York, 2002, p. 237

would no longer tolerate or legalize racism or religious oppression; instead it would *finally* revert back to its original moorings to protect the inalienable rights of all men and women, regardless of race and regardless of religion. *Finally,* these liberties would be protected by the strong and upright central government with the support of law abiding state governments.

The refining fire of war produced another new birth of freedom by cleansing America of the shameful blemish articulated and ratified by the Supreme Court's Dred Scott Decision in 1857, in which whites were proclaimed to be superior to blacks and that as such, the blacks would be viewed and treated by whites as an inferior race, unworthy of the freedoms guaranteed to all men in the Declaration of Independence. This Supreme Court decision granted all white Americans the right to practice open discrimination and racism under the protection of the law as a political perk for being white. But thanks be to God, the governmental recognition and protection of this notion was drowned in the baptism of the Civil War and with the course correcting Thirteenth and Fourteenth Amendments. Both Joseph Smith and Abraham Lincoln prophesied that specific corrections to our sacred Constitution had to be made to ensure that freedom would prevail in America and in most of the world. By the hand of the Almighty God, those modifications were made, but at great cost through His true and righteous judgments for our erring ways.

Thus began the progression of public thought, inspired by Joseph Smith and Abraham Lincoln through the 1840s and 50s, that this great chastisement and humiliation infused into this people by the war, would now set their primary allegiance to the Republic. Over the coming decades, Americans would internalize the concept that they were now truly united as one nation and under God's approbation; their state allegiance remaining important but secondary to the Union. The war brought a new birth of freedom in this nation with common freedoms *and* individual responsibilities, transforming it into a powerhouse for good around the world because it now possessed a complete and unsullied Constitution governing the strongest nation in the world. Lucifer had no more embedded contaminating influence in the Constitution nor could he overpower it through outside interventions or invasions.

The gravity of the war for the South and the passing of time extinguished the Southern indifference for the Declaration of Independence and its self-evident and inalienable truth that all men are created equal. There was just no more wind for that sail as survival became the concern of the day for the depleted post-war South. In the ensuing decades following the war, disdain for these sacred documents was replaced by reverence, patriotism and gratitude for the abundant blessings of freedom that these documents provide. Religious expression became more fully acknowledged as a protected right.

The Pledge of Allegiance

The Pledge of Allegiance, formally adopted by Congress in 1942 illustrates the shift in public opinion of pre-Civil War American and post World War II America. Many pre-Civil War Americans would not have joined in this pledge of national patriotism.

"I pledge allegiance to the flag of the United States of America and to the Republic for which it stands."

The zeal for states' rights that was a precipitator of the Civil War was strong throughout America but more prominently in the South. Their allegiance was to their state; many were wary of a strong central government and would not pledge their allegiance to the Republic or its flag.

One nation,

No. Many Americans in this era wanted two nations and were willing to go to war over this sophism.

Under God,

This, most pre-Civil War Americans would agree with. Not so much today, however.

Indivisible,

No. Many still preferred two nations.

With liberty and justice for all.

No. Liberty and justice for all *except* Blacks and Mormons.

Although the World War II era's level of patriotism and love of country was unprecedented in America, those values have waned again in the past few decades.

Civil and Religious Freedom

As described earlier, both Joseph Smith and Abraham Lincoln led separate, yet remarkably similar campaigns calling for respect for established Constitutional law and the order that it inspired. They also raised their voices in a call for reverence for the civil and religious liberties guaranteed therein. Their messages on these subjects would be applicable to our day as we find that these same freedoms are again being challenged, as the following examples illustrate

Proclamation

In August 1861, President Lincoln issued his first of eleven proclamations to America. In deep humility and power, he described the reason for the war was God's punishment for the nation's sins. He then made it clear that the fight with the Southern rebellion was to restore the gift of *civil and religious freedom*.

And whereas, when our own beloved country, once by the blessing of God, united, prosperous and happy, is now afflicted with faction and civil war, it is peculiarly fit for us to recognize the hand of God in this terrible visitation, and in sorrowful remembrance of our own faults and crimes as a nation and as individuals, to humble ourselves before Him, and to pray for His mercy—to pray that we may be spared further punishment, though most justly deserved; that our arms may be blessed and made effectual for the re-establishment of *law, order and peace*, throughout the wide extent of our country; and that the inestimable boon of *civil and religious liberty*, (emphasis added) earned under His guidance and blessing, by the labors and sufferings of our fathers, may be restored in all its original excellence...[5]

In May 1843, the Prophet Joseph Smith introduced the first issue of the *Nauvoo Neighbor*. The theme of his message was that of religious and civil freedom.

We have had and may have to defend ourselves against the oppressions, persecutions and innovations of men. And if this should be the case, we shall not shrink from the task, but shall fearlessly and unflinchingly *defend our rights*, sustaining that liberty which our glorious constitution guarantees to every American citizen, for which our fathers jeopardized their liberty, their lives, and their sacred honor.[6]

Continuing, the Prophet emphasized religious freedoms:

We look upon all men that would abridge us or others in their religious rights as enemies to the constitution, recreant to the principles of

---

5. Abraham Lincoln, *Proclamation of a National Fast Day,* August 12, 1861
6. *History of the Church,* Salt Lake City, 1973, vol 15, p. 380

republicanism; and whilst they render themselves despicable, they are striking a secret but deadly blow at the freedom of this great republic. *We will always contend for our religious rights*[7] (emphasis added).

Today's Apostles stand in Defense of Religious Freedom

This common message of Abraham Lincoln and Joseph Smith in defense of religious freedom in their day, is similar to a message being carried by Church leaders today. As of August 2018, Church leaders including a number of the Quorum of the Twelve Apostles, have been, like Joseph Smith and Abraham Lincoln, "contending for our religious rights."[8] At least six members of the Twelve have addressed the topic of religious freedom more than forty times throughout the world in the last few years. Some of these messages have been to Church congregations but many others have been to governing bodies, community organizations and interfaith religious groups around the world. Their common theme is that the right to free expression of religious beliefs and practices is once again being threatened. Lucifer is unrelenting in his final push for the suppression of thoughts about and faith in the Great God of Heaven.

In September of 2016, LDS Church launched a new webpage entitled religiousfreedom.lds.org. This website contains resources for defending the principle of religious liberty and a call to members of the Church and people of all faiths to stand firm, with kindness and civility in defending this right.

This quote by Elder Robert D. Hales, is highlighted in this website,

---

7. *Ibid.*, p. 382
8. *Ibid.*, p. 382

The faithful use of our agency depends upon our having religious freedom. We already know that Satan does not want this freedom to be ours. He attempted to destroy moral agency in heaven, and now on earth he is fiercely undermining, opposing, and spreading confusion about religious freedom...

Introducing this new website, Elder Dallin H. Oaks of the Quorum of the Twelve Apostles said, "We hope that what we say here will explain why members of The Church of Jesus Christ of Latter-day Saints must be committed to maintaining the free exercise of religion, and why all citizens of this nation should be supportive of this effort."[9]

Assaults on religious beliefs and practices are increasing in elementary school settings as well as graduate level university courses, in the workplace and in social media. Meanwhile, this movement is noted for the rise in the number of Americans who profess no faith or who staunchly support nondiscrimination rights and bristle at assertions of religious belief.

Elder Oaks elaborated on why it so important to the LDS Church and its members today.

> Latter-day Saints are committed to the free exercise of religion because the fulfillment of God's Plan of Salvation is only possible under the free exercise of religion guaranteed in our God-inspired Constitution.
>
> Thus, for us, the free exercise of religion is not just a basic and cherished principle of our Constitution. It is essential to God's Plan of Salvation. The free exercise of religion allows all

---

9. *The Deseret News*, Salt Lake City, Sept, 10, 2016

men and women to choose to develop faith in God, to worship him and to act on their beliefs and choices.

Powerful forces, including political correctness, are trying to weaken the free exercise of religion or place it under siege, seeking to replace it with other rights or priorities, such as the powerful emerging right of nondiscrimination.[10]

In the September 2016 *Ensign,* Elder Ronald A. Rasband speaks to this same topic:

Some of you may struggle with an understanding of religion's role in society, politics, and civic issues. Some of you may wonder why religious groups are involved in politics in the first place... In recent years the collective voice of groups who feel that religion should not play a role in political deliberation has grown louder.

The opportunity to be involved in the political process is a privilege given to people in most nations. We need every individual in society to take an active role in engaging in civic dialogue that helps frame laws and legislation that are fair for everyone.

So what is the position of the Church on religious freedom? I can assure you that apostles and prophets, under the inspiration of heaven, have given significant consideration to this issue. We believe in creating a space for everyone to live their conscience without infringing on the rights and safety of others. When the rights of one group collide with the rights

10. The Deseret News, Salt Lake City, Sept, 10, 2016

of another, we must follow the principle of being as fair and sensitive to as many people as possible. The Church believes in and teaches fairness for all.[11]

Protecting conscience is about safeguarding the way someone thinks and feels and safeguarding that person's right to act on those beliefs. I am talking about someone telling you that the thoughts, feelings, and beliefs you have are not allowed, valued, or acceptable because your views are not popular. A war in heaven was fought for agency, and it is a gross violation of that agency to force you to betray your conscience because your views do not align with the crowd.

Elder Rasband continues,

A recent example of the Church's "fairness for all" approach occurred in January 2015, when the Church held a press conference with three Apostles and a member of the Young Women general presidency to remind our members, the community, and the Utah state legislature that the Church favors a balanced approach that secures the rights of all people. Elder Dallin H. Oaks of the Quorum of the Twelve Apostles had this to say at that press conference:

"We call on local, state and the federal government to serve all of their people by passing legislation that protects vital religious freedoms for individuals, families, churches and other faith groups while also protecting the rights of our LGBT [lesbian, gay, bisexual, and transgender] citizens in such areas as

---

11. Ronald A. Rasband, Of the Quorum of the Twelve, Faith, Fairness, and Religious Freedom, Ensign, September 2016, p. 30

housing, employment and public accommodation in hotels, restaurants and transportation—protections which are not available in many parts of the country."[12]

With the passage of protections for both LGBT and religious people six weeks later, our Church leaders and others congratulated the LGBT community. It was encouraging to see them protected against eviction, housing discrimination, or being fired from a job because of their sexual orientation or gender. We also congratulated our religious friends of other denominations, seeing them similarly protected in the workplace and in the public square.

Utah—and the Church—received national news coverage and praise for such a historic compromise. Now, note that no doctrinal or religious principles were sacrificed. No changes were made to God's moral law or to our belief that sexual relations should occur only within marriage between a man and a woman. The outcome was fair to all and reflected a consistency in moral standards and teachings and in respect for others.

Most important, we need you to engage in dialogue regarding the complexities of this issue and find solutions for how to best extend fairness to everyone, including people of faith. These

12. Ronald A. Rasband, Of the Quorum of the Twelve, Faith, Fairness, and Religious Freedom, Ensign, September 2016, p. 31

conversations need to be occurring in our schools, in our homes, and in our relationships with friends and co-workers.

When you have these conversations, please remember these principles: see others through a lens of fairness, treat them with respect and kindness, and expect the same treatment in return.[13]

On September 9, 2016, Columnist Joe Davidson of the *Washington Post* reported on a disturbing development against religious freedom by a branch of our Federal government. The U.S. Civil Rights Commission had been deliberating for an extended time to establish their position on the growing conflict between civil liberties vs. religious freedom. Here is their conclusion:

> Religious exemptions to the protections of civil rights based upon classifications such as race, color, national origin, sex, disability status, sexual orientation, and gender identity, when they are permissible, *significantly infringe upon these civil rights,* the report said. The chairman of the commission, Martin R. Castro, elaborated on their troubling conclusion, "The phrases 'religious liberty' and 'religious freedom' will stand for nothing except hypocrisy so long as they remain code words for discrimination, intolerance, racism, sexism, homophobia, Islamophobia, Christian supremacy or any form of intolerance."[14]

In response to this stunning display of religious intolerance by the U.S. Civil Rights Commission, Roger Severino, director of the De-

---

13. Ibid., pp. 27-34.
14. Joe Donaldson, *The Washington Post,* September 9, 2016

Vos Center for Religion and Civil Society at the conservative Heritage Foundation, described the particularly troubling aspect of the report as,

> The attempt to discredit sincere religious believers as being motivated by hate instead of faith and the implied recommendation that religious groups should change their beliefs on sexual morality to conform with liberal norms for the good of the country. I would expect to see such a slanted and anti-religious report come out of China or France perhaps, but am disappointed to see it come from the U.S. Commission on Civil Rights.[15]

Elder Oaks addressed this U.S. Commission on Civil Rights report, which prompted The Washington Post columnist Joe Donaldson to conclude that the Commission has "determined that sexual liberty trumps religious liberty."[16]

> As the powerful emerging right of non-discrimination has been accommodated in the law, many rank it above the constitutional guarantee of free exercise of religion, contending that religious freedom must be curtailed wherever it conflicts with non-discrimination. To such I say please respect the laws that provide unique protections for believers and religious institutions.[17]

He said some public policy advocates have tried to intimidate people of faith from influencing or making laws, arguing that religious people are trying to impose their views on others. Elder Oaks asks a question:

> These arguments leave me wondering why any group of citizens with secular-based views are free to seek to persuade or impose

---

15. Columnist Joe Davidson of *The Washington Post*, September 9, 2016
16. Ibid., Davidson *The Washington Post*
17. Tad Walsh, Deseret News Faith, September 10, 2016

their views on others by a democratic law-making process, but persons or organizations with religious-based views are not free to participate in the same democratic law-making process?[18]

Elder Oaks repeated the consistent themes of several talks he's given over the past three years. First, that the LDS Church's position is one of "fairness for all, including people of faith." Second, that all should proceed with respect and civility for all people, avoiding contentious communication. Continuing, he clarifies:

We are here to talk about how to preserve religious freedom while living with the differences that exist in our society, among friends and neighbors, and even within our families. We are also here to consider how to explain our goals and efforts without encouraging the misunderstandings that detract from our common desires to live in an atmosphere of goodwill and peace.[19]

He also repeated themes on religious freedom as a strong force for peace, and stability, dignity, charity, moral progress, social good, checking government, service and economic development. Said he:

The weakening of any part of the First Amendment weakens it all. Religion has an honored and uniquely favored place in our public life. The First Amendment framers' guarantee of 'free exercise of religion' rather than just 'freedom of conscience' shows an intent to extend its unique protections to *actions* in accordance with religious belief.[20]

---

18. Ibid., Walsh, Deseret News
19. Ibid., Walsh, Deseret News
20. Ibid., Walsh, Deseret News

Elder Lance B. Wickman urged true Constitutionalists to rally around Elder Oaks' message.

> Tonight, we have heard a clarion call from an apostle of the Lord to also be citizens in defense of our most basic civil rights —the freedom to practice our faith, the freedom to trumpet our beliefs in the public square and the freedom to live according to our core principles in every aspect of our lives. I sometimes fear that we have relied too much on the Constitution to do the hard work of citizenship for us. The Constitution—including the First Amendment—was never intended to make us lazy citizens, to absolve us from the duty and imperative to be vigilant in defense of our religious rights and interests.[21]

On March 25, 2016, as the keynote speaker at the 2016 Mormon Studies Religious Freedom Conference at Claremont Graduate University in California, Elder Oaks declared:

> Many of the most significant advances in Western society have been motivated by religious principles... Examples include the abolition of the slave trade in England and the Emancipation Proclamation in this country. Also the Civil Rights Movement—they were driven primarily by persons who had a clear religious vision of what was morally right.

> George Washington's farewell address: "Of all the dispositions and habits, which lead to political prosperity, religion and morality are indispensable supports. Reason and experience

---

21. Ibid., Walsh, Deseret News

both forbid us to expect that national morality can prevail in exclusion of religious principle."

I also maintain that religious values and political realities are so inter-linked in the origin and perpetuation of this nation that we cannot lose the influence of religion and religious bodies in our public life without seriously jeopardizing our freedom and prosperity.

Religion is surely under siege by forces of political correctness that seek its replacement by other priorities.[22]

In a *Deseret News* article on January 15, 2017 entitled Finding Fairness for All, Kelsey Dallas describes the dilemma:

. . .gridlock that's taken hold in compromise efforts that have involved LGBT activists, national corporations, religiously affiliated colleges, small-business owners and other groups with a stake in the LGTB rights versus religious freedom debates taking place in state legislatures around the country.

Robin Fretwell Wilson, director of the family law and policy program at the University of Illinois College of Law said,

We think...the view that nondiscrimination protections must crowd out every other value is wrong, but we have different visions of the right. Wilson is a leader of what has been labeled the "Fairness for All" camp, working with lawmakers across the country to enact laws, like the Utah Compromise, that balance sexual orientation and gender identity, or SOGI, antidiscrimination laws, with exemptions to protect the con-

22. *Church News*, Week of April 3, 2016

science of rights of faith communities and religious business owners.

Passed in March 2015, Utah's (Compromise) law protected members of the LGTB community from discrimination in housing and employment, while also ensuring the rights of faith groups and government officials with deeply held religious beliefs. It succeeded with the support of the dominant Church of Jesus Christ of Latter-day Saints and other religious stakeholders in the state, as well as representatives of local and national LGTB rights groups

The LGBT community has succeeded in enacting strong LBGT protections in large and small cities throughout the nation. 'These SOGI statutes often pass without religious exemptions."[23]

There have been some disturbing trends leading up to today's assault on religious freedom. Over the years there are certain points of religious expression that have been deemed improper and therefore, forbidden. On the issue of school prayer, those who disagree with it have successfully prohibited its practice instead of reaching a compromise that is fair for all. Leaving those who believe in prayer barred from expressing it where their children are educated. Americans are divided in their beliefs about the origin of life, creationism and evolution. Instead of both views being considered, only one is prohibited in schools—the teaching that God created this world. The Biblical version is held captive and may not be discussed or even considered by our children in school.

---

23. Kelsey Dallas, *The Deseret News,* January 15, 2017

Many Americans believe that it is against God's law to engage in premarital sex and homosexuality. These views are at times berated and decried instead of being allowed as first amendments rights. The pattern here is the muffling of religious beliefs in favor of secular interpretations. The success in this may have emboldened those who resent religious beliefs and practices in America to pursue further quieting of religious expression.

Elder Quentin L. Cook reminded students at a BYU Devotional on February 12, 2017, of the numbing effect of this offensive against religious beliefs:

> . . . in the United States alone there are as many abortions every two years as was the number of Jewish children killed in the Holocaust, during the Second World War. We are so numbed and intimidated by the immensity of the practice of abortion, that many of us have pushed it to the back of our minds and try to keep it out of our consciousness.[24]

Satan Unrelenting in Obtaining Captivity of the Soul

The pattern of today is strikingly similar to Lucifer's strategy from the beginning where he proposed to the Father of Us All to enforce compliance to the laws of God through the denial of agency or the ability to choose whom God's children would serve. Because Lucifer "sought to destroy the agency of man"[25] he was cast down.

> And he became Satan, yea, even the devil, the father of all lies, to deceive and to blind men, and to lead them captive at his will, even as many as would not hearken unto my voice.[26]

24. Church News, Week of February 12, 2017
25. The Pearl of Great Price, Book of Moses 4:3
26. Ibid., Moses 4:4

Satan's efforts to curtail the liberty to choose right from wrong continues today by his systematic and relentless removal of the option to choose righteously, leaving only one remaining option—his bondage and captivity.

Satan has not given up his desperate fight against the agency of man. No longer has he been able to find a political power like the Roman Empire to persecute Christians, or a great church to sponsor the horrific European Inquisitions to oppress and torture true believers. His dramatic attempt to sabotage the Declaration of Independence and the U. S. Constitution with the abominable practice of slavery, also narrowly but soundly failed. His assault continues against the liberties proffered in these two sacred and God-given documents of freedom, whose principles have been embraced worldwide.

But his relentless chipping away at these freedoms has achieved restrictions on religious expression and created a clear and present danger, as the Latter-day apostles have recognized and warned. Elder D. Todd Christofferson declared:

> There are concerted efforts to shame and intimidate believers who have traditional moral values and to suppress religious viewpoints and practices regarding marriage, family, gender and sexuality. Worst of all, governments sometimes joins in these efforts.[27]

Russia is a case in point regarding laws that prohibit or restrict religious freedoms:

On July 20, 2016, Russia's new anti-terrorism laws, which restrict Christians from evangelizing outside of their churches, went into effect.

The "Yarovaya package" requires missionaries to have permits, makes house churches illegal, and limits religious activity to registered church buildings, among other restrictions. Individuals who disobey

---

could be fined up to $780, while organizations could be fined more than $15,000.

> The new laws will "create conditions for the repression of all Christians," wrote Russia's Baptist Council of Churches in an open letter. "Any person who mentions their religious view or reflections out loud or puts them in writing, without the relevant documents, could be accused of 'illegal missionary activity.'"[28]

In his October General Conference address in 2013, Elder Quentin L. Cook gave his message entitled, Lamentation of Jeremiah, Beware of Bondage. In it he explained how this is happening now:

> The most universal subjugation in our day, as it has been throughout history, is ideology or political beliefs that are inconsistent with the gospel of Jesus Christ. This is emblematic of our own day where gospel truths are often rejected or distorted to make them intellectually more appealing or compatible with current cultural trends and intellectual *bondage*.

> Forces that cause righteous people to violate sincerely held religious principles can result in bondage, he said. "Our challenge is to avoid bondage of any kind, help the Lord gather His elect and sacrifice for the rising generations. If we are true to His light, follow His commandments, and rely on His merits, we will avoid spiritual, physical and intellectual bondage as well as the lamentation for wandering in our own wilderness for He is mighty to save.[29]

28. http://www.christianitytoday.com/gleanings/2016/july/russia-ban-evangelism-effect.html
29. Quentin L. Cook, General Conference Address, Ensign, November 2013

Defenders of Religious Freedom—Joseph Smith and Abraham Lincoln

Early in his presidency and before the Civil War had escalated into the horror that it was, Lincoln's concern was for the civil and religious freedoms now in peril. In a letter, he thanked a group of Evangelical Lutherans for their support in the looming conflict:

> [We face] an important crisis which involves, in my judgment, not only the civil and religious liberties of our own dear land, but in a larger degree the civil and religious liberties of mankind in many countries and through many ages...[30]

In an important way the Civil War was a pivotal point in the restoration process. It was a much more epic event than an armed conflict in a divided nation. It was a colossal collision of four hundred years of God's preparations for the ushering in of the Dispensation of the Fullness of Times and Lucifer's machinations to stop it. It was the promised avenging of the persecuted Latter-day Saints, "that the cry of the saints, and of the blood of the saints, shall cease to come up into the ears of the Lord of Sabbath, from the earth, to be avenged of their enemies."[31] Finally, it was the fight for civil and religious freedoms to allow the unhindered dissemination of the *Book of Mormon* that had been hidden for centuries, and out of Satan's reach. Translated by the Prophet Joseph Smith by the power of God, without a trace of Lucifer's contaminations in it, nor governmental interferences.

The Priesthood and the keys of this dispensation had been bestowed on Joseph Smith, and Lucifer was powerless to prevent the transfer, al-

---

30. Phillip L. Ostergard, *The Inspired Wisdom of Abraham Lincoln*, Tyndale House Publishers, Inc., Carol Stream, Illinois, 2008, p. 199

31. Doctrine and Covenants 87:7

though. He was determined to destroy the foundations upon which God built His global latter-day kingdom—a promised land, a land of freedoms, a land "choice above all other lands,"[32] the Declaration of Independence and the Constitution, and of course, the Restored Gospel. Had the South prevailed in the Civil War or if Lincoln had been unsuccessful in preserving the Union and repairing the Constitution, Lucifer would have regained the power he possessed during all of the previous dark ages. But thanks be to Almighty God, whose works are never frustrated, only the works of men.

In his journey by rail, as the newly elected President of the United States, Abraham Lincoln gave a number of brief speeches along the way. He often ended these speeches with a sobering question: "Shall the Union and shall the liberties of this country be preserved to the latest generation?"[33]

Lincoln's faithful and prayerful leadership guided this nation through its baptism of fire and into a "new birth of freedom"[34] that would bring America back to its original foundation documents, the Declaration of Independence and the Constitution. These divine gifts were inspired through our Founding Fathers, whom God raised up for the purpose of creating a government where all men would be treated equally and with justice, and where civil and religious freedom would prevail.

Once the world saw Lincoln's successful defense and rescue of the Constitution, that it could withstand "a formidable internal attempt to overthrow it"[35], governments throughout the world began to follow the

32. 2 Nephi 1:5
33. Abraham Lincoln, Speech in Indianapolis, February 11, 1861
34. Abraham Lincoln, *The Gettysburg Address*, November 19, 1863
35. Abraham Lincoln, *First Address to Congress*, July 4, 1861

United States lead in establishing their own Constitutions to protect civil and religious freedom in their own lands.

This inspired constitutional influence would eventually cover the globe, opening the way for religious freedom and the fulfillment of God's declaration that the restored gospel would be preached to the ends of the earth. The power in the U.S. Constitution was epic and continues to have no equal in the secular history of the world. Nevertheless this inspired set of governing principles has remained in the crosshairs of the Adversary since its Civil War recovery and repair—the assaults continue today.

Who among us will muster even a particle of the courage exhibited by the two greatest figures of the 19th Century by doing all in our power to ensure that these same precious freedoms are preserved for our own posterity, even unto the latest generation?

About the Author

Ron L Andersen has been a noted career management consultant for thousands of clients throughout the United States and Latin America.

Along with his writing, Mr. Andersen has been a dynamic and compelling public speaker throughout the country on the remarkable similarities and contributions of Joseph Smith and Abraham Lincoln. In these presentations he draws his audiences into the life and world of these great American patriots, revealing their incomparable leadership, unwavering faith in God and their enduring legacies.

He maintains a following of thousands of loyal Abraham Lincoln admirers through his Lincoln Leadership Society, which he founded in 2009. *Defenders of Religious Freedom* is Andersen's fourth book on the monumental and lasting influence of Joseph Smith and Abraham Lincoln upon the entire world. His previous books are:

Abraham Lincoln—God's Humble Instrument 2009
Abraham Lincoln and Joseph Smith—How Two Contemporaries Changed the Face of American History 2014
Ingenious Abe 2016

Ron served on the Young Men General Board for the Church of Jesus Christ of Latter-day Saints from 2009-2015; promoting integrity and faith in the lives of over 600,000 youth in nearly every country in the world. He also served in two stake presidencies and as a bishop. He and his wife, Kathleen reside in Bountiful, Utah.